Understanding
and Managing Stress:
A Book of Readings

Understanding
and Managing Stress:
A Book of Readings

Edited by
John D. Adams

University Associates, Inc.
8517 Production Avenue
P.O. Box 26240
San Diego, CA 92126

CONTENTS

INTRODUCTION   1

I   UNDERSTANDING STRESS   7

CHAPTER 1:   STRESS AND THE RISK OF ILLNESS
              John Adams   9

CHAPTER 2:   THE HOLISTIC HEALTH REVOLUTION
              George Leonard   21

CHAPTER 3:   THE LIFE EVENTS INVENTORY: A MEASURE
              OF THE RELATIVE SEVERITY
              OF PSYCHO-SOCIAL STRESSORS
              Raymond Cochrane and Alex Robertson   37

CHAPTER 4:   ORGANIZATIONAL STRESS AND
              INDIVIDUAL STRAIN
              John R.P. French, Jr., and Robert D. Caplan   45

CHAPTER 5:   ANDROGYNY AS
              A STRESS-MANAGEMENT STRATEGY
              Alice G. Sargent   85

CHAPTER 6:   CORRELATES OF JOB STRESS AND
              JOB SATISFACTION FOR MINORITY
              PROFESSIONALS IN ORGANIZATIONS
              David L. Ford, Jr., and Diane S. Bagot   93

II   MANAGING STRESS   105

CHAPTER 7:   EMERGENT AND CONTEMPORARY LIFE
              STYLES: AN INTER-GENERATIONAL ISSUE
              Frank Friedlander   107

CHAPTER 8:   THE AFFLUENT DIET:
              A WORLDWIDE HEALTH HAZARD
              Erik Eckholm and Frank Record   123

CHAPTER 9:   CHOOSING THE RIGHT EXERCISE
              Jane E. Brody   139

CHAPTER 10:   MEDITATION HELPS BREAK
              THE STRESS SPIRAL
              Daniel Goleman   147

CHAPTER 11:   DEVELOPING AND USING
              A PERSONAL SUPPORT SYSTEM
              Charles Seashore   155

CHAPTER 12:   ON CONSUMING HUMAN RESOURCES:
              PERSPECTIVES
              ON THE MANAGEMENT OF STRESS
              John D. Adams   161

CHAPTER 13:   IMPROVING STRESS MANAGEMENT:
              AN ACTION-RESEARCH-BASED
              OD INTERVENTION
              John D. Adams   179

III   MAKING PERSONAL LIFE-STYLE CHANGES   199

CHAPTER 14:   GUIDELINES FOR STRESS MANAGEMENT
              AND LIFE STYLE CHANGES
              John D. Adams   201

APPENDICES

APPENDIX 1:   A VARIETY OF IDEAS
              FOR RESPONDING TO STRESS   211

APPENDIX 2:   SUGGESTED READINGS   215

INTRODUCTION

Stress is a necessary, positive force. We cannot work effectively or even maintain good health and a sense of well-being without a fair amount of it; in other words, if we have insufficient stress in our lives, we may "rust out." However, stress becomes a major problem when we are overstimulated or bombarded with too much work or too many disruptions and surprises. When we experience this situation, we may "burn out." The stress-management task each of us faces is one of maintaining life and work styles that avoid both rusting out and burning out.

It is an acknowledged fact that too much stress over too long a period is a major factor in illness. Many physicians have stated that at least 70 percent of the ailments they treat are stress related. The various chapters of this book explain the connection between stress and illness and present a variety of ways to manage stress both on and off the job.

All types of stress, regardless of the source, cause the same physical reactions; for example, getting married and getting fired trigger the same physiological response involving the autonomic nervous system and the endocrine-gland system (especially the pituitary, thyroid, and adrenal glands). Under normal circumstances, these systems work to maintain our bodily processes (heart rate, blood pressure, metabolism, and so on) in a physiological equilibrium. When we experience stress, the equilibrium is disrupted because these systems start equipping our bodies to either fight or take flight from the stressors we encounter. Fighting and/or running away were appropriate responses to most stressors experienced by prehistoric humans, but they are seldom appropriate for us today. Because we in modern society have no complete outlet for our stress responses, eventually we experience undesirable manifestations of strain, such as hypertension, increased smoking or drinking, irritability, depression, sleep problems, and so on. Living with these evidences of strain over a prolonged period lowers our resistance to illnesses and decreases our morale and our effectiveness at work.

The major illnesses we are anxious about these days, such as cancer, heart disease, ulcers, or alcoholism, have no single causes. They also probably have no single cures, as evidenced by the persistence of these diseases despite the billions of dollars spent searching for cures; instead, these illnesses have multiple causes consisting of psychological, physiological, and social factors. In other words, stress is often largely responsible for these diseases because it lowers our resistance and enhances our predispositions to certain illnesses.

Each of us has such predispositions; some may be due to heredity, others to past history, and still others to personality. For example, research indicates that competitive, achievement-oriented, aggressive behavior is a risk factor in coronary heart disease (Friedman & Rosenman, 1974). Speculation and increasing data also suggest that personality plays a role in the risk of cancer and other diseases as well (McQuade & Aikman, 1975; Pelletier, 1977). Whatever our predispositions, we pay the price when our resistance to illness is lowered for a prolonged period.

The stress response can be illustrated as follows:

```
                Fight                            Illness
Stressor ──────▶ or  ──────────▶ Strain ──────▶ Dissatisfaction
                Flight                           Lowered productivity
```

In summary, this chain of events is moderated (alleviated or heightened) by our personalities, past histories, and heredities; how well we take care of ourselves; how we relate to other people; and how our places of work operate. In addition to understanding the stress response, we should also learn proven stress-management techniques. The purpose of this book of readings is to describe the stress response in greater detail and to outline certain methods for managing stress and for protecting ourselves from its adverse consequences.

The chapters that follow are organized into three parts that parallel the structure of *Understanding and Managing Stress: A Workbook in Changing Life Styles.*

PART I—UNDERSTANDING STRESS

Six chapters are included in Part I. Chapter 1 provides a basic understanding of the stress response and the relationship between stress and illness. In Chapter 2 Leonard reviews the growing holistic health movement, which advocates a life style that can buffer against the effects of excessive stress; because those of us in poor physical, mental, and spiritual health are more likely to succumb to stress, a conscious focus on the maintenance of good health in each of these three areas is a valuable stress-management technique.

Chapter 3 by Cochrane and Robertson and Chapter 4 by French and Caplan explain two major types of stress. Cochrane and Robertson deal with *episodic* stressors, or critical incidents of stress; French and Caplan are concerned with *chronic* stressors, or ongoing, stressful conditions.

Chapter 5 by Sargent and Chapter 6 by Ford and Bagot introduce ways of looking at stress that have not previously received enough attention. Sargent examines the stress-moderating effects of "masculine" and "feminine" behaviors and calls for the development of androgynous behavior patterns for stress alleviation. Ford and Bagot raise a variety of important questions for further research about organizational stress as experienced by minorities.

PART II—MANAGING STRESS

Part II consists of seven chapters that reflect the major areas of concentration for effective stress management: self-management (Chapters 7 through 10), the development of supportive relationships (Chapter 11), and the management of work-related stress (Chapters 12 and 13). The basic message conveyed in Part II is that it is necessary for each of us to take personal responsibility for managing stress; also, organizations must take positive action in removing avoidable stressors and in supporting organizational members in their handling of unavoidable stressors.

Self-Management

The first dimension of self-management dealt with is self-awareness. Because stress and its management are unique for each of us, we must develop our self-awareness and thereby learn which situations cause us stress, how we tend to react to stress, and which stress-management techniques work for us individually. Friedlander's discussion of life-style orientations in Chapter 7 provides one approach to increasing self-awareness. He discusses the ways in which we tend to relate to each other as indications of our personal preferences. For example, some of us may have a high sociocentric orientation, which means that we rely heavily on our peers, friends, family, or neighbors for guidance and direction in our lives. Those of us with this type of focus might be gregarious by nature but employed in work situations that require us to be isolated from others; the discrepancy between such a natural inclination and the actual life situation may cause stress.

A second aspect of self-management involves developing sound nutritional practices. We cannot cope effectively with stress if our bodies are improperly nourished and thus predisposed to illness during highly stressful periods in our lives. In Chapter 8 Eckholm and Record provide a solid review of the undisputed basics of good nutrition as compared with the poor nutritional practices currently associated with our affluent life styles.

A third approach to self-management is the establishment of a program of regular, vigorous exercise. Such a program increases overall health and fitness, thereby enabling the body to better withstand the pressures placed upon it by stress. In Chapter 9 Brody outlines a variety of exercise programs and compares their benefits with regard to achieving fitness.

A fourth self-management technique, meditation, is propounded by Goleman in Chapter 10. Goleman emphasizes the ways in which meditation can increase our abilities to relax, to handle the hectic pace of modern life, and to deal with stress serenely.

Development of Supportive Relationships

High-quality relationships with others constitute another important stress-management resource. Those of us who maintain such relationships are able to use them to our advantage for support and guidance, particularly during periods of excessive stress. In Chapter 11 Seashore discusses the value, creation, and use of personal support systems.

Management of Work-Related Stress

Stress in the organizations in which we work is the subject of Chapters 12 and 13. Chapter 12 explores the stress-producing effects of the extreme organizational emphasis on the short-term achievement of objectives. Chapter 13 presents a case review of an action-research project that investigated organizationally caused stress and suggests ways in which organizations might work toward the alleviation of such stress.

PART III—MAKING PERSONAL LIFE-STYLE CHANGES

Much of the stress we experience is a result of our life styles, and any workable stress-management plan incorporates the necessity for making certain life-style changes. Chapter 14 presents a systematic approach to effecting such changes; if followed, the guidelines provided can facilitate our attempts to develop life styles that are inherently less stressful and that equip us to handle unavoidable stressors.

APPENDICES

The two appendices provide additional information that might be found useful. Appendix 1 specifies a variety of stress-management techniques that have proven helpful for others, and Appendix 2 comprises a list of readings that promote further stress education.

REFERENCES

Friedman, M., & Rosenman, R.H. *Type A behavior and your heart.* New York: A.A. Knopf, 1974.

McQuade, W., & Aikman, A. *Stress.* New York: Bantam, 1975.

Pelletier, K.R. *Mind as healer mind as slayer.* New York: Delacorte, 1977.

PART I
UNDERSTANDING STRESS

CHAPTER 1

STRESS AND THE RISK OF ILLNESS

John Adams

Transitions, regardless of what sort they are, represent a disruption in one's routines. Hence, they cause a disruption of equilibrium. Even positive, carefully planned transitions lead into new areas for the individual and to the disruption of that person's routines to some extent. The stress response ("strain") is a major factor to consider in the study of transitions because transitions are always, to a greater or lesser degree, strain inducing.

Modern living is stressful. Society is changing rapidly causing changes in values, life styles, career patterns, family expectations and so on. Over the past few years, popular and professional books, magazines and journals have focused increasingly on stress and its impact on people. On any newsstand one can find books on stress and how to escape from it. Likewise, professional publications in the behavioural sciences are dealing with the same issue. While "strain" may be defined somewhat differently from one publication to the next, the clear trend is towards defining it as a non-specific physiological response to disruption, and towards relating the chronic experience of this response to the risk of various illnesses and other health changes (e.g. accidents). To a growing number of doctors and behavioural scientists, strain is becoming the basic bridge between psychology and medical pathology.

Strain is the body's physical, mental and chemical reaction to disruptions, which prepares one to handle the unfamiliar or the frightening. It is both good and bad. Strain is needed for alertness and the performance of high quality work. In emergencies, it is needed as a source of increased energy and strength. On the other hand, chronic or

Reprinted from: J. Adams, J. Hayes, and B. Hopson, *Transition: Understanding and Managing Personal Change.* London: Martin Robertson, 1976. (New York: Universe Books, 1977.) Used with permission.

prolonged strain can cause or heighten the effects of a vast array of diseases. For example, in *Stress* (McQuade & Aikman, 1974) the table of contents reads, in part:

PART TWO: What Stress Can Do To You
  Chapter 1: The Cardiovascular System:
          Heart Attack, Hypertension, Angina, Arrhythmia, Migraine
  Chapter 2: The Digestive System:
          Ulcers, Colitis, Constipation, Diarrhea, Diabetes
  Chapter 3: Stress and the Immunity Screen:
          Infections, Allergies, Auto-immunity, Cancer
  Chapter 4: The Skeletal-Muscular System:
          Backache, Tension headache, Arthritis, the Accident-prone

In each case, the authors make a detailed accounting of case examples and population studies which suggest strongly that prolonged exposure to stress can cause or heighten each of these conditions. The authors describe the differing personality characteristics of persons prone to different diseases and show how stress eventually leads to bodily breakdown.

An improved understanding of one's own transitions or the intention to help others manage their transitions more effectively must be accompanied by an understanding of stress and of how chronic strain increases the risks of illness. The next section of this chapter describes the non-specific stress response in greater detail. Following that, some historical and current perspectives relating stress to illness are developed. A third section reviews the relationship between organisational variables (as stressors) and illness and begins to indicate ways of alleviating or buffering the impact of stress.

THE STRESS RESPONSE

If one's body is invaded by a certain kind of virus, one's lymphatic system will send out a tailor-made kind of cell, called an antibody, which will attack that particular virus, almost like fitting a key to a lock. Following the success of the antibody in overcoming the virus, the antibody remains in the system and the person remains, at least for a time, immune to further attacks by the same virus (e.g. measles). Since the "common cold" is made up of a great many combinations of viruses, it is one illness we don't seem to become immune to. In any event, this is an example of our body's making a specific response to a specific invasion. The stress response is always the same, regardless of the invasion.

The stress response triggers the autonomic nervous system, which ordinarily serves to keep our bodies in equilibrium through controlling our metabolism and growth rates. It does this through acting on our thyroid and pituitary glands, telling them when to release hormones into our bodies. It is called the autonomic nervous system because it is autonomous. That is, it normally is beyond our conscious abilities to control it. The autonomic nervous system also is set off frequently by disruptions from outside, and this is the beginning of the stress response. In other words, it is other people and events out in the environment we must relate to that set off the stress response. With this in mind, we can view stress not as a bad thing to be avoided but as a fact of our lives.

Doctors and psychologists are becoming concerned, however, because of the number of times events disrupt our sense of continuity and set off the stress response. Surprises set it off most often—things like getting fired, having an accident, or being asked for a divorce. But changes we decide to make—like looking for a new job or adopting a new career—also cause disruptions that set off the stress response. And now we are learning that normal life developments like menopause or turning thirty create their own turbulence and therefore set off the stress response too!

The chemical reactions occurring during the stress response are meant to equip the body to fight or take flight, by increasing blood pressure and metabolism rate, increasing the production of cholesterol, and producing adrenalin. Society has made it less necessary for us to fight or flee with any great frequency, but our bodies have not evolved as fast as has society, and the disruptions of everyday living still set off the stress response cycle once needed for survival. Over a period of time, if we set the stress response off regularly, there is a cost to be paid. The list of diseases, as we saw above, looks somewhat like the table of contents from a basic pathology text. The eventual wear and tear of chronic stress responses lowers resistance to these maladies and also seems to intensify their impact.

There is a tremendous difference between people both physically and in terms of their personalities. While much is yet to be learned, it is fairly clear that these differences greatly affect our eventual reactions to chronic stress.

Different people are either born with or develop different equipment than their neighbours. Some of us have inherited weaknesses like poor eyesight or weak livers because those things run in our families. Others of us acquire weaknesses through accidents, illnesses, or personal neglect or abuse. All of us have some weak links, physically, which are susceptible to the gradual wear and tear of chronic stress.

People also develop different personalities. Psychiatrists tell us that we learn very early in life whether or not it is "permissible" to experience and express feelings. For example, if we are raised in an environment where it is not all right to cry or not all right to be angry, we learn very quickly to hold our breath when we have such feelings, and therefore develop shallow breathing habits. This can make one's respiratory system susceptible to breakdowns.

We also learn very early in life what sorts of relationships to have with people. For example, boys are taught that men are self-reliant and do not have intimate relationships with other men or with very many women. Society tends to say we should develop one intimate relationship and does not encourage us to develop a network of support systems which, we shall see later, probably can help alleviate strain.

What all of this adds up to is that many of the stress-related diseases listed above tend to have clusters of behavioural characteristics that differentiate them from the others. For example, coronary prone people typically tend to be highly competitive and driven; they fall easily into conflict with authority figures; and they are determined to out-do their parents. Very active and energetic people tend to be coronary risks (see, for example, Friedman & Rosenman, 1974).

Ulcer patients typically also are go-getters, but under the surface they are holding down a strong need to be nurtured. They tend to have a lot of hostility in their systems which is blocked from expression by their need to be loved. Ulcer patients also tend to get into marital troubles quite readily (see, for example, Wolf, 1965).

Cancer patients are different. They have often had a life of loneliness and exhibit deep-seated melancholy, despair, disappointment and hopelessness. The onset of cancer often follows shortly after a severe disruption to or termination of a crucial relationship (see, for example, LeShan, 1966).

Arthritic patients tend to be more domineering people and yet are often socially shy at the same time. They express their feelings in aggressive actions. Many athletes fit this category. As they get older and have less energy, they are less able to utilise these outlets and tend to develop arthritis in one or more of their joints (see, for example, Brooke, 1960).

It is thus indicated that people who tend to "come down with" these different diseases have different physical make-ups and different personalities. To reiterate, we all have our weak links.

When these diseases are induced or maintained by stress, they are not easily cured. As an example, thirty people in a recent study had surgery done on their ulcers. During the next year, seventeen developed new ulcers, seventeen developed physical signs of anxiety like tics and phobias, five became asthmatic, four developed high blood pressure and one contracted tuberculosis (Silverman, 1968). There is no complete medical cure for diseases where a major stress factor is involved.

HISTORICAL AND CURRENT PERSPECTIVES ON RELATING STRESS AND ILLNESS

Claude Bernard, the famous nineteenth-century biologist, thought that the "seeds" of disease were all around and inside us all of the time. The diseases, or dis-eases, did not have an effect on one's body unless one's body was in a state to "receive" one of them. Most frequently, according to Bernard, our bodies maintain an equilibrium that resists disease and the seeds therefore cannot grow.

During the same period, however, microbiologists like Louis Pasteur were receiving more attention from the medical world as they identified and learned to destroy pathogenic microbes, like those causing diphtheria. Over the years, conquered diseases have disappeared or become rare, but others have always replaced them. We are still building and expanding hospitals. We still do not know for sure why people get sick.

The pendulum, however, seems to be swinging from "Pasteur" back towards "Bernard." Pasteur, when near death, reputedly said that "Bernard was right. The microbe is nothing, the terrain (state of the body) is everything." However, Pasteur's achievements outlived his dying words and have strongly influenced the practice of medicine.

Bernard's work was revived in the 1930s by Walter Cannon, a Harvard physiologist who described a "wisdom" of the body that sets off adjustments to change and disruption. Cannon noted that the same adaptive responses were triggered by a wide variety of intrusions.

Even earlier, around the turn of the century, Johns Hopkins psychiatrist Adolf Meyer recognised that the human organism's adaptive system can become overloaded and break down. He kept life-charts or biographies of his patients which showed that people became ill shortly after clusters of major changes in their lives much more frequently than chance would predict. Harold G. Wolff, a psychiatrist at Cornell, studied these phenomena and began to relate life settings and emotional states to specific diseases.

Thomas H. Holmes, formerly a co-worker of Wolff's at Cornell and now at the University of Washington, took the work of Meyer and Wolff even further in developing a scale for predicting one's susceptibility to stress diseases. By 1965, Holmes and his colleagues had evolved their Social Readjustment Rating Scale to its present widely known form (see Holmes & Rahe, 1967). After being discussed by Alvin Toffler in *Future Shock*, this scale has appeared in the *New York Times, Reader's Digest* and nearly every popular and professional book concerned with relating stress to illness susceptibility.

This scale consists of 43 life-change events. Each event has been assigned a number of points (through an extensive research process), which represents the average relative amount of readjustment required to restore one's equilibrium after experiencing that event. A great many studies have been conducted and are now being conducted using the Social Readjustment Rating Scale. While the results vary from one study to the next (due to different populations and differing research designs) one thing remains constant across these studies—the more readjustment points one amasses during a period, the greater one's likelihood of becoming ill in the not too distant future. And, according to Holmes, the higher the total points, the more severe that illness is likely to be!

This section is concluded with a few brief mentions of a variety of specific studies that have related stress and illness.

Jay M. Weiss (1972) of the Rockefeller University in New York subjected two rats in each experiment simultaneously to the same physical stressors (electric shock) while varying the psychological stress (predictability of the shock). While an audible signal told one rat when to expect the shocks, the second rat heard the signal randomly. A third rat was confined in the same manner as the other two but received no shocks or signals. The control rat (no shocks or signals) developed very few ulcers. The rat that heard the audible signals randomly developed ulcers five times larger than the rat that heard warning signals! In these experiments, *unpredictability* emerged as the key factor. That is, the less expected the disruption, the greater the impact of the stress response.

Seligman's (1975) work on the phenomenon of "learned helplessness" demonstrates clearly in animals and humans that distress and depression are generated when a subject does not have control over his environment. If responses are rewarded randomly instead of being contingent upon certain behaviour, then "learned helplessness" appears and continues to affect the subject even in future tasks where in actuality he now has control.

John C. Cassel of the University of North Carolina has been studying the experiences of first time mothers. For those experiencing a high degree of stressful readjustment during their pregnancies, 30 per cent of those who received a great deal of love and support during the readjustment period prior to delivery experienced complications in childbirth; while 90 per cent of those who received little warmth and support experienced childbirth complications (from Lamott, 1975, p. 10).

Cassel has also found changed hormonal levels in people deprived of warmth and support. In a related study, he found that divorced men have a death rate three to five times as high as married men of the same age (ibid.).

Lawrence E. Hinkle and William N. Christensen looked for "Asian flu" among twenty-four women by examining samples of their blood for the presence of the influenza virus. The women had varying concentrations of the virus, but the amount of virus was uncorrelated with the onset of influenza. In nearly every case, the women who succumbed were those who had recently gone through a bad emotional experience (ibid., p. 13).

In 1949, Franz Alexander noted that while hypertension was virtually unknown among African blacks, it was an exceedingly widespread disease among American blacks. Black psychiatrists William H. Grier and Price M. Cobb attribute the high incidence of hypertension among black ghetto dwellers to "being black, and perpetually angry, and unable to express it or do anything about it." Similarly, Ernest Harburg, of the University of Michigan, tested the blood pressures of blacks in high and low stress areas in Detroit. He found that, all other things being equal, 32 per cent of the people tested in the high stress area had hypertension while 19 per cent of the people in the low stress area had hypertension (ibid., pp. 31–2).

S. L. Syme, of the University of California, has investigated the relationships between social changes (transitions) and heart disease. The data he has collected have led him to three conclusions:

1. Men whose adult life setting is different from that in which they grew up (typically rural to urban) are three times as likely to have a coronary as those whose life setting remains the same.
2. The more often a person changes a job, the more likely he or she is to have a coronary.
3. As rural areas become urbanised, the incidence of heart disease increases (ibid., p. 36).

These are but a few of an almost endless list of studies which have been conducted linking stress and physical illness. Readers interested in further such examples are referred to W. McQuade and A. Aikman (1974) and K. Lamott (1975). Both of these books are easily read and themselves contain further references for investigating the relationships between stress and illness. As a means of summarising the studies cited above, the following conclusions can be drawn:

1. The incidence of illness is positively correlated with the amount of life change or transition one undergoes.

2. Unpredictable disruptions cause more severe stress-related diseases than predictable disruptions.

3. Lack of feedback on the success of attempts to cope with strain-inducing events causes more severe stress-related diseases than when relevant feedback is present.

4. Interpersonal warmth and support during stressful periods seem to reduce the impact of the stress response.

5. Viruses alone do not cause all illnesses. The incidence of bad emotional experiences seems to upset the body and allow the viruses to take over.

6. Hypertension occurs much more often in environments characterised by high stress and few ways to respond to that stress.

7. The more major life changes (jobs, location, etc.) the higher the risk of coronary heart disease.

ORGANISATIONAL STRESS AND ILLNESS

John R. P. French, Jr., and his colleagues in the Institute for Social Research at the University of Michigan have for several years been involved in a series of research efforts investigating the consequences of various organisational factors on the health and emotional well-being of the members of organisations. Their findings not only corroborate the relationships between stress and illness mentioned above, but also begin to point the way towards comprehensive ways of buffering oneself from the impact of strain-inducing events.

One of their major studies was conducted at the Goddard Space Flight Center of NASA (French & Caplan, 1972). The theory they tested in this study is that occupational stressors, as modified by individual differences, induce psychological and physiological strains which, in turn, induce coronary heart disease. This is represented in Fig. 3.1. Their findings indicate the extent of the impact of modern working life on organisational members. The findings are reviewed here by looking briefly at physiological and psychological strains related to each of the proposed organisational stressors. Each of the strains in their study has been shown in previous studies to be a risk factor in coronary heart disease.

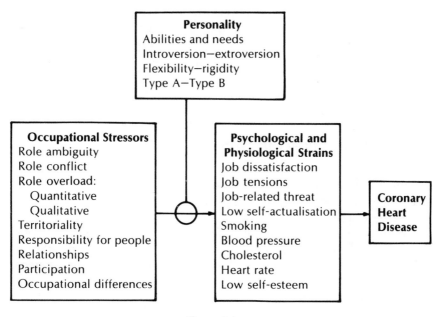

Figure 3.1

Role ambiguity: lack of clarity in one's work resulted in dissatisfaction, threat, under-utilisation and a sense of futility.

Role conflict: conflicting demands or apparently overlapping responsibilities resulted in dissatisfaction, tension, threat, and increased heart rate.

Quantitative and qualitative role overload: when one had too much to do or work that was beyond one's capabilities, the result was dissatisfaction, lowered self-esteem, threat, raised cholesterol levels, and increased smoking and heart rate. Interestingly, subsequent studies have shown the opposite conditions (too little to do and unchallenging work) to have similar outcomes.

Territoriality: when one had to cross organisational boundaries regularly, such as being an administrator in a scientific setting, one experienced quantitative and/or qualitative overload and the attendant strains.

Responsibility for people: more or less responsibility for others than was desired led to increased smoking, blood pressure and cholesterol levels.

Relationships: poor relationships were a prime cause of role ambiguity and role conflict.

Participation: high authentic participation resulted in low psychological strain, positive attitudes towards work and high productivity.

Occupational differences: administrators in the scientific community (NASA) were found to have the highest incidence of quantitative role overload and the most occasions to cross organisational boundaries. They also experienced coronaries at three times the rate of scientists in the same research centre.

Alleviating the Impact of Stress

One might now ask what can be done to alleviate stress or to buffer its effects. While there are not yet any clear-cut answers, we do have some clues from the French, et al. research findings (1972), which are summarised here.

With a focus on the findings involving participation and relations with others, and on the organisational stressors themselves, two paths for buffering stress are apparent: (i) develop supportive working relationships; (ii) examine organisational dynamics found to be stressors and make changes that will alleviate the strains.

An extension of the first path, which is related to the need for warmth and support during stressful periods reported above, would be for people to develop their personal support systems more fully. As mentioned, our society does not encourage us to develop support networks. There is mounting evidence, however, that effective use of one's supportive relationships can alleviate strain. One of the best ways to get through a stressful period is to talk it out. In depth. With feeling. Yet how many people do this with a friend, a clergyman, or a doctor? Most people have very few friends they feel close enough to, to turn to for counselling. Often one's few close friends are so much like one that they cannot offer a different perspective in any event. We all need others to help us focus; help us test reality; help us find intimacy, self-worth and perspective; help us take responsibility for ourselves.

The second path is organisational change. The norms or ways of doing things in organisations induce a lot of strain in people. As was described above, unclear responsibilities or mixed messages from one's superior can set off one's stress response. So, too, can too much work or too little work. Even having to work with people trained in a different area can be strain-inducing! People in organisations can examine their ways of working and make changes to reduce ambiguities, to balance work loads and to develop good working relations. For some time, organisational psychologists have pointed out that such changes can improve productivity and satisfaction. Now doctors and psychiatrists are beginning to say these changes may help us live longer or in better health.

A third pathway should be mentioned in closing, that of taking care of one's self. As was pointed out, some of us do not take very good care of ourselves, and all of us have developed characteristics of which we are at best only partly aware. Research indicates that good nutrition, exercise and relaxation habits help alleviate the impact of stress. We can also manage our strain more effectively if we are aware of our preferences, needs and peculiarities. For example, if a person has high needs to work in a cohesive group, he or she will find assembly line work stressful; whereas someone who would just prefer to "do his thing" and not worry about a group may not find the same assembly line job to be stressful.

REFERENCES

Brooke, J. W. (1960) *Arthritis and You*, New York: Harper.

French, J. R. P. & Caplan, R. D. (1972) "Organisational stress and individual strain" in A. J. Marrow (ed.) *The Failure of Success*, New York: AMACOM, pp. 30–66.

Friedman, M. & Rosenman, R. H. (1974) *Type A Behavior and Your Heart*, New York: Alfred Knopf.

Holmes, T. H. & Rahe, R. H. (1967) "The Social Readjustment Rating Scale," *Journal of Psychosomatic Research, 11*, pp. 213–8.

Lamott, K. (1975) *Escape from Stress*, New York: G. P. Putnam.

LeShan, L. (1966) "An emotional life-history pattern associated with neo-plastic disease," *Annals of the New York Academy of Science*, New York.

McQuade, W. & Aikman, A. (1974) *Stress*, New York: E. P. Dutton & Co.

Seligman, M. E. P. (1975) *Helplessness*, Reading: W. H. Freeman/San Francisco: W. H. Freeman.

Silverman, S. (1968) *Psychological Aspects of Physical Symptoms*, New York: Appleton-Century-Crofts.

Weiss, Jay M. (1972) "Psychosocial factors in stress and disease," *Scientific American*, June, pp. 104–13.

Wolf, S. (1965) *The Stomach*, New York: Oxford University Press.

CHAPTER 2

THE HOLISTIC HEALTH REVOLUTION

George Leonard

As a veteran of the consumer wars, I considered myself beyond being shocked by the ravages of inflation. But then my 1976 Blue Cross bill arrived. Last year, my bill was $374.40. Now, it was $484.40. Ten years ago, the service would have cost $158.28.

That rise itself was enough to unsettle a grizzled campaigner. But there was something more, something peculiar and chilling about the communiqué that came with the bill. "The cost for hospital and medical care," the note began, "is rising twice as fast as the cost of living." A few examples of increased costs followed, but not one word about the *cause* of these disproportionate increases. I searched the note in vain for some explanation, some expression of regret, some hint of hope for the future. "Because of rising costs and updated benefits, we must raise the subscription charge for your program." Just that. For all I could tell, the increases might go on forever.

But *why?* What's going on here? Against the fact that our medical care costs have gone up 330 percent in twenty years while the price index has risen by only 74 percent, we are offered only disclaimers. Physicians' fees, we are told again and again, are not a factor. The price of drugs, pharmaceutical firms remind us, has stayed in line with the cost of living. And it's certainly not that the nation's health is improving due to our extravagant investment in the present medical system. Life expectancy for American adults has improved little or none since the 1920s, and in many ways we are becoming more sickly than ever. Something simply doesn't make sense.

In his often-quoted book, *The Structure of Scientific Revolutions,* Thomas Kuhn argues that every dominant science eventually oversteps itself. Its very successes take it out to extreme positions and practices that hasten its fall, its replacement by another approach. In its final stages, according to Kuhn, the old science enters a period of crisis and anomaly. In other words, things don't work and things don't make sense. Could it be that our present medical science—the provenance of miracle drugs and heart transplants, the habitat of *Marcus Welby, M.D.*—has entered just such a period? And if so, what is the New Medicine that will take its place?

I got a pretty good idea when I visited the Wellness Resource Center of Mill Valley as a client. The experience was an eye-opener, and I'll describe it in some detail. But first, a little perspective is in order:

Conventional modern medicine, the Old Medicine, must be given its due. The miracles are real, the triumphs truly dramatic. For what it's good at, the Old Medicine is superb. If you are hit by a truck or contract a severe bacterial infection or have an attack of appendicitis, you are fortunate indeed to be in the hands of a Marcus Welby. But the Old Medicine has little to offer in the way of promoting good health. And its practices are now *causing* a great deal of sickness and suffering—more, according to some critics, than they are curing.

Doctor-prescribed drugs, for example, have become one of the nation's major causes of death. Adverse drug reactions probably total at least 3 million a year. Estimates of hospital deaths due to drugs range up to 140,000 a year. Taking the rather conservative figure of 29,000 deaths from the Boston Collaborative Drug Study, you will have adverse drug reaction as the eleventh most deadly killer in the United States, just behind bronchitis, emphysema, and asthma. Combine these drug reactions *in* hospitals with the estimated 300,000 people *admitted* to hospitals every year because of doctor-prescribed drugs, and you have an added hospital care cost of $4.5 *billion* annually.

Hospitals are indeed dangerous places. In addition to the perils of drugs, there are the particularly resistant strains of bacteria that lurk where antibiotics are the common diet. And there are the side effects of surgery and radiation, as well as inevitable human error on the part of hospital employees, who find themselves overburdened in spite of their great and ever-increasing number. Fifteen years ago there were two hospital employees for every patient; now there are three. Between 1965 and 1975, the total number of people in the health-care field increased from 3.3 million to 4.4 million. And yet, as more and more reinforcements are called up, the situation continues to worsen.

The Old Medicine has created its own Frankenstein's monster. Potent drugs, futuristic technology, and heroic procedures now exist, and thus, in the name of "saving" even the hopelessly ill, must be used. The cost is staggering; the results are questionable. Dr. Alexander Leaf of Harvard Medical School has cited one study group of 40 patients with ruptured aortic aneurysms. The combined hospital bills of these people came to more than a million dollars, an average of better than $25,000 each. Only one of the 40 left the hospital alive. Such expensive exercises in futility are naturally reflected in our health insurance bills.

More of the same—more drugs, more hospitals, more technology, more spectacular operations—is obviously not the answer. Under present conditions, medical science has probably gone about as far as it can go. This once-radical point of view is now reverberating in academic and professional circles. "No one is saying that medicine is good for nothing," observed Professor Aaron Wildavsky of the Graduate School of Public Policy at Berkeley, "only that it is not good for everything. Thus the marginal value of one, or one billion, dollars spent on medical care would be close to zero in improving health." Though it's a bitter pill for some physicians to swallow, more and more of them are now owning up to the limitations, as opposed to the god-like omnipotence, of their profession. "What it all comes to," editorialized Dr. Irvine H. Page, editor of *Modern Medicine,* "is that a host of factors in daily living influence health far more than all the medical care that could be administered."

As the Old Medicine grinds painfully toward the end of the era of "modern medical miracles," a New Medicine is in the process of being born. This New Medicine, sometimes known as "holistic health," is the creation of a large and colorful cast of characters, ranging from established medical professionals to psychic healers and Indian shamans. Like most experimental movements, it is centered on the West Coast, though its practitioners are scattered around the nation. Its growth is spectacular (a symposium on healing at the University of California, Santa Cruz, last spring drew an unexpected overflow crowd of 1,500), and its results are already promising enough to attract substantial academic, foundation, and governmental support. Though New Medicine practitioners are a diverse lot, most of them share common assumptions:

1. *Positive wellness, not just the absence of disease, is the goal.* The conventional physician considers a person well if he has no symptoms and falls within the normal range in a series of diagnostic tests. Yet, this "well" person might smoke heavily, take no exercise, eat a bland, sweet, starchy diet, and impress all who meet him as glum, antisocial, and emotionally repressed. To a New Medicine practitioner, such a person is

quite sick, the carrier of what biologist René Dubos calls "submerged potential illness." In the New Medicine, the absence of overt disease is only the starting point, beyond which a whole world of *good health* beckons. Psychology entered a new era when Abraham Maslow began studying people who are at their peak mentally and emotionally, rather than pathological individuals, who had always preoccupied that science. In the same way, medicine is transformed when it begins looking at above-average physical fitness, extraordinary alertness and awareness, and the tingling sense of well-being that affords high resistance to disease.

At the Langley Porter Neuropsychiatric Institute in San Francisco, Dr. Kenneth R. Pelletier and his colleagues are currently studying the responses of exceptionally healthy people. These people are hooked up to a battery of biofeedback devices that measure brain waves, muscle tension, constriction of the small blood vessels, the pattern of heartbeat and respiration, and skin conductivity. From the way these internal systems return to normal after stress, Pelletier's group is able to draw a profile of the ideally healthy individual. "These people seem to have a high degree of mind-body integration," Dr. Pelletier said. "They may be rare in our culture, but then again, we've never really bothered to look."

2. *The causes of most illness are to be found in environment, life-style, and emotional/sensory balance.* This assumption of the New Medicine is only partly new. The environmental origin of many diseases has long been known, but the true dimensions of the problem are only now coming to light. Recent studies suggest that 80 to 90 percent of all cancers may be triggered by environmental factors, especially the pesticides, plastics, food additives, and other pollutants that have flooded our environment since World War II. One distinguished bio-chemist, who asked that his name not be used, fears that we may be in for a veritable plague of cancer, during which up to one out of four adults in the United States would be stricken. Such a plague would be particularly insidious, since the lead-time for environmentally caused cancer is ten to twenty years.

Life-style as a crucial factor in sickness and health—a cornerstone of New Medicine belief and practice—is also gaining impressive validation. Some of the venerable truisms of good, clean living, in fact, are now popping up in large-scale health surveys. Dr. Lester Breslow, Dean of UCLA's School of Public Health, compared the actual health of 7,000 California adults with seven old-fashioned "health habits":

No smoking
Moderate drinking

Seven or eight hours sleep per night
Regular meals with no snacks in between
Breakfast every day
Normal weight
Moderate, regular exercise

The survey showed, with amazing consistency, that the health of people with seven of the habits was better than the health of those with six, those with six better than those with five, and so on down the line. The average number of years of life remaining at age 45 for men with zero to three good health habits was 21.6 years compared with 33.1 years for those with six or seven—a difference of 11.5 years. A study of 2,000 long-lived people conducted by Dr. Robert Samp of the University of Wisconsin came up with similar results, and with additional findings that related good health with personality traits such as moderation, serenity, optimism, interest in others, and interest in the future.

The connection between disease and personality is a bit more controversial. There's no question about the emotional factors involved in such ailments as ulcers and spastic colon. But New Medicine practitioners go much further, arguing that *all* disease is related to personality, with the way you handle your emotions. Environmental causes may trigger cancer, they feel, but the person with a fluid, well-balanced personality is far more likely to ward it off. A number of researchers, in fact, have independently arrived at what might be called a "cancer personality," observing that cancer patients tend to be rather rigid, self-sacrificing people, who repress their feelings and hold onto resentments. More conventional researchers reject this thesis. They may agree with the environmental genesis of cancer, but tend to believe, with curious disregard for scientific causation, that pure chance, the roll of the dice, determines who actually develops the disease. In any case, the link between personality type and a variety of serious ills is becoming increasingly well-defined. The driven, aggressive, goal-oriented personality, for example, is rather clearly associated with increased risk of heart attack.

3. *Prevention of illness, according to the New Medicine, lies less in the annual physical than in the transformation of your life.* "Subjecting people with no medical complaints to a complete battery of screening procedures every twelve months is probably ridiculous," Dr. Stuart O. Schweitzer was quoted as saying in a recent interview in *Family Practice News*. Dr. Schweitzer, who is doing a federally funded study on the cost-effectiveness of routine medical tests, points out that the chances of

finding something wrong during an annual checkup on a person without symptoms is very, very low—and extremely costly.

The most effective and least expensive preventive measures have little or nothing to do with medical science as we have known it. "Health care in the future will be based on a far broader base," Dr. Philip R. Lee said. "Changes in life-style, for example, can make truly fantastic improvements in the nation's health." Dr. Lee, Professor of Social Medicine at the University of California School of Medicine and one of the nation's most distinguished health-care experts, suggested a thought experiment to dramatize the possible effects of social and personal transformation. "If all abuse of tobacco, alcohol, and automobiles could be magically erased with the snap of a finger," he said, "at least half of all hospital beds in this country would suddenly be empty."

The New Medicine concerns itself not just with the abuse of tobacco, alcohol, and cars, but with all the tragic and ingenious ways we have learned to abuse the gift of life.

4. *Healing of many chronic diseases, which are only ameliorated by the Old Medicine, may be possible after all.* We rarely stop to consider how many of our common ills are beyond the power of our present medicine to heal. Potentially dangerous drugs are often used just to mask symptoms and provide temporary relief. Television commercials offer us aspirin and stomach remedies and backache salves, but don't promise that the headache or indigestion or backache won't be back tomorrow or next month or next year. In the same way, certain prescription remedies may arrest or slow the course of arthritis, diabetes, emphysema, and the like, but lack the power to improve the situation. New Medicine practitioners believe, to a greater or lesser degree, that long-term healing may take place in the case of some otherwise hopeless chronic ailments, without the use of powerful drugs.

Dr. William Gray, a Mill Valley, California, physician who turned to the practice of homeopathic medicine "because I like results," relates a number of startling cures from his own practice. Homeopathy is based on the ancient principle that *like cures like*. The practice consists of giving tiny, drastically diluted doses of the substance that would, if taken full strength, cause the precise symptoms of the sickness in question. Dr. Gray tells of one thirteen-year-old girl who was severely crippled by juvenile rheumatoid arthritis. For ten years she had been taking heavy doses of cortisone along with up to 30 or 40 aspirins a day. She was entirely bedridden until a warm waterbed made it possible for her to get up about two hours a day. Six different medical specialists had given up on her case when she came to Dr. Gray. He interviewed her for 45 minutes to learn her symptoms and personality, then gave her a single dose of homeopathic medicine. As expected, her joints felt worse for a week. After that, the pain started disappearing from the top down. When she visited Dr. Gray a month after the treatment, there was only moderate pain in the knees and ankles. The pain was totally gone a month later. Now, after eight months, she goes to school, engages in after-school activities, and leads a normal life.

"Homeopathy is purely empirical," Dr. Gray said. "I have no idea how it works. But it does work."

All healing practiced by the New Medicine may be seen, ideally, as self-healing.

5. *Illness is not necessarily bad.* According to New Medicine practitioners, every outbreak of illness is an expression of some imbalance in your life. Thus, it provides important information that can be used for creative growth. Rather than attacking every disease with all the force that can be mustered, the New Medicine practitioner is prepared, in noncritical cases, to let the malady run its course, allowing the body, mind, and spirit (the three aren't seen as separate) to achieve balance, perhaps at a higher level than before the illness.

6. *Responsibility for your health lies not with your physician, but with yourself.* The New Medicine holds that you are not a mere physical object, vulnerable to random attacks by germs and viruses and other mysterious agents of disease. You are a capable, self-aware being with considerable command of all your interactions in this world. Doctors and medical technicians may assist you in your quest for good health, but *the buck stops with you.*

This simple, radical shift of responsibility, and power, underlies every aspect of the New Medicine. It also points the way toward a solution to the current crisis in the Old Medicine.

To find out what the New Medicine looks like from the inside, I visited the Wellness Resource Center of Mill Valley, California, as a "client." (There are no "patients" in the New Medicine.) The director of the center, John Travis, is a young (33), lanky (six-foot-five, 165-pound) physician with solid credentials (M.D. at Tufts, residency in preventive medicine and a Master's in public health at Johns Hopkins). An exceptionally sober and gentle man despite a rather flamboyant red beard, Travis took a gamble in opening his center, sharing in the considerable costs of remodeling a gracious old Mill Valley house for his office space. The effect is lovely; liquid green light from surrounding redwoods filters into the offices to blend with the soothing ambience of redwood beams, hanging plants, and thick carpeting. I dropped by the first time just to pick up a descriptive folder, a battery of questionnaires, and a Client-Staff

Agreement that wastes no time in blowing the old medical game out of the water. For its part, the staff agrees to provide information on achieving wellness, recommendations for life-style changes, and energy and support in making the changes. The client's agreement is reprinted here in full:

I, as a client:

1. acknowledge full responsibility for myself. I realize that my health state (me) is a manifestation of my habits, actions, and behavior.

2. am aware of the futility in blaming others for my experiences in life.

3. am aware that as a result of my growth, I may decide to change friends, job, spouse, or life-style.

4. am willing to enter into open, trusting communication and will use any feedback to benefit my growth.

5. will meet my financial obligations promptly and understand that a charge will be made for all time reserved unless cancelled 24 hours in advance.

Signed _____

Two of the questionnaires were to be completed and turned in at least a week before my appointment with Dr. Travis, since they would go to a computer center for analysis. The Health Hazard Appraisal asks questions related to the ten most common statistical causes of death, questions about smoking, drinking, driving, mental depression, medication, and such obvious symptoms as rectal bleeding. The Nutritional Evaluation Profile requires a detailed description of your diet. I turned in these two, then settled down at my leisure to fill out the remaining forms, a process that was to take almost two hours. They were: Medical History (including the health of all close relatives), a survey of Recent Health Problems, an Eating Habits Survey ("Do you hide or sneak food?"), a Life Change Index, Life Goals Index, and, finally, Travis's own Wellness Inventory.

I worked slowly, pausing to consider the implications of the questions. Frequently, I realized I was being invited to get my life together, to take charge of my own health. This was especially true on the last three questionnaires.

The Life Change Index is based on the pioneering work of Dr. Thomas Holmes, who has studied the case histories of over 5,000 people to show that *any* significant change in life increases your chances of getting sick. The scale ranges from "Death of Spouse" (100 points) down to "Minor Violation of the Law" (11 points). Even change for the better is stressful. Thus, "Trouble with Boss" rates at only 23 points, while "Outstanding Personal Achievement" costs you 28 points. "Personal Injury or Illness" rates at 53 points, just slightly above "Marriage," at 50. Even "Vacation" and "Christmas" show up on the index, at 13 and twelve points respectively. It isn't that change has to be avoided, only that the stress accompanying it should be acknowledged and dealt with. Then, too, a person who, say, has just divorced (73 points) and noticed a change in sleeping habits (16 points), might think twice before remarrying (50 points) and making a business readjustment (39 points).

The Life Goals Index examines questions of goals, personal freedom, and the meaning of life and death. At the end, you are asked to "Write a paragraph describing in detail your aims, ambitions, goals in life. How much progress are you making in achieving them?"

Aims, ambitions, and goals as an aspect of good health? The New Medicine says, "yes."

The Wellness Inventory, John Travis's own creation, takes the boldest leap yet past the boundaries of the Old Medicine. There are 100 questions in all, ranging from "Productivity, Relaxation, Sleep" to "Community Involvement" and "Creativity, Self-Expression."

On the day of my office visit, I turned in the questionnaires with a somewhat satisfied feeling. (I could answer "yes" to each of the questions and most of the others.) After all, I had been at least peripherally involved in the New Medicine movement all along, through my practice and teaching of aikido and energy awareness.

While Travis studied my answers, I was ushered into a small, quiet room with a reclining chair by a young woman named Lynda Berkley. She attached electrodes to my forehead (to measure electrical impulses of muscle tension) and a sensitive themister to my left index finger (to measure the temperature of one of my extremities). She told me to relax, and I watched the temperature needle on a biofeedback machine climb steadily, from 82 degrees to 93, indicating that the blood vessels in my hands were dilating. This is a particularly good measure of overall bodily relaxation.

With the muscle tension in my forehead, it was a different matter. The biofeedback machine gave off a rapid clicking sound, like a Geiger counter—the more clicks, the more tension—and there was also a needle moving back and forth on a scale of from one to seven microvolts. Two on the scale might have been a fairly relaxed reading. Mine was hovering between six and seven, and the machine was giving off the sound of an angry hornet. I tried to bring it down, at which the hornet buzzed even more angrily. Then I tried to stop trying, and that didn't work either. After about ten minutes of exasperation, I had to give up—at which the needle dropped to three. The lesson was clear enough, but I couldn't seem to get it at the time.

Released from the electrodes, I accompanied John Travis into his office, where we began going over the forms. Travis showed me a computer print-out of my Health Hazard Appraisal. With my actual age

A WELLNESS INVENTORY

INSTRUCTIONS: Please put a mark in the box before each statement which is true *for you.*

WHAT IS WELLNESS AND WELL MEDICINE: The ideas of measuring wellness and helping people attain high levels of wellness are relatively new. Most of us think in terms of illness and assume that the absence of illness indicates wellness. This is not true . . . .

Many people lack physical symptoms, but are bored, depressed, tense, anxious, or generally unhappy with their lives. These emotional states often lead to physical disease through the lowering of the body's resistance. The same feelings can also lead to abuse of the body through smoking, drinking, and overeating. These behaviors are usually sub-stitutes for other more basic human needs such as recognition from others, a stimulating environment, caring and affection from friends.

Wellness is not a static state. It results when a person begins to see himself as a growing, changing person. High level wellness means taking good care of your physical self, using your mind constructively, express-ing your emotions effectively, being creatively involved with those around you, being concerned about your physical and psychological environment.

SCORING: Every box checked is a point toward "wellness."

It should be understood that this is only a sampling of three out of ten sections from the complete questionnaire used by the Wellness Resource Center of Mill Valley, California. Dr. John Travis of the Center deempha-sizes the idea of scoring per se, and uses the questionnaire together with other tools for diagnosis.

As a guide, however, consider that a score of 19 for this sample is average.

PRODUCTIVITY, RELAXATION, SLEEP

☐ I usually enjoy my work.

☐ I seldom feel tired and run-down (except after strenuous work).

☐ I fall asleep easily at bedtime.

☐ I usually get a full night's sleep.

☐ If awakened, it is usually easy for me to go to sleep again.

☐ I rarely bite or pick at my nails.

☐ Rather than worrying, I can tem-porarily shelve my problems and enjoy myself at times when I can do nothing about solving them immediately.

☐ I feel financially secure.

☐ I am content with my sexual life.

☐ I meditate or center myself for fifteen to twenty minutes at least once a day.

ENVIRONMENTAL AWARENESS

☐ I use public transportation or car pools when possible.

☐ I turn off unneeded lights or appliances.

☐ I recycle paper, cans, glass, clothing, books, and organic waste. (Mark true if you do at least three of these.)

☐ I set my thermostat at 68 degrees or lower in winter.

☐ I use air-conditioning only when necessary, and keep the thermostat at 76 degrees or higher.

☐ I am conscientious about wasted energy and materials both at home and at work.

☐ I use low-phosphate detergent.

☐ My car gets at least eighteen miles per gallon. (If you don't own a car, check this statement as true.)

☐ I have storm windows and adequate insulation in attic and walls. (If you don't own your home or live in a mild climate, check this statement as true.)

☐ I have a humidifier for use in winter. (If you require little winter heat, check this statement as true.)

EMOTIONAL MATURITY AND EXPRESSION OF FEELINGS

☐ I am frequently happy.

☐ I think it is okay to feel angry, afraid, joyful, or sad.

☐ I do not deny my anger, fear, joy, or sadness, but instead find constructive ways to express these feelings most of the time.

☐ I am able to say "no" to people without feeling guilty.

☐ It is easy for me to laugh.

☐ I like getting compliments and recognition from other people.

☐ I feel okay about crying, and allow myself to do so.

☐ I listen to and think about constructive criticism rather than react defensively.

☐ I would seek help from friends or professional counselors if needed.

☐ It is easy for me to give other people sincere compliments and recognition.

---

being 52, the computerized form gave my "Appraisal Age" as 48 and my "Attainable Age" as 45. My risk of death, compared with the average person of my age, race, and sex, was listed as .7. On three of the ten most important causes of death—cirrhosis, motor vehicle accident, and pneumonia—I showed up somewhat above average. The computer has decided this from one of my answers: On the question about alcoholic beverages, I had checked the box marked "7 to 24 drinks a week." I complained that the computer must have overreacted to an occasional beer, especially in light of Dr. Breslow's finding that moderate drinkers live longer than either heavy drinkers or nondrinkers.

"It's strictly statistical, based on medical records of deaths," Travis told me. "The appraisal is a nice link between the Old Medicine and the New. It's not as significant for you as for high-risk people. For them, it can be very dramatic."

He showed me the print-out for a 60-pounds overweight smoker who took no exercise. His actual age was 51, his Appraisal Age 60, and his Attainable Age—if he were to change his habits for the better—was 52. His risk was 2.1 times average.

"A person in this category," Travis said, "gets a clear picture of the relationship between his behavior and his health."

As John Travis and I went over the remainder of the questionnaires, a pattern began to emerge. In many ways, my health pattern seemed ideal. I got plenty of exercise (maybe *too* much, if there's any such thing), ate comparatively well, didn't smoke, drank very moderately, and (when I wasn't traveling) lived a rather well-balanced life. But my answers revealed a certain disproportion in energy given and received. Travis pointed out that my energy expenditure was high, and that I seemed unable or unwilling to ask for assistance and support from others. This going-it-alone syndrome was probably reflected in my increased muscle tension.

Thus, his "prescription" recommended that I "develop a support structure—people you can get support from when your reserves are low, a kind of credit union." Travis also recommended that I take five biofeedback sessions devoted to reducing muscle tension.

I asked for clarification on a few points in the questionnaires. For example, what does voting regularly have to do with good health?

"Well, you might say voting is a gross measure of how you relate to your environment. Disease is a function of life-style, and if you're cut off from the social system—withdrawn into yourself—you're likely to be less healthy. You can't be a well person contributing to a sick environment. Eventually, it will make you sick directly."

In addition to biofeedback training, Travis offers Life-Style Evolution Groups, which use techniques from transactional analysis, Gestalt, and body awareness to integrate the biofeedback with clients' own needs, and help them take control of their own lives. He also refers them to the rich and diverse resources that are available in books and other publications, and in the New Medicine subculture throughout Northern California.

With his lovely quarters, expensive biofeedback equipment, and computer analyses, Travis seems rather expensive ($75 for the complete

Wellness Evaluation, $25 an hour for biofeedback sessions), but is really quite cheap compared with the price of actual time spent with conventional doctors. He has more than enough clients, most of them well-to-do suburbanites, to keep him and his staff quite busy.

Hundreds of New Medicine groups and practitioners, however, offer their services for lesser costs, ranging all the way down to barter. For example, the Wholistic Health and Nutrition Institute (WHN), also located in Mill Valley, gives a wellness evaluation similar to Travis's for $48. In addition, WHN provides an umbrella for consultations and classes in an almost unimaginable variety of New Medicine techniques. To list only a few: Self-Healing with Visualization, Herbal Studies, Physical Fitness and Consciousness Training, Applied Meditation, Iridology (reading the eyes for knowledge of internal body conditions), Auto-Hypnosis, Reflexology, Massage and Centering, and the Psychic Process of Healing.

"These techniques or systems are optional and experimental," Dr. Rich Shames said. Shames keeps a foot in both medicines, serving half-time as director of WHN and half-time as county clinic physician for Marin County. "If people should begin to think that any technique alone can solve their problems from the outside, then we're back in the Old Medicine again. That would be like doing yoga postures to cure a backache rather than creating a yoga of life. What we really want to do is help people become so strong that illness will be taken care of before it manifests."

Though Shames, like Travis, is a medical doctor (which is by no means a prerequisite for the New Medicine), his holistic health practice stands entirely outside the traditional medical establishment. Only a few efforts have been made to reform from within. The Institute for the Study of Humanistic Medicine, a spin-off from Esalen Institute, introduces doctors and other medical personnel to some of the practices of the New Medicine, carries on research in the field, and runs a publishing program. By moving cautiously and keeping a low profile, the Institute has gained considerable inside respectability.

The precise role of traditional medicine in the emerging field is yet to be defined. In the words of Dr. Leonard Duhl of the Health and Medical Sciences Program at Berkeley: "Doctors haven't been trained for health, but somehow have been held responsible for it. That's not right. Health is the responsibility of the society. Doctors should be connected to holistic health, but shouldn't control it."

"I'd hate to see the holistic health field entirely taken over by the medical profession," added Jerry Green, an attorney who specializes in medical malpractice. "Health is the job of the whole culture and the specific responsibility of the individual. To solve the malpractice problem

TAKING THE NEW MEDICINE:
A SAMPLER

To name the hundreds of individual New Medicine practitioners in California would be impossible. What follows is a sampling (not a definitive list) of centers that bring together the various elements of the field.

Wellness Resource Center, 42 Miller Avenue, Mill Valley, California 94941 (415 383-3806). *Wellness evaluation, individual consultation, biofeedback, life-style evolution groups.*

Wholistic Health and Nutrition Institute, 150 Shoreline Highway, Mill Valley, California 94941 (415 332-2933). *Wellness evaluation, consultation, and classes in a wide variety of New Medicine techniques and practices.*

Devta, 122 Ward Street, Larkspur, California 94939 (415 924-0406). *Concentrates on massage, meditation, and body work.*

Lomi School, 2250 Bush Street, San Francisco, California 94115 (415 931-5924). *Nutrition, body work, energy healing, Gestalt groups.*

Wholistic Childbirth Institute, 1627 10th Avenue, San Francisco, California 94122 (413 664-1119). *Offers several alternative ways of assisting in "healthy" childbirths.*

Esalen Institute, 1793 Union Street, San Francisco, California 94123 (415 771-1710), and Big Sur, California 93920 (408 667-2335). *Though not devoted specifically to the New Medicine, the original growth center sponsors numerous workshops.*

Optimal Health Associates, 2035 9th Street, Los Osos, California 93402 (805 528-2148). *Workshops and classes in many self-help techniques, biofeedback, massage.*

Center for the Healing Arts, 11081 Missouri Avenue, Los Angeles, California 90025 (213 477-3981). *Workshops and classes in theory and practice of holistic health with emphasis on professional participation.*

Meadowlark, 26126 Fairview Avenue, Hemet, California 92343 (714 927-1113). *A retreat center with two-week minimum residence. Health evaluation, homeopathy, nutrition, psychosynthesis, and transpersonal groups.*

San Andreas Health Council,
531 Cowper Street, Palo Alto,
California 94301 (415 324-9350).
Classes, workshops, and consultation in a wide variety of practices; biofeedback, weekly lecture demonstrations, senior citizens' groups.

Association for Wholistic Health,
Box 23231, San Diego, California
92123.
Working with universities to create a functional model in the New Medicine, including certificate program in holistic health at University of California, San Diego, Medical School. Will open pilot clinic in Santa Monica this month, followed by San Diego and San Francisco—stressing evaluation, prevention, and personal responsibility. **—G.L.**

and relieve the overall crisis, the Old Medicine should stop taking responsibility for people's health and start doing just what it's good at— the treatment of trauma and pathology. As it is now, doctors spend a tremendous amount of time taking unwarranted responsibility and practicing defensive medicine—giving unnecessary tests, doing unnecessary procedures, using unnecessary technology, and calling in unnecessary specialists—just to defend themselves in case of lawsuits. All this makes medicine more and more impersonal, technical, and expensive. Which causes more resentment. Which causes more defensive practice. And so on. Break this circle, and doctors themselves will be healthier and happier."

But can the circle be broken? Organized medicine has proven itself particularly resistant to basic reform. And it is powerful: The so-called "health-care" industry represents 8 percent of our total GNP, and it is not simply going to disappear. John Travis and other "well" doctors tell their clients that, in case of sickness, they should go to conventional physicians. Ideally, these doctors, too, would be aware they are treating persons, not mere patients. Here, the old-fashioned family doctor serves as a model: More and more medical students these days are turning toward general family practice.

In any case, the current situation—the crisis in the Old Medicine, the emergence of a New—bears watching simply because it provides such a clear, extreme example of the larger social challenge. If purely technological, impersonal, specialized, manipulative solutions will no longer work, what will? The answer may well lie in a new understanding of the wholeness of life, the ultimate power of personal responsibility.

The New Medicine will draw its share of charlatans. Trivial, faddist practices will masquerade under the name "holistic." But the energy behind this movement comes from a need—perhaps a historical necessity—that will outlast any fad. It is simply that we have given too much of our time and money to sickness. At best, the New Medicine turns us toward something we may have almost forgotten: the tingling feeling of being totally alive and aware and at home in the world.

THE LIFE EVENTS INVENTORY: A MEASURE OF THE RELATIVE SEVERITY OF PSYCHO-SOCIAL STRESSORS

Raymond Cochrane and Alex Robertson

Holmes and Rahe [1] describe an instrument—the Schedule of Recent Experiences (S.R.E.)—which has been widely used for measuring life stresses retrospectively. It consists of a check list of events with spaces for subjects or patients to indicate which, if any, of the events have happened to them in a stated period of time—usually the past year. Each event is assigned a weighting which is supposed to reflect the degree of disruption that would be caused should that event befall an average

---

Notes:

(1) Many of the items on the S.R.E. were not completely appropriate to a general measure of recent life stresses. Some were trivial (e.g., *Christmas*). Others were only relevant to a small number of people (e.g., *Major business readjustment*—merger, reorganization, bankruptcy, etc.). Still others were ambiguous (e.g., *Major change in financial state*—a lot worse off or a lot better off than usual). With items of this latter type, it appeared more reasonable to distinguish between a deterioration and an improvement in the condition in question.

(2) The S.R.E. was not at all comprehensive or consistent in the items included. The original events were said to have been "empirically derived from clinical experience," (Ref. [1], p. 213). It was felt this list could be supplemented by other items obtained from a systematic inquiry into the kind of stressful events that befall people, to produce a more comprehensive measure of recent life stresses.

(3) No published weights derived from groups on which the instrument was most often used were available. Although, as already mentioned, agreement was obtained between the weights assigned by various samples of convenience, weights were not available from patients or from other groups most likely to have extensive experience of the amount of stress the events cause.

person. These weights are expressed in "life change units" (L.C.U.'s); an individual's score on the S.R.E. being the sum of the L.C.U.'s of the events he reports having experienced.

The original weights were obtained in a somewhat arbitrary fashion. Originally, samples of convenience were asked to act as judges and to assign a number between 1 and 100 to each event on the S.R.E. to indicate the amount of "turmoil, upheaval and social readjustment" that would be occasioned by its occurrence. One of the items, usually *Marriage* was assigned an arbitrary weight of 50; the intention being that this would establish an anchoring point at the middle of the scale that would act as a common frame of reference for all judges. When judged by the criterion of interjudge agreement this procedure has been quite successful. Even when groups that vary on age, ethnicity and cultural backgrounds are used as judges, good agreement about the weights to be assigned to each event is obtained [2-7].

The instrument has been shown to be reasonably reliable [5] and has been extensively used in studies of the antecedents of illness [6-12]. To some extent this wide use may be more indicative of the lack of a suitable alternative measure of recent life stresses, than of the inherent quality of the S.R.E. The work reported here was undertaken to remedy what were seen as three important deficiencies that reduced the usefulness of the S.R.E. as a research tool.

METHOD

Stage 1

After an initial process of editing and revising, a modified version of the S.R.E. was administered to 125 psychiatric patients in Edinburgh. Eighty-five of these patients were admitted to hospital following an unsuccessful suicide attempt, the remaining 60 being consecutive admissions to five wards of a general mental hospital. Schizophrenic, depressive, neurotic, alcoholic and personality disordered groups were represented in the sample. Following the administration of the questionnaire, patients were asked if any other events had happened to them in the previous year. They were encouraged to report as many events as possible, and were asked to give sufficient detail so that the events could later be considered for inclusion on a revised schedule. A total of 59 new events which had happened to one or more patients was collected in this way. Many events were not relevant either because they may have been symptomatic (e.g. loneliness, depressed) or because they were very rare occurrences (e.g. raped by father). It was possible, however, to incorporate many of the events in the new schedule by adding items which covered the specific event in a more general way; for example a specific incident—extra-marital affair discovered by lover's wife—was subsumed under the general item: *Problems related to sexual affair.*

Stage 2

Weights for items on the revised schedule were derived from three sources. A group of university students to correspond with Holmes' "sample of convenience"; a group of psychiatrists and psychologists; and a group of patients. The psychiatrists and clinical psychologists were obtained from several sources including personal contacts and published lists. Most were sent a questionnaire by mail and were asked to return it in the same way. One hundred were approached in this way and a total of 60 usable replies was received. Patients were obtained from the sources described earlier, there being a small overlap between the two groups. As the task of assigning relative weightings to a large number of items proved quite complex, about 30 per cent of patients interviewed were unable to complete the questionnaire. For all three groups instructions were identical:

> Would you please rate the amount of "turmoil, upheaval and social readjustment" that would follow each of the events listed below. Rate each item on a 1-100 scale with 100 standing for maximum disruption. The item *marriage* is assigned an arbitrary score of 50, so please rate the others on a comparative base with this. Thank you.

Following these two procedures a second process of editing and revising was undertaken. This led to some events being deleted and others having wording changed to make them more explicit. A new instrument emerged—The Life Events Inventory (L.E.I.)—which, it is hoped, is a comprehensive measure of recent life stresses equally suitable for use with all sections of the population. Weights for items added at this stage were obtained from a second sample of students ($N=60$). This procedure was assumed to be valid because of the high inter-group agreement on weightings which are described below.

RESULTS

Table 1 contains the items on the Life Events Inventory together with the mean weightings obtained from three groups, and the overall mean taken from the three groups combined. Items in Section 1 are relevant to all subjects; those in Section 2 to "ever-marrieds"; married, separated, divorced or widowed; those in Section 3 to the "never-marrieds."

Table 1. Weights Obtained from Several Groups
for Items on the Life Events Inventory

	Psychiatrists $N=60$	Patients $N=42$	Students $N=75$	Total $N=177$
Section 1. All				
1. Unemployment (of head of household)	67	73	66	68
2. Trouble with superiors at work*	35	48	39	40
3. New job in same line of work	23	39	29	31
4. New job in new line of work	40	47	50	46
5. Change in hours or conditions in present job	20	40	28	31
6. Promotion or change of responsibilities at work*	32	43	40	39
7. Retirement*	62	45	52	54
8. Moving house	36	46	41	42
9. Purchasing own house (taking out mortgage)	26	58	40	40
10. New neighbours	18	23	16	18
11. Quarrel with neighbours	25	32	23	26
12. Income increased substantially (25%)	25	39	35	35
13. Income decreased substantially (25%)	61	65	60	62
14. Getting into debt beyond means of repayment	58	74	67	66
15. Going on holiday*	14	35	27	29
16. Conviction for minor violation (e.g. speeding or drunkenness)*	23	37	20	34
17. Jail sentence*	81	72	72	75
18. Involvement in fight	30	47	31	38
19. Immediate family member starts drinking heavily	63	70	63	65
20. Immediate family member attempts suicide	62	73	66	66
21. Immediate family member sent to prison	66	62	56	61
22. Death of immediate family member*	68	73	67	69
23. Death of close friend*	46	69	54	55
24. Immediate family member seriously ill	56	71	55	59
25. Gain of new family member (immediate)*	37	50	42	43
26. (Problems related to alcohol or drugs)				59

*Item derived from Schedule of Recent Experiences.

Items in parentheses or brackets were added after the main study. Weights obtained from a second group of students ($N=60$).

Table 1 (cont.)

Section 1. All (cont.)	Psychiatrists N=60	Patients N=42	Students N=75	Total N=177
27. Serious restriction of social life	40	60	45	49
28. [Period of homelessness (hostel or sleeping rough)]				51
29. Serious physical illness or injury requiring hospital treatment	71	59	63	65
30. (Prolonged ill health requiring treatment by own doctor)				48
31. Sudden and serious impairment of vision or hearing	63	56	58	59
32. (Unwanted pregnancy)				70
33. (Miscarriage)				65
34. (Abortion)				63
35. Sex difficulties*	52	62	58	57
Section 2. Ever-Married Only				
36. Marriage*	50	50	50	50
37. Pregnancy (or of wife)*	43	50	49	49
38. Increase in number of arguments with spouse	44	67	52	55
39. [Increase in number of arguments with other immediate family members (e.g. children)]				43
40. Trouble with other relatives (e.g. in-laws)	35	45	28	38
41. Son or daughter left home*	44	59	46	44
42. (Children in care of others)				54
43. (Trouble or behaviour problems in own children)				49
44. Death of spouse*	89	82	83	86
45. Divorce*	78	73	70	75
46. Marital separation*	72	73	65	70
47. Extra-marital sexual affair	54	66	56	61
48. (Breakup of affair)				47
49. Infidelity of spouse	62	67	70	68
50. Marital reconciliation*	44	60	53	53
51. Wife begins or stops work*	25	42	31	34
Section 3. Never-Married Only				
52. (Breakup with steady boy or girl friend)				51
53. (Problems related to sexual relationship)				54
54. [Increase in number of family arguments (e.g. with parents)]				43
55. (Breakup of family)				77

Eighteen of the fifty-five items are taken over from the S.R.E. These are marked with an asterisk in Table 1.

Spearman rank correlation coefficients were calculated between the rank-order of the mean weightings assigned by the three groups. As in previous studies, good agreement was found even between quite disparate groups of judges. The coefficients are: patients and psychiatrists 0-82; patients and students 0-74; and psychiatrists and students 0-94. The coefficient of concordance for all three groups is 0-89. All four coefficients are significant beyond the $p<0.001$ level.

DISCUSSION

What began as an attempt to improve an existing measure culminated in the production of a new instrument. The Life Events Inventory can be used both as a supplement to the clinical interview and a standardized measure of the amount of stress that has been present in a person's immediate environment in the preceding year. It is important to note that the L.E.I. is intended as a stimulus measure. The response that any individual makes to the events is determined by other factors which require to be measured separately. The quantification of events on the L.E.I. is intended to indicate the amount of stress that would be caused *on average* by their occurrence.

The high level of agreement obtained between three groups of judges when assigning weights to items on the L.E.I. is indicative of the reliability of estimates of the relative severity of the events. No significance is attached to the absolute weight given to each event. In fact, the three groups pitched their weights at somewhat different levels. Patients tended to assign generally higher weights across all items (mean = 55·65) than did psychiatrists (46·21) or students (47·86). The relative position of the items remained quite constant across the three groups.

Two further points should be made about the L.E.I. Inspection of Table 1 shows that not all the events will necessarily be accompanied by negative affect. Items such as *Marriage* and *Going on Holiday* are, presumably, pleasant events. Others such as *Moving House, New Job in New Line of Work* and *Pregnancy* may be either pleasant or unpleasant, or even neutral events. The L.E.I. is designed to quantify the amount of "turmoil, disturbance and upheaval" that people are subject to, rather than just unpleasant experiences. The degree and direction of the affect associated with the events is a property of the individual's response rather than the stimulus itself. A response measure, such as the Affect Balance Scale [13,14] might well be used in conjunction with the L.E.I. to provide a more complete picture of the degree of stress subjectively experienced.

The events on the L.E.I. also vary along another dimension; the degree to which they are under the control of the subject himself. Some of the events are clearly brought about, at least in part, by the subject— *Marriage, Abortion, Moving House* for example. Others are clearly outside his control—for example, *Death of Spouse, New Neighbours.* A large group of events remain where it is impossible to decide upon a definite locus of responsibility—*Unemployment* and *Divorce* for example. Certain of the events which are under the control of the subject may, sometimes, be symptomatic or indicate responses to stress. In certain conditions it may be preferable to score these events separately. This would seem to apply to items 26-35 in particular. It was felt, however, that although events such as *Sex difficulties* and *Problems related to alcohol or drugs* may have originated as responses to stress, they acquire stress producing properties in their own right and may correctly be regarded as stimulus events which require a further response.

Finally, as somewhat different versions of the L.E.I. are used with married and unmarried subjects, the maximum score obtainable by these two categories of subjects differs. A number of items on the Inventory refer to family and marital problems which are irrelevant to the unmarried. As there is no reason to suppose that married individuals are subjected to more stress than their unmarried counterparts this could produce some biassing of results. It is therefore important to match for this characteristic when comparing groups using the L.E.I.

SUMMARY

The development of a measure of recent life experiences is reported. The Life Events Inventory has three distinct advantages over the Schedule of Recent Experiences: it is more comprehensive; more consistent in the kind of events included, and has weights derived from groups most likely to have experience of the events involved. Weights for the items on the L.E.I. were derived from psychiatrists and psychologists ($N = 60$), psychiatric patients ($N = 42$) and students ($N = 75$). Close agreement was found between the relative weights assigned by all three groups.

REFERENCES

1. Holmes T. H. and Rahe R. H. The social readjustment rating scale. *J. Psychosom. Res.* 11, 213 (1967).
2. Komaroff A. L., Masuda M. and Holmes T. H. The social readjustment rating scale: a comparative study of Negro, Mexican and white Americans. *J. Psychosom. Res. 12,* 121 (1968).

3. Rahe R. H. Multi-cultural correlations of life change scaling: America, Japan, Denmark and Sweden. *J. Psychosom. Res. 13*, 191 (1969).

4. Ruch L. O. and Holmes T. A. Scaling of life change: comparison of direct and indirect methods. *J. Psychosom. Res. 15*, 221 (1971).

5. Casey R. L., Masuda M. and Holmes T. H. Quantitative study of recall of life events. *J. Psychosom. Res. 11*, 239 (1967).

6. Rubin R. T., Gunderson E. K. E. and Arthur R. J. Life stress and illness patterns in the U.S. Navy—V. Prior life change and illness onset in a battleship crew. *J. Psychosom. Res. 15*, 89 (1971).

7. Thurlow H. J. Illness in relation to life situation and sick-role tendency. *J. Psychosom. Res. 15*, 73 (1971).

8. Thomson K. C. and Hendrie H. C. Environmental stress in primary depressive illness. *Archs. Gen. Psychiat. 26*, 130 (1972).

9. Rahe R. H., Meyer M., Smith M., Kjaer G. and Holmes T. H. Social stress and illness onset. *J. Psychosom. Res. 8*, 35 (1964).

10. Hendrie H. C., Parkaskevas F. D., Baragar F. D. and Adamson J. D. Stress, immunoglobulin levels and early polyorthritis, *J. Psychosom. Res. 15*, 19 (1971).

11. Rahe R. H. and Lind E. Psychosocial factors and sudden cardiac death: a pilot study. *J. Psychosom. Res. 15*, (1971).

12. Theorell T. and Rahe R. H. Psychosocial factors and myocardial infarction—I. An inpatient study in Sweden. *J. Psychosom. Res. 15*, 25 (1971).

13. Bradburn N. M. *In Pursuit of Happiness*, National Opinion Research Centre, Chicago (1963).

14. Phillips D. L. Social class and psychological disturbance: the influence of positive and negative experiences. *Social Psychiatry 3*, 41 (1968).

ORGANIZATIONAL STRESS AND INDIVIDUAL STRAIN

John R. P. French, Jr.
Robert D. Caplan

The large, bureaucratic organization, like other settings, exerts its own set of unique forces on the individual. Through the application of these forces, the organization is able to channel the individual's behavior toward certain goals and to direct his interactions toward certain people and away from others. This conformity to organizational norms is, of course, purchased at a price most often thought of in terms of salary or wages. But there are often other prices which the organization incurs for insisting that its members adhere in certain ways to certain goals—costs which are rarely, if ever, tallied in the quarterly reports of modern organizations; they are costs in the form of job-related pathologies of the people who make the organization run. These pathologies can manifest themselves in forms ranging anywhere from passive apathy, job dissatisfaction, and depression to violent acts directed against the organization. In some cases, the individual may even suffer a disabling ulcer or heart attack which forces him to withdraw from an active life in the organization before his full value as a human asset (Brummet, Pyle, & Flamholtz, 1968) has been realized. Thus, both mental and physical health may be affected by the continual pressures of the job over a period of years.

Although there are many clinical observations on the effects of job stress on mental and physical health, there has been very little systematic quantitative research. Accordingly, in 1957 the Institute for Social Research at the University of Michigan organized a program of research on the effects of the social environment, especially the effects of large organizations, on individual strain (including job dissatisfaction and tension, poor adjustment, physiological disturbances such as high blood pressure or elevated cholesterol, and diseases which are related to stress).

It is the purpose of this chapter to present some of the findings from this program of research, with particular emphasis on organizational stresses which produce psychological and physiological strains leading to coronary heart disease. We focus on this disease because it is so important in terms of death rates, disease rates, and costs. All forms of heart disease (including strokes) accounted for more than half of all deaths in the United States in 1963; about a quarter of the persons in the population between the ages of 18 and 79 had definite or suspected heart disease; and the costs (the sum of direct costs for medical care plus losses of output by members of the labor force due to heart disease) amounted to $22.4 billion, or 4 percent of the GNP in 1963 (The President's Commission on Heart Disease, Cancer and Stroke, 1964). By far the largest part of this burden of total heart disease is attributable to coronary heart disease, a disease which is more common in men than in women and has an especially high incidence in the age range of most business managers.

Our focus on coronary heart disease does not imply that there is a large body of dependable medical knowledge on the effects of organizational stress on this disease; on the contrary, we wish to warn the reader that many of our findings are new and have not yet been confirmed by other researchers. They deserve further research, but they also deserve attention from management.

Before describing our results, we will present an outline of the theory and research strategy which guided the studies and which can serve as a summary of the main findings. This outline, presented in Figure 1, can serve as a map to guide the reader through a complex set of findings. Then we will present our research grouped according to the following organizational stresses: role ambiguity, role conflict, role overload, organizational boundaries, responsibility for people, relations with others, participation, and occupational differences in stress, strain, and heart disease. Finally, we will speculate a bit about what management might do to reduce heart disease where organizational stress is a contributory cause.

Our theory, as presented in Figure 1, starts with occupations or roles as loci of stress in organizations. Public health statistics in England and in the United States show that there are large differences among occupations in rates of coronary heart disease. Studies by Russek (1960, 1962, 1965) reveal that different specialties within a profession have different rates of heart disease; for example, the general practitioner has higher rates than the dermatologist or radiologist. Similar differences are found for lawyers, dentists, and other occupations. However, these data do not

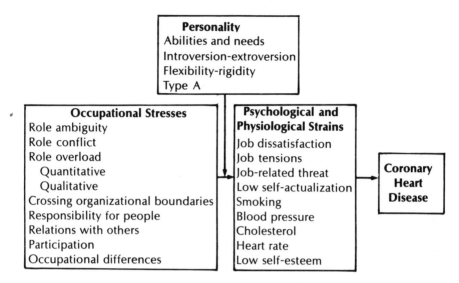

Figure 1. An outline of a theory about how organizational stresses affect individual strains contributing to coronary heart disease. The horizontal arrows show the effects of environmental stresses on individual strain which in turn affects heart disease. The vertical arrow shows the conditioning effects of personality variables.

tell us *why* one occupation has more disease than another. We have attempted to discover some of the specific variables which might account for such occupational differences. The occupational stresses listed in the first box of Figure 1 are the major ones which we have found to be related to individual strain.[1]

The first horizontal arrow represents our central set of hypotheses concerning the effects of each of the job stresses on one or more of the measures of psychological and physiological strain. These strains, in turn, are hypothesized to be risk factors (contributory causes) in heart disease, as indicated by the second horizontal arrow. Some of these—for example,

---

[1]Both the occupations and the specific job stresses associated with them are descriptions of the person's social environment. In our program of research, we have generally distinguished between the *objective* social environment and the *subjective* social environment, as it is perceived by the person. Where perception is veridical, the two environments coincide and the distinction may be disregarded. We have chosen to omit the distinction generally in this chapter in order to simplify a complex set of findings.

smoking, blood pressure, and cholesterol—are generally accepted as risk factors. Heart rate is strongly implicated by two recent studies (Hinkle et al., 1970; Stamler et al., 1969). Our own research suggests that job dissatisfaction may be a risk factor. Job tension and low self-esteem remain plausible hypotheses, but there is no direct evidence that they are risk factors in heart disease.

Finally, we must qualify our central hypothesis about the effects of stress on strain. How a person reacts to job stress—that is, whether he shows strain or not—is a function of both the stress he encounters and the type of person he is. In other words, we assume in our model that part of the effects of organizational stress on the individual are determined by his personality. Thus, the top box in Figure 1 contains characteristics of the person which have this conditioning effect on the influence of stress on strain. For example, the influence of a heavy work load on job tension is very strong for persons low in the abilities necessary to do the work, but the same work load produces minimal tension in persons high in these abilities. It is the *goodness of fit* between the demands of the job and the abilities of the person which will determine the amount of strain. Similarly, the goodness of fit between the needs of the person and the degree to which these needs are satisfied in the job environment will also affect the strain. Other aspects of personality, such as the hard-driving Type A coronary-prone syndrome, are expected to have similar conditioning effects.

In order to test our theory about the effects of job stress on heart disease, we have chosen to deal with strains that are known risk factors in heart disease (for example, cholesterol and blood pressure). This strategy has been adopted for reasons of efficiency. One can demonstrate, using twenty men, that work overload influences cholesterol, but it would require 2,000 men to prove that work overload influences coronary heart disease because the disease is so rare.[2]

Now, with our model from Figure 1 in mind, let us turn to the evidence which links stress in modern organizations to coronary heart disease and other indicators of individual strain.

---

[2]Although the theory outlined in Figure 1 does not show any causal relations among the various forms of individual strain, we do in fact assume that psychological strains affect heart disease by means of some intervening physiological strains. Also, one physiological strain such as heart rate may affect another physiological strain such as blood pressure. These mechanisms of the disease will not be discussed further because an understanding of them is not necessary to our major concern with the effect of environmental stress.

STUDIES OF ROLE AMBIGUITY

In order for us to perform our jobs well in an organization, we have to have a certain amount of information regarding what we are expected to do and not do. We need to know our rights, obligations, and privileges—essentially our "areas of freedom" (Maier, 1965). Usually, we would also like to have some information regarding the potential consequences of anything we do in carrying out our jobs. Furthermore, we often want to know what the consequences will be for ourselves, other members of the organization, and the organization itself (Kahn et al., 1964). Typically, however, we have less than all the information we need, and so we may experience some degree of *role ambiguity*. In asking people to indicate the amount of ambiguity they have experienced, we have asked men to rate items such as the following:

1. The extent to which their work objectives are defined.
2. The extent to which they can predict what others will expect of them tomorrow.
3. The extent to which they are clear on what others expect of them now.
4. How clear the scope and responsibilities of their job are.

In other words, role ambiguity is a state in which the person has inadequate information to perform his role. Our particular interest in role ambiguity stems from its negative effects on the well-being of individuals in organizations, its potentially harmful consequences for the organization, and its prevalence in today's work settings.

Our findings on role ambiguity are based on data drawn from a wide variety of occupations. We started our research with an intensive study of the effects of role ambiguity on job satisfaction and job-related psychological tensions in six large business organizations in the United States (Kahn et al., 1964). Fifty-three persons were interviewed at length about various aspects of stress and strain in their jobs. The major findings of this study showed that men who suffered from role ambiguity experienced lower job satisfaction and higher job-related tension.

We found further support for these findings in a later study carried out at Goddard Space Flight Center, one of NASA's bases. In the Goddard study, 205 male, volunteer administrators, engineers, and scientists filled out a lengthy questionnaire describing various aspects of stress and strain in their jobs. As part of this study, we obtained blood samples from the men and took measures of blood pressure and pulse rate for later analysis as indicators of physiological strain. We will be reporting on the findings regarding physiological strain in a later section of this chapter. Our major findings with regard to role ambiguity showed that it was again significantly related to low job satisfaction ($r = -.42$)[3] and to feelings of job-related threat to one's mental and physical well-being ($r = .40$). In addition, we found that the more ambiguity the person reported, the lower was his utilization of his intellectual skills and knowledge ($r = -.48$), and the lower was his utilization of his administrative and leadership skills. This lack of utilization also adversely affected satisfaction and increased job-related threat.

The latter two findings regarding low utilization of personal abilities suggest that people are unable to make their best contribution to an organization partly because the channels for utilization are unclear or ambiguous. Thus, an organization which is fraught with role ambiguity may suffer because it gets less than full use of its human resources. The individuals tend to see little opportunity for their own advancement in the organization ($r = -.44$), again because there is ambiguity about how to get ahead. This means that a person who wants to advance or improve himself in his job may feel that his efforts are quite futile. While we have no data on turnover from the Goddard study, it seems reasonable to assume that turnover is likely to be high in settings where people who want to advance feel unsure of what they should be doing, see themselves as being underutilized, and see no clear channels for advancement.

The upshot of all this is that role ambiguity may have far-reaching consequences beyond the strain which the individual experiences—

---

[3] r is an index of correlation between two variables; that is, it measures the extent to which two such variables are related to each other. Such correlations can mathematically vary only from $+1.00$ to -1.00. A correlation of $+1.00$ would indicate that two variables are perfectly and positively related to each other. A correlation of -1.00 would indicate a perfect *inverse* relation. A .00 correlation ($r = .00$) would mean that the two variables are completely unrelated to each other. A perfect correlation is rare in research in the social sciences; in this chapter the correlations range from .22 to .68. The following table may help to interpret these correlations:

$r = .20-.29$ is a very weak relation
$r = .30-.39$ is a weak relation
$r = .40-.49$ is a moderate relation
$r = .50-.59$ is a substantial relation
$r = .60-.69$ is a strong relation

All findings presented here are statistically significant at $p < .05$ or higher unless otherwise noted. That is, it is highly improbable that they represent chance findings due to "luck" since they could not occur by chance more than five times out of one hundred. Our general rule has been to present only those findings which have been confirmed in two or more studies.

consequences such as turnover of personnel and poor condition which directly affect the efficiency and operating costs of any modern organization.

While role ambiguity is generally stressful for people, there are individual differences in how much ambiguity a person can tolerate. Persons with a high need for structure and a low tolerance for ambiguity are more likely to experience job-related tension than persons low on these needs when they are faced with ambiguity in their work (Kahn et al., 1964).

How prevalent is role ambiguity in our organizational society? Data obtained from another study, a national survey of 725 male wage and salary workers (Kahn et al., 1964), show that 34.7 percent reported role ambiguity. In the Goddard study, 60 percent reported some form of role ambiguity. These figures and others on the prevalence of stresses (to be discussed later) are presented in Table 1.

Table 1. The Prevalence of Several Major Types of Job Stress

Type of Stress	Percent Reporting Stress	
	Goddard[a]	Kahn et al., 1964[b]
Role ambiguity	60.0	34.7
Role conflict	67.1	48.0
Subjective quantitative overload	72.6	44.0
Subjective qualitative overload	53.8	—

[a]These percentages represent people whose average scores are equivalent to at least the "some" category on the measuring scale used.

[b]From a national survey of male wage and salary workers (n = 725).There is substantial, but not perfect, overlap between the measures of stress used in the Kahn et al. study and the measures of stress used in the Goddard study.

Figure 2 graphically depicts the findings. In summary, role ambiguity, which appears to be widespread, (1) produces psychological strain and dissatisfaction, (2) leads to underutilization of human resources, and (3) leads to feelings of futility on how to cope with the organizational environment. It is worthy of attention because it tells a great deal about the behavior of people in organizations.

ROLE CONFLICT AND STRAIN

If role ambiguity reflects a situation where there is a lack of information, role conflict reflects a situation where the information

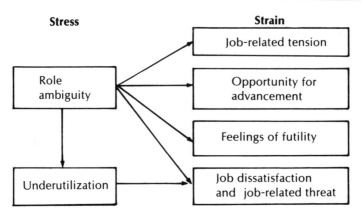

Figure 2. The Effects of Role Ambiguity on Stress and Strain in Organizations

arouses conflict. The following items about the conflicts people experience are typical of those we have asked members of organizations to rate:

1. Being torn by conflicting demands.
2. The pressure of "having to get along" with people.
3. Differences of opinion between oneself and one's superiors.
4. Difficulties in handling subordinates, secretaries, and others.
5. Having to do things one really doesn't want to do, such as certain administrative duties.

The phrase "torn by conflicting demands" rings true to many employees, even in America's best-managed organizations. The very essence of an organization is the division of labor among jobs or roles and a clear agreement on who should do what. Nevertheless an interview survey of a national sample of male wage and salary employees revealed that 48 percent are sometimes caught in the middle between two sets of people who demand different kinds of behavior on the job. Fifteen percent of these employees report that such role conflict is a frequent and serious problem (Kahn et al., 1964).

Some organizations have more role conflict than others. Compared to the national average of 48 percent, we found that 67.1 percent of male employees at Goddard Space Flight Center reported some role conflict.

Similarly, some jobs in an organization have more role conflict than others. At Goddard, administrators suffer more role conflict than engineers and scientists. The administrator has more opportunity for conflict because he spends less time than the others working alone (34 percent of his time against 38 percent and 57 percent).

What are the effects of these variations in role conflict? Our first studies of role conflict examined the consequences for psychological strain and mental health, and it was only later that we included measures of physiological strain and physical health. We started with an intensive study of the effects of role conflict on job satisfaction and on job-related tensions in six large business organizations (Kahn et al., 1964). Fifty-three focal persons were interviewed, each of whom named an additional six or eight co-workers who were "role senders," that is, who defined the focal person's job, who made demands upon him, and who told him how he should perform his role. Next we interviewed all these role senders to find out what demands, instructions, expectations, and requests they sent to the focal person. From the interviews with co-workers we constructed a measure of role conflict which reflected the conflicting demands from these co-workers. The major finding showed that men who suffered more role conflict had lower job satisfaction and higher job-related tension.

This study also showed that how a focal person reacted to conflict depended on the type of position he held relative to his role senders. The greater the power of the role senders over him, the greater the job dissatisfaction and sense of futility produced by the role conflict. It is worse to receive conflicting messages from two superordinates than from two subordinates.

We say that any role senders who depend heavily on the focal person to complete some task in order for them to discharge their own responsibilities are *functionally dependent* on the focal person. To take an example, you may be unable to submit a report unless one of your subordinates does the job of gathering certain necessary information. In that case, you are functionally dependent on your subordinate.

Functional dependence, interestingly enough, creates some unique problems for the focal person as well as for the people who are dependent on him. When the focal person experiences role conflict, the fact that he has others who are dependent on him apparently makes it more difficult to resolve the conflict. Thus, in the interview study, we found that persons experiencing role conflict report high feelings of job dissatisfaction and futility in trying to deal with their organizational environment; but this is only true if these people have role senders who are functionally dependent on them for getting work done.

We also find that the personality of the individual is an important determinant of how he reacts to role conflict. Specifically, role conflict produces greater job-related tension in introverts than in extroverts. The findings show that introverts are less social, that is, they enjoy interaction with other persons less than extroverts, and they are more independent than extroverts. Thus, it may be that the introvert has more difficulty in coping with conflict because it occurs in social situations and threatens his independence.

Similar findings also appear for flexible people, who show greater job-related tension under conditions of conflict than do rigid individuals. Kahn et al. note that flexible people are characterized by their tendency to blame themselves when things go wrong, while rigid people tend to externalize blame and assume that the fault lies within the environment. Thus, it would seem that the flexible person, when confronted with conflict situations, would turn the blame for conflict inward and consequently experience more job-related tension than the rigid person.

An interview survey of a national sample of male wage and salary workers confirmed the finding that role conflict is associated with job dissatisfaction and tension.

Another study of over 800 salesmen examined the relationship between role conflict, measures of job satisfaction, and job-related tension. It was found that among managers, role conflict decreases satisfaction ($r = -.54$) and increases job-related tension ($r = .39$). In this study role conflict is weakly related to physical symptoms of anxiety as measured by eight questions about insomnia, nervousness, clammy hands, hard breathing, and so forth.

Although conflicting role pressures have their source in organizational variables, such as the conflicting goals of different departments, they have their expression in the demands which are made on a person. When these demands conflict, at least one of them must be rejected or ignored. It would not be surprising if such a rejection were resented and taken personally. In the study at Goddard we did indeed find that high role conflict goes with poor relationships with one's peer group ($r = .24$) and with dissatisfaction with one's subordinates ($r = .35$). Role conflict is also associated with job-related threat: the person under role conflict feels that this stress threatens his health, his feelings of pride, freedom from tension, and so on ($r = .29$). Given poor interpersonal relations and feelings of threat, persons under more role conflict experience a greater need for better relations with subordinates ($r = .35$).

Finally, we have some preliminary evidence that role conflict is related to physiological strain. In a study of twenty-two men in NASA headquarters we telemetered and recorded the heart rate of each man for a two-hour period while he was at work on his regular office job. We found that mean heart rate was strongly related to the man's report of role conflict on a questionnaire ($r = .61$). However, in another study this same seven-item measure of role conflict was not related to pulse rate when a single, thirty-second, casual reading of pulse was taken instead of a two-hour-long measure as the person worked in his office.

Some major findings from these five studies of role conflict are summarized in Figure 3. The figure shows that this form of job stress produces a variety of psychological strains, but these effects of stress on strain vary depending on the personality of the individual and his relationships with others in the organization.

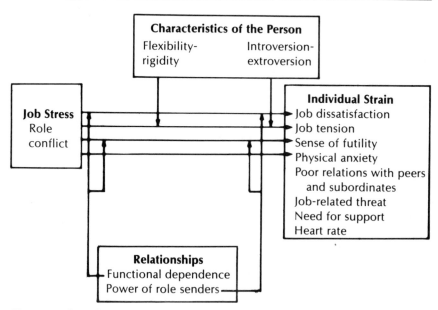

Figure 3. The Effects of Role Conflict on Psychological and Physiological Strain

ROLE OVERLOAD

We have talked about role conflict as a situation in which a person finds, in essence, diametrically opposed demands being made on him. But very often a person is asked to work on one assignment when he already has some other assignments which also must be completed. If he is to work on the new assignment, he may have to stop what he is doing at the time. This is also a form of conflict, and it leads to a situation known as *overload*. When the issue concerns merely the sum total of work that must be done, irrespective of its difficulty, we talk about *quantitative* overload—the person has more work than can be done in a given period of time. When the work is overloading because it requires skills, abilities, and knowledge beyond what the person has, then we talk about *qualitative* overload.

Quantitative overload lies on a continuum running from "too little to do" to "too much to do." The continuum for qualitative overload runs from "too easy work" to "too difficult work." Either extreme on these continuums represents a bad fit between the demands of the environment and the ability of the organization member. A good fit would reside at that point on both scales of work load where the demands of the job just match the abilities of the person.

In our research, quantitative overload has been measured in a variety of ways. Our questionnaires contain items on "overwhelming work load," "not enough time," "the quantity of work you are expected to do," and others. The number of hours that a man works per week (as reported by the man and by his wife) is another measure. The frequency and severity of deadlines is still another measure. In order to avoid the biases in self-reports, we have actually observed the number of meetings, office visits, and phone calls; these form an index of work load since, at best, each event takes up time which could have been used in other work and, at worst, each event may mean the person receives additional work assignments. All these measures make sense as indicators of quantitative overload, all of them tend to hang together, and in general, they show similar effects of overload on strain.

The measures of qualitative overload are primarily qestionnaire items referring to "the quality of work you are expected to do," "the demands of the job for training or knowledge," and "the difficulty of assignments."

The conceptual overlap between role conflict and overload is, of course, not surprising. Indeed, we have found in a reanalysis (Sales, 1969) of some of the findings from the study of role conflict that a good deal of the relationship between role conflict and job-related tension could be explained by a subset of three items in our measure of conflict which dealt specifically with quantitative overload. These items correlated .60 with job tension.

Overload is one of the concepts which receives a good deal of attention from general systems theorists. Miller (1960), for example, has shown that excessive overload leads to general breakdown in a system no matter what the level of the system is. That is, the finding holds true for systems ranging from single biological cells to individuals to organizations to states. Recent research has also indicated that overload resulting from excessive rates of change in the complexity of the environment (Terreberry, 1968) also leads to system breakdown. This process of "complexification" appears to be associated with systems dysfunctions at various levels ranging from individual suicide to bankruptcy of a business organization.

Quantitative overload is prevalent in our achievement-oriented society (McClelland, 1961). Even though their jobs do not demand it, university professors in one of our studies work fifty-seven hours per week. In the national sample survey, 44 percent of male white collar employees reported some degree of overload on our questionnaire measure. On the same measure, 45 percent of our small sample at NASA headquarters and 72.6 percent at Goddard Space Flight Center reported some degree of overload. On the average the men at Goddard spend about half their time working under moderate to extreme deadline pressure. At both NASA installations, persons who are high on the questionnaire measure of quantitative overload also spend more time in meetings, on office visits, and on the phone and correspondingly less time working alone.

The prevalence of qualitative overload is also high; 54 percent of the men at Goddard report at least some. This appears to be lower than the prevalence of quantitative overload in the same sample. In our sample of college professors, we also found more quantitative overload (a mean of 2.39) than qualitative overload (a mean of 2.13).

One of our initial studies of overload looked at the nature of quantitative as well as qualitative overload in a large university (French, Tupper, and Mueller, 1965). Questionnaires, interviews, and medical examinations to obtain data on risk factors in coronary heart disease were administered to 122 professors and university administrators. In order to see whether quantitative and qualitative overload were two different factors, as we had conceptually predicted they would be, we factor-analyzed the responses to the questionnaire items. This analysis confirmed our expectation that quantitative and qualitative overload are two distinct and separate variables.

Both quantitative overload and qualitative overload, as reported by the professors, were related to the same index of job tension which we used in the studies of role conflict ($r = .41$ and $.58$, respectively). These findings were supported when the overload was reported by the wife, although the correlations were not quite as high. These results together with the parallel findings in our studies of role conflict give us confidence that work overload is generally associated with job tension. One must be cautious in inferring causes from correlations. There are always three logical possibilities. In this case they are: (1) overload causes job tension; (2) job tension causes overload (perhaps because tension so interferes with performance that the man can't get his work done); (3) both overload and tension are caused by some third factor (for example, a harsh and demanding boss), and so there is a correlation between overload and tension even though neither causes the other. Our hypothesis states that overload causes tension, but we cannot rule out the other two possibilities on the grounds that they are implausible. So what we need is an experiment in which we systematically vary work overload while holding all other factors constant and observe the resulting variation of job tension. Such experiments are reported below.

Some professors did not understand the interview question that asked how difficult it is to "meet the demands of your job," because they did not experience their work as a response to demands from others but as self-induced activities (such as research, study, and serving on committees) which they were free to do or not do. When the meaning of "demands" was explained to him, one professor replied, "Oh, I could do that with one hand tied behind my back!"

Then what induces some professors and administrators to overload themselves, to work sixty or even seventy hours per week? In an effort to answer this question, we coded the intensive interviews for "achievement orientation," a syndrome which includes engaging in multiple activities, pushing oneself to achieve, reported achievement, taking leadership in accomplishing goals, and so on. As expected, this measure correlated .42 with the number of hours worked per week and .25 with our factor score on quantitative overload. More surprising, achievement orientation correlated very highly with serum uric acid ($r = .68$ in the first half of the sample, and $r = .66$ when cross-validated in the second half of the sample; Brooks & Mueller, 1966). This surprising finding was well replicated in a second study of professors, so the association between achievement orientation and serum uric acid may be taken as a fact. This substance in the blood is best known for its association with gout, and it has been observed long ago that gouty men often achieve eminence. Serum uric acid has also been considered a possible risk factor in coronary heart disease, but its causal connection is uncertain. It is known that serum uric acid tends to be high in occupational groups who are high in achievement, such as business executives; and we have found it to be low in a sample of unemployed men.

These facts suggested that serum uric acid might be the biochemical basis for achievement motivation. However, in a special study of this question we could find no relation between serum uric acid and two projective measures of achievement motivation. In another study of male high school students, a connection between serum uric acid and motivation to achieve was suggested: those who attempted college but dropped out had higher serum uric acid than either those who completed college or those who never tried to go to college. Within the group who attempted college (in spite of poor high school grades) those with higher serum uric acid persisted longer before dropping out (Kasl, Brooks, & Cobb, 1966).

The finding that overload is related to low self-esteem is confirmed in the total sample at Goddard. Qualitative overload is correlated with two measures of low self-esteem ($r = .27$ and $.30$); however, quantitative overload is not related to either. This effect is found primarily in the scientists, whose role is most like that of a professor. Among scientists as among professors, qualitative overload strongly lowers self-esteem ($r = .58$) while among administrators and engineers there is no significant effect.

Finally, we found at Goddard that both quantitative and qualitative overload correlate with job-related threat ($r = .22$ and $.29$, respectively). The number of cigarettes smoked, a much publicized risk factor in heart disease, also increases with increases in the actual number of phone calls, office visits, and meetings a person has (as tallied by each person's secretary). The correlation between cigarette smoking and this measure of quantitative overload is .58.

Having strong evidence that work overload is related to several forms of psychological strain, it was only natural to hypothesize that overload would produce physiological strains. Several studies have reported an association of work overload with cholesterol level, but in these studies only crude indicators of overload have been used: a tax deadline for accountants (Friedman, Rosenman, & Carroll, 1958) and an impending examination for medical students (Dreyfuss & Czaczkes, 1959; Grundy & Griffin, 1959; Horwitz & Bronte-Stewart, 1962; Thomas & Murphy, 1958; Wertlake et al., 1958). Accordingly, a preliminary field study at NASA headquarters tested the hypothesis that overload increases both cholesterol level and heart rate.

NASA was chosen as a research site because the Division of Occupational Medicine wanted to develop measures of job stress which would be useful in a computerized system for the early identification of those men who had a high risk of heart disease. NASA also seemed an appropriate site for the research, because the organization was reported to have strong deadline pressures and work overload.

Twenty-two white collar males were observed at work for a period of two to three hours on each of three days. A team of two observers recorded coordinated data on events occurring in the job environment and heart rate responses to these events. The heart rates were obtained by means of a pocket-sized telemetry device which did not interfere with the employee's freedom of activity and movement. On the same day of the observations, blood samples were drawn so the cholesterol determinations could be made. On the third day of observation each subject filled out a questionnaire which yielded a factor score on quantitative overload. This subjective measure could be compared with an objective measure constructed from the observer's report of incoming phone calls and office visitors. The two measures showed substantial agreement. Those men who reported that they were generally overloaded on their jobs were observed to suffer more interruptions from phone calls and visitors ($r = .64$).

As predicted, both objective and subjective overload were substantially related to heart rate ($r = .39$ and .65, respectively). Both were also related to cholesterol ($r = .43$ and .41, respectively). All the above findings are based on correlations across individuals; but analyses within individuals show that increases in work load were accompanied by increases in heart rate, a fact which supports our hypothesis that stress produces the observed physiological strain.

Although the association of overload with physiological strain has been strongly demonstrated in this study at NASA, it still does not prove that overload causes strain. In order to prove more conclusively that the stress of work load produces physiological strain, we conducted two controlled laboratory experiments. In the first experiment we found that men who were subjected to qualitative overload, as compared with those who received easy tasks, not only suffered psychological strain such as embarrassment and loss of self-esteem, but also showed more physiological strain as measured by the basal skin resistance level (Modigliani, 1966). In the second experiment those subjects who were given a substantial quantitative overload, as compared with those who were underloaded, showed lower self-esteem, made more errors, and had higher heart rates. During the one hour of working on the task, the level of cholesterol increased most for overloaded subjects. Together the two experiments prove that qualitative and quantitative work overload are the causes rather than the effects of physiological as well as psychological strains. When overload is reduced, the strain decreases.

In summary, our findings from several studies show that the various forms of work load produce at least nine different kinds of psychological and physiological strain in the individual (see Figure 4). Four of these (job dissatisfaction, elevated cholesterol, elevated heart rate, and smoking) are risk factors in heart disease. It is reasonable to predict that reducing work overload will reduce heart disease.

ORGANIZATIONAL TERRITORIALITY

Robert Ardrey's armchair excursion into the world of *The Territorial Imperative* reveals the significance of territories for the behavior of animals and suggests the potential importance which personal space and

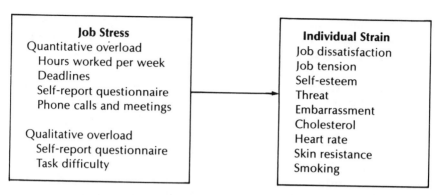

Figure 4. A Summary of the Effects of Quantitative and Qualitative Overload on Various Forms of Individual Strain

territory may play in the everyday activities of man. To what extent is territory important to people in modern organizations? Do people develop feelings of ownership with respect to their offices or their own departments? Shouldn't the time a person spends in other territories prove to be a source of stress for the individual? What types of strains, such as insecurity, do people show when they cross the boundary between their own section of the organization and other sections—or move out from their own organization completely, as the salesman does routinely? Indeed, every time a person moves out of his territory, he invades the territory of someone else, potentially putting the other person as well as himself under stress.

What is the nature of territories and boundaries in organizations? These are essentially two. In addition to the external boundaries which separate the organization from its environment, there is a set of internal boundaries corresponding to the functional division of labor among divisions, departments, and the like. NASA, for example, is broken down into various bases spread across the country, and a base, such as Goddard, is further divided hierarchically as follows: directorates, divisions, branches, and sections. In order to achieve the goals of the organization, it is necessary to coordinate the activities of all these "territories." Likert (1961) pictures the manager at each level as a "linking pin" who has primary responsibility for such coordination. The manager is the leader of his own unit and at the same time he is a subordinate in his boss's larger unit; he has a special responsibility for coordinating the work of the two units. Nonmanagerial employees may also have contacts across organizational boundaries. The salesman, for example, has contacts across the external boundaries of the organization, and he may find that his customers make demands on him which conflict with those from his superior.

There has been little research on organizational territories, and we are just beginning to explore the stresses and strains which may be involved. Here we will report on two variables which seem to belong to the domain of territorial behavior: having to make work contacts across organizational boundaries, and having your job located in a territory where the dominant occupation is different from your own (for example, the engineer who works in an administrative department where there are few other engineers).

Contacts across organizational boundaries are quite prevalent in organizational life. In our national sample survey 43 percent of the employees reported that they sometimes, rather often, or nearly all the time had contacts outside the organization; the corresponding figure for contact across departmental boundaries was 47 percent. Our sample at Goddard spent more than half their time "interfacing," as they call it, with other sections of the organization.

Contact across organizational boundaries, we discovered in our intensive study of role conflict in business organizations, is associated with role conflict. Those who are located on either the external or the internal boundaries of the organization have substantially more role conflict. Among internal contacts, those interactions with more distant departments are more stressful because the role senders have a less adequate understanding of the key person's job and hence they make more unreasonable demands. At Goddard, too, contacts with more distant organizational units are more difficult and they involve greater deadline pressures. The amount of deadline pressure decreases with the increase in amount of time spent in contacts within one's own branch $(r = -.31)$. On the other hand, these deadline pressures increase with increasing amounts of time spent in contacts with other bases or centers $(r = .39)$. The still more distant contacts involved in monitoring contracts with outside companies have other attendant stresses. The more time people spend in contract monitoring, the heavier is their actual work load in the form of meetings, office visits, and phone calls $(r = .61)$.

Given all these stresses associated with interacting across organizational boundaries, it is not surprising to find that such interfacing also produces strain. Frequent boundary contacts are associated with high job-related tension in our national sample and with low self-actualization in our Goddard sample. In Goddard the amount of interfacing is associated with low self-actualization (that is, low utilization of one's best abilities and leadership skills), whereas the amount of time spent in contact with persons in one's own work unit is associated with high self-actualization.

We turn now to the effects of having one's job located in an alien environment. At Goddard our sample of administrators consisted of two subgroups: those in an administrative environment and those in an engineering environment. Similarly, there were subsamples of engineers in each of the same two environments. For each occupation, therefore, we could compare men in an alien environment with men in a better-fitting environment where most of the employees shared the same occupations.

As predicted, the men in an alien environment showed more stress and strain: (1) administrators in an engineering unit showed more quantitative overload, more qualitative overload, a larger percentage of time under great deadline pressure, higher systolic and diastolic blood pressure, and a faster pulse rate; (2) engineers in an administrative unit showed more incoming and outgoing phone calls, greater deadline pressure from their own branch, more contacts across organizational boundaries and less within their own unit, less opportunity to do the kind of work they preferred, less opportunity for advancement, and lower self-actualization.

It seems that crossing an organizational boundary and working in an alien territory entails stress and strain and poses a threat to one's health.

RESPONSIBILITY FOR PEOPLE

The responsibilities a person has constitute another frequent stress in organizations. In our research we have found it useful to categorize responsibilities into two types: responsibilities for persons and responsibilities for things. Responsibility for persons includes their work, their careers and professional development, and their job security. Responsibility for things includes budgets, projects, and equipment and other property.

In the Goddard study about 59 percent of the respondents reported at least some degree of responsibility for people, and about 59 percent of the respondents reported at least some degree of responsiblity for things. We found that responsibilities for persons increase as one moves up the hierarchy of the organization (measured by government salary level in this study; $r = .44$). Responsibilities for things also increase as one moves up the status ladder, but the relationship between impersonal responsibilities and organizational status is not as great ($r = .26$). Thus, responsibilities for persons are fairly prevalent in Goddard and an increase in status is more likely to mean an increase in responsibilities for persons than in responsibilities for things.

People who have great responsibility for others at Goddard seem to pay the price in terms of large amounts of time spent interacting with people in meetings and on the phone, and in reduced amounts of time working alone ($r = -.47$). It is not surprising that such people also end up reporting they spend a good deal of time under great deadline pressure, often to the point where they can just barely keep up with their schedules ($r = .34$). Responsibility for things, on the other hand, has little or no effect on these other stresses.

We further found that the responsibility for people can hardly be considered conducive to good health and low risk of coronary heart disease. First, the more time the person spends carrying out responsibility for the work of others, the more he smokes ($r = .31$). Second, the more responsibility he has for the work of others, the higher his diastolic blood pressure ($r = .23$). On the other hand, the more responsibility he has for things, the lower his diastolic blood pressure ($r = -.32$).

Finally, when a person has either more responsibility for the work of others than he wants or less responsibility for the work of others than he wants, his serum cholesterol level tends to be higher than when he has exactly as much responsibility as he wants (the index of nonlinear association equals .23).[4]

If there is any truth to the adage that "man's greatest enemy is himself," it can be found in these data—it is the responsibility which organizational members have for other organizational members, rather than the responsibility for impersonal aspects of the organization, which constitutes the more significant organizational stress.

POOR RELATIONS WITH OTHERS

Psychologists and students of organizations have paid a good deal of attention over the last twenty years to the quality of working relations people have with one another. Many organization theorists have, in fact, suggested that good relations between organization members can be a key factor in improving organizational health (for example, see Likert, 1961, 1967; Argyris, 1964; and McGregor, 1960).

In the Goddard study we have examined the quality of the relations people have with their immediate superior, their colleagues or peers, and their subordinates as important sources of organizational stress. Poor relations have been defined as those which include low trust, low

---

[4]In this latter condition the goodness of fit between the person and his environment is perfect. That is, the person demands so much of his environment, and the environment provides just that amount. In the case of poor fit, the environment has either some deficiency or some excess of the desired supply. Additional research, not reported on here, also suggests that other conditions of poor fit between the person and his job environment produce strain in the individual.

supportiveness, and low interest in listening to and trying to deal with the problems that confront the organization member.

Poor relations with one's superior, colleagues, and subordinates are likely to occur whenever the person experiences a good deal of ambiguity about what he should be doing as part of his role in the organization (the correlations range from .23 to .46). These findings are in keeping with those from another study, the intensive interview study of job stress by Kahn et al. (1964). In that study mistrust of the persons one worked with was positively associated with high role ambiguity ($r = .38$). Lack of information apparently leads to misconceptions about people and how one should interact with them. As we might expect, poor relations with the people one works with are also likely to occur when conflicts arise over how jobs should be done and over what the priorities are for carrying out such jobs ($r = .24$). Often in an organization, the decisions on conflicts such as these are not easily resolvable by facts, and the decisions may rest on the weight of one person's subjective opinion against another's. It is quite conceivable that such conflicts often develop into sources of interpersonal friction with a consequent deterioration in relations between the persons involved.

Poor relations perhaps generated by factors such as conflict or inadequate communication between people, go on to produce psychological strain in the form of low job satisfaction (r's range from .25 to .47) and feelings of job-related threat to one's well-being. Interestingly enough, poor relations with one's subordinates do not seem to affect feelings of threat ($r =$ only .12), whereas poor relations with one's colleagues and immediate superior do affect threat (r's = .44 and .41, respectively). Apparently an individual's feelings of threat are more likely to be reduced by improving his relations with his superior and colleagues than with his subordinates.

In summary, then, poor relations with other members of an organization may be precipitated by conditions of ambiguity—conditions where adequate information regarding roles and responsibilities and information necessary to carry them out are not provided. The misunderstandings and conflicts that may occur as a result of all this may in turn negatively affect the quality of trust, supportiveness and willingness to listen to organization members' problems. Finally, these poor interpersonal relations generate dissatisfactions with the job and feelings of threat.

PARTICIPATION

Participation refers to the extent to which a person has influence on decision processes of the organization. To the extent that people's knowledge, opinions, and wishes are excluded from such decision processes, we say that they have low participation. Of course, there is nothing inherently bad about being a nonparticipant. It all depends on the context. For example, you and I are often glad to be excluded from decision making because we do not have either the time to participate or the need to. We are concerned here, however, with decisions which the person might want to participate in, such as decisions about how he should do his job.

Early experimental research has shown that lack of opportunities to participate in such decisions can create strain in the person and even adversely affect productivity. One study of participation in a sewing plant (Coch & French, 1948) examined groups experiencing three different degrees of worker participation in making a major decision about a change in work procedures. The findings showed that the greater the degree of participation, the greater was the subsequent productivity, the higher the job satisfaction, the lower the turnover, and the better the relations between the workers and the managers. These findings were later replicated in a study in a Norwegian factory (French, Israel, and Ås, 1960). This line of research has also been extended to the study of the effects of employee participation in work-appraisal interviews. Such participation, when coupled with supportive supervisory practices, has produced improvements in relations between the employee and his boss and subsequent improvement in performance.

The findings on participation seem to hold across a very wide range of organizations. In Yugoslav factories, operated under a system of Workers' Councils, we also find that participation is associated with job satisfaction (Obradović, French, & Rodgers, 1970). Even more different from our large American organizations are the very small factories and poultry branches in the kibbutzim of Israel. Our study of forty-four such organizations revealed that high participation was associated with high satisfaction with the job and the organization, high self-esteem, low alienation, high commitment to work and to the organization, more innovation for better ways of doing the job, doing more extra work, reading more books and magazines related to work, a higher performance evaluation by one's manager, and lower absenteeism (Levitan, 1970).

Field experiments of the kind cited above have indicated that lack of participation can be a major source of stress. In the Goddard study high participation was accompanied by better relations with the person's immediate superior, colleagues, and subordinates (r's range from .24 to .52). We might expect that by participating in what is going on, a person reduces his ambiguity regarding relevant information for performing his work. This is in fact the case. High participators report low role ambiguity

($r = -.55$). As a result of lowered ambiguity, we would expect that people who participate a lot would utilize their skills and abilities more since they would have more information on how to best apply their talents. In fact, we found that high participation is positively related to high utilization of both administrative ($r = .50$) and nonadministrative ($r = .52$) skills and abilities.

Potential benefits to the organization may accrue from all of this. The attitude toward work by the high participators is quite positive. They tend to prefer more rather than less work than they already have ($r = .34$), which suggests that the involvement generated by participation makes people more willing to take on added tasks. High participators, compared with low participators in our sample of Goddard administrators, engineers, and scientists, also perceive greater opportunities for advancement in the organization ($r = .47$). This means that the organization is less likely to have turnover problems with these employees since they are less likely to be attracted to competing organizations.

We expect that with the right to participate in decisions goes the responsibility to enact and carry out those decisions. Our Goddard findings offer support for this expectation. The more a person participates, the more responsibility of all kinds he reports having, irrespective of his organizational status (measured here by government salary level; $r = .61$).

In the study at Goddard we found that people who report high opportunities to participate in decisions affecting the work they do tend to report both high satisfaction ($r = .50$) and low job-related feelings of threat ($r = -.51$). People who participate a lot also have high feelings of self-esteem or self-worth ($r = .32$). Thus, in terms of psychological well-being, our high participators are much better off than our low participators.

We have already mentioned a variety of other stresses, in addition to that of low participation, which are also accompanied by low job satisfaction and/or job-related threat. These stresses include poor relations with others, role conflict, role ambiguity, and quantitative and qualitative overload. Of all the stresses we have considered, low participation has the greatest harmful effect on job satisfaction and threat. This means that participation is a relatively important determinant of psychological well-being.

Since participation is also significantly correlated with low role ambiguity, good relations with others, and low overload, it is conceivable that its effects are widespread, and that all the relationships between these other stresses and psychological strain can be accounted for in terms of how much the person participates. This, in fact, appears to be the case. When we control or hold constant, through statistical analysis techniques, the amount of participation a person reports, then the correlations between all the above stresses and job satisfaction and job-related threat drop quite noticeably. This suggests that low participation generates these related stresses, and that increasing participation is an efficient way of reducing many other stresses which also lead to psychological strain.

We have discussed direct relationships between participation and its effects on organizational members. There is some additional evidence which suggests that the effects of participation on the person and his work may differ as a function of his personality or as a function of the nature of the decision he participates in making. Thus, if the person is given the opportunity to participate in trivial decisions or decisions unrelated to how work is done, satisfaction and productivity might remain unaffected. We have not gone into the specific findings here on the role of these *context* factors, because there have been only minor amounts of research in these areas.

Figure 5 summarizes our findings on participation. People who report high levels of participation are less likely to experience mental strain in the form of job dissatisfaction, job-related threat, or low self-esteem. The lack of role ambiguity which accompanies participation apparently enables the person to better utilize his skills and abilities in performing his work. High participation also is accompanied by high responsibility in our samples.

The high morale of the participators is seen in their positive attitudes toward their work. They prefer to take on more rather than less work, and they see the organization as a place where they have a good opportunity to advance. Some of our research indicates that under conditions of high participation one can expect to find low turnover, high productivity, and high performance improvement when employees participate in decisions on ways to improve their performance.

OCCUPATIONAL DIFFERENCES IN STRESS AND STRAIN

We have already noted that public health statistics, as well as specific studies by other investigators, have revealed large occupational differences in coronary heart disease. At Goddard we became interested in stress and strain differences between administrators, engineers, and scientists because NASA administrators have over three times as much heart disease as engineers and scientists. Our model of the effects of stress on strain, presented in Figure 1, suggests that there should indeed be such occupational differences in heart disease. First of all, different occupational groups are likely to experience different quantities of the

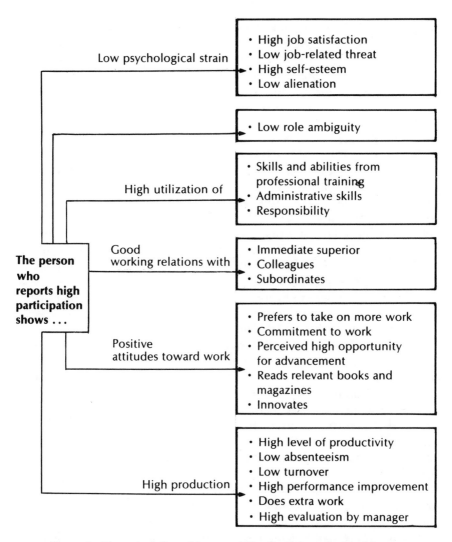

Figure 5. Characteristics of Persons Who Participate in Decisions Which Affect Their Work

same stress (for example, five deadlines per year versus five per month). Second, different occupational groups are also likely to experience different forms of stress (such as responsibility for the work of others versus responsibility for budgets). Third, occupational groups may differ in terms of the amount of strain they experience. Thus, recent research by Sales and House (1970) has shown that these occupational differences in heart disease are highly correlated with differences in the amounts of psychological strain (job dissatisfaction) that are encountered ($r = .49$). These findings hold especially for white collar occupational groups. Finally, different groups may react with different forms of strain (one group may develop coronary heart disease while the other group may experience low self-esteem).

An interesting example of these differences in stress and strain in occupations comes from a study of administrators and professors in a large Midwestern university (French, Tupper, & Mueller, 1965). Administrators experienced different stresses than did university professors, and each group's feelings of psychological strain were related to different types of stress. Administrators experienced more *quantitative* overload than professors. Professors experienced more *qualitative* overload than administrators. Quantitative overload produced feelings of low self-esteem in administrators ($r = -.65$) but not in professors. On the hand, qualitative overload produced feelings of low self-esteem in professors but not in administrators. Thus what was psychological "poison" for one group was not so toxic for the other group and vice versa. Administrators would apparently rather do all their tasks sacrificing a bit on quality, while professors would rather sacrifice on quantity and do a high-quality job on a smaller number of tasks.

When we did the study of administrators, engineers, and scientists at Goddard we were curious to see if the scientists and engineers were like university professors in their concern with the quality of their work, and if the Goddard administrators were like the university administrators with regard to the quantity of work they had. This, in fact, turned out to be the case. The scientists reported the most qualitative overload while the administrators reported the least. On the other hand, the administrators reported the most quantitative overload while the scientists reported the least. In fact, the administrators scored the highest on a whole series of indicators of high quantitative work load including the number of phone calls, office visits, and meetings per week. They even took the longest, on the average, to return their questionnaires, suggesting that they indeed had many more items demanding immediate attention on their desk compared to the engineers and scientists.

We also found that administrators were highest on another important stress linked with coronary heart disease—namely, responsibilities for persons. The administrators reported spending the greatest amount of time, compared with the engineers and scientists, in responsibilities for the work of others and for others' futures. Our administrator group also reported the most role conflict.

Finally, we found that administrators, compared with engineers and scientists, spend the most time in contact with persons outside their own immediate part of the organization (that is, in other territory). They spend

more time interfacing with persons in other branches, divisions, directorates, and bases. As a result of such contact across boundaries, they report
greater stress from these other areas of the organization than do engineers and scientists.

We have already noted that quantitative overload and responsibility
for persons are related to risk factors in coronary heart disease such as
pulse rate, diastolic blood pressure, and number of cigarettes smoked.
The next quesion, then, was whether we would find the administrators to
be highest on these three risk factors. We did, although the differences in
pulse rate and diastolic blood pressure were not statistically significant.
The administrators also turned out to have the highest systolic blood
pressures.[5]

Occupational Differences in Personality and Their Relevance to Heart Disease

In our theoretical model of organizational stress and its effects on
individual strain, personality plays a very special role. If you look back at
Figure 1, you will see that there is no arrow from personality to the risk
factors. Instead the vertical arrow depicts personality as having a conditioning effect. If there is a particular stress such as quantitative overload,
then we hypothesize that the Type A person will react by showing a good
deal of strain (such as raised cholesterol, faster pulse, or more cigarettes
smoked); on the other hand, the person who lacks the Type A traits will
be relatively unaffected by the stress (that is, his cholesterol, pulse, or
smoking behavior will remain unchanged).

The reader can probably think of everyday examples where personality plays this special role. Some people, for example, when faced with a
good deal of job stress, become immobilized, make mistakes, or lose their
tempers; others, under the same conditions, calmly go about the work
before them. We usually think of these two types of people as differing in
some relatively stable traits or personality dispositions. The stress is the
same, but their reactions to the stress are a function of their respective
personalities.

A good deal of research on the role of personality traits as a factor in
coronary heart disease has already been carried out. Research by Friedman, Rosenman, and their colleagues (Rosenman et al., 1970; Rosenman
et al., 1966) has shown that one can predict with some success the
occurrence of coronary heart disease on the basis of the presence of a
personality pattern known as Type A. These longitudinal studies have

---

[5]These physiological findings are age corrected.

been carried out over a period of four and a half years using 3,182 males from a wide range of occupational groups. The Type A personality pattern includes traits such as high involvement in one's work (Involved Striving), a liking for deadlines and other job pressures (Positive Attitude Toward Pressure), a tendency to feel overburdened by one's work (Environmental Overburdening), and a tendency to take on roles of considerable responsibility—perhaps for the work of others (Leadership).

Having found that our Goddard administrators score highest on stresses commonly associated with coronary heart disease, we might wonder whether they would also be higher than engineers and scientists on the Type A personality traits. This is indeed the case. The findings are presented in Table 2. Administrators score highest on involved striving, positive attitude toward pressure, environmental overburdening, leadership, and on an overall measure of Type A called "What I am like." They also score highest on flexibility, a personality trait which, as we noted earlier, increases the effect of role conflict on job tension. All of these occupational differences in personality are statistically significant.

That the administrators score highest on the Type A personality traits means they are likely to react to certain stresses in ways which produce elevations in risk factors in coronary heart disease. On the other hand, since the engineers and scientists score lower on these measures of Type A, they are less likely to react to the same stresses in ways which will elevate their smoking, pulse rates, cholesterol, and blood pressure.

Table 2. Occupational Differences in Personality

Measure	Occupation			
	Administrator	Engineer	Scientist	P
Rigid personality (flexibility-rigidity scale)	2.3[a]	2.4	2.5	.01
Involved striving	5.2[b]	4.8	5.0	.05
Positive attitude toward pressure	5.2	4.9	4.8	.05
Environmental overburdening	5.6	5.1	5.4	.05
Leadership	5.0	4.3	4.2	.05
What I am like (Type A)	3.5[c]	3.3	3.2	.05

[a]These values are based on a four-point scale where 1 = flexible and 4 = rigid.

[b]The values for involved striving and the next three traits in the table are based on a seven-point scale where 1 = low on the personality trait and 7 = high on the personality trait.

[c]These values are based on a five-point scale where 5 = Type A and 1 = the opposite.

Our studies at Goddard provide some concrete examples of the difference personality makes in how a person reacts to stress. We found, for example, that persons who are high on involved striving show increases in diastolic blood pressure and cholesterol as the percent of time they spend in responsibilities for others' futures increases. These people, who are so high on involved striving, apparently take their responsibilities for others' futures quite seriously. Persons who are low on involved striving don't appear to be affected by such responsibilities. As we have noted, administrators are the highest occupational group with regard to involved striving, responsibility for others' futures, and diastolic blood pressure.

There are similar findings of this type involving each of the other personality traits that characterize the administrators. In each case, the person who is high on the trait, compared with the person who is low, shows greater physiological strain in the face of some job stress.

In summary, people with different jobs encounter different kinds and amounts of stress. Consequently, they experience different kinds of strain. Our own research shows that administrators, for example, are far more likely to develop coronary heart disease both because they experience different types of organizational stress linked to risk factors in the disease and because they experience more of those types of organizational stress than do engineers and scientists. It is important to consider the role personality plays in all of this. People with Type A personality traits are more likely to show strain reactions when they encounter organizational stress than are people who do not have these traits. Thus occupations (such as administration) which, for one reason or another, attract people with these personality traits will be higher risk groups for coronary heart disease than occupations which do not attract such persons.

PROTECTING OUR HUMAN RESOURCES

The research we have reviewed clearly indicates that the stresses of today's organizations can pose serious threats to the physical and psychological well-being of organization members. When a man dies or becomes disabled by a heart attack, the organization may be partly to blame. But the assignment of guilt will not prevent people from dying or prevent the organization from incurring large losses in terms of the investments required to recruit and train replacements. What is needed, instead, is a program of organizational diagnosis and prevention aimed at curtailing the loss of human resources to an organizational enemy known as coronary heart disease.

As we begin to discuss prevention, some perspective is needed on what might be accomplished if we were to institute the ideal prevention program, given what we now know about coronary heart disease. First of all, if one reviews the medical literature, one finds that the known risk factors in coronary heart disease account for about 25 percent of the variation in the disease. This means that if you could perfectly control cholesterol, blood pressure, smoking, glucose level, serum uric acid, and so on, you would have controlled only about one-fourth of coronary heart disease.

Furthermore our data suggest that a perfect control of job stresses would control only a small part of the variation in these physiological risk factors. However, it may be that job stress also affects heart disease by means of other mechanisms which we have not studied. Thus there is positive evidence that the control of job stress should have a small effect on heart disease, but there is a possibility that it could have a substantial effect. This latter possibility is still a big unknown. We know just enough to justify thinking about programs of prevention and planning research to explore their feasibility.

We should point out that although our notions about prevention are concerned primarily with coronary heart disease, there is some evidence to suggest that reduction in job stresses may also lower the incidence of other work-related illnesses, such as ulcers (Dunn & Cobb, 1962). The fact that dispensary visits tend to increase under increased responsibility (Kasl & French, 1962) gives support to the notion that a wide variety of illnesses, such as respiratory ailments, headaches, anxiety attacks, and nausea, might be prevented by reducing job stress.

What should be done to prevent coronary disease and psychological strain in organizations? To answer that question, we must change hats and switch from the role of social scientist to that of consultant and adviser. This is a difficult switch for us to make, and we want the reader to understand the difficulties so that he can properly evaluate the nature of our recommendations.

For one thing, very little research has been done on experimental programs of prevention. It is one thing to know, on the basis of careful research, some of the organizational stresses which influence heart disease and its risk factors; it is quite another thing to know how to control these stresses. Although we will utilize the available research, our advice must often rely on interpretations which go beyond the established facts. We will not hesitate to use our experience in organizations and our creative imagination in trying to invent programs of prevention. In this section, therefore, we can no longer adhere to our standards of scientific reporting, namely, that we report only those findings where we can assess their probable truth and where the chances are at least 95 in 100 that the findings are true. Instead, we will try to generate a variety of suggestions for prevention which are implied by our research but whose feasibility must be judged by the reader. The ultimate effectiveness of these suggestions must, of course, be determined by trying them out along with a careful research evaluation.

A second difficulty which faces us as consultant but not as social scientist is that we must now pay attention to a whole series of constraints. Any prevention program designed to improve health must not cost too much, must not conflict with other organizational goals, must not violate existing policies, must be feasible to carry out with the available (or obtainable) personnel, and so forth. Our suggestions will try to take account of these constraints even though we do not have space to discuss each of them.

However, one constraint is too important to bypass: Will the prevention program interfere with productivity and profits? Our general answer to this question is no. The research underlying systems of management such as the one proposed by Likert (1961, 1967) shows that high productivity often (although not always) goes together with high morale and job satisfaction. Some aspects of this system of management seem well adapted to reduce organizational stress and individual strain. It seems possible to design programs that will reduce heart disease and in the long run improve organizational performance. Nevertheless, there can be cases, especially in the short run, where organizational goals and individual well-being are in conflict. An ambitious Type A man, for example, may voluntarily take on an extremely heavy work load and contribute greatly to the performance of the organization, but eventually he may die of a heart attack.

A third problem facing us in the consultant role is the fact that every organization has its own special environment, its own unique structure and procedures, and its own pattern of stresses. Just as stress and disease differ greatly from one occupation to another, so too they differ from one organization to another. As consultants we are in a position similar to the doctor who is asked to make a diagnosis and prescribe a cure without seeing the patient. The first step in devising a program of prevention must be to make an accurate diagnosis of the stresses and strains in the particular organization. Such a diagnosis would include answers to the following questions: (1) How is heart disease distributed among the different divisions, departments, and other organizational units and among occupations? (2) How are psychological and physiological strains distributed among organizational units, among occupations, and among individuals? (3) What are the patterns of stress in the various organizational units and occupations and on individuals?

Given the answers to these questions, we can concentrate preventive programs on those organizational units, occupations, and individuals where the risks to health are greatest. For example, we know that at NASA we should focus on administrators rather than on engineers and scientists. At a more sophisticated level of analysis, we might aim our program at those places in the organization where there is high overload and heavy deadline pressures, high role conflict and role ambiguity, many contacts across organizational boundaries, and a heavy load of responsibility for other people. Finally, this information would enable us to devise programs designed to alleviate particular kinds or patterns of stress.

We believe that the research methods we have employed can be adapted as useful instruments for the kind of diagnosis that will permit each organization to devise its own tailor-made program of prevention. In the absence of such information, the reader should recognize that our suggestions here must be rather general and, of course, cannot be specific to the special conditions in his own organization.

One can distinguish three methods of preventing the bad effects of disease: (1) primary prevention—that is, preventing the stresses from reaching the person; (2) once the noxious elements of the environment have reached the person, preventing the disease by, for example, early elimination of strain; (3) once the disease has broken out, preventing a later disability by proper treatment. Our emphasis will be on the first two of these, for they seem more desirable and more appropriate for action by management. The third method, the treatment and management of the cardiac patient, will not be discussed here because it is the special province of the physician.

In this discussion we shall be dealing with two broad classes of preventive actions which stem from our two main findings. The first main finding is that various organizational stresses produce strains in the individual which may eventually result in heart disease. This finding suggests a kind of primary prevention—the elimination or reduction of these stresses in the environment so that they do not impinge upon the person. The second main finding is that the effects of stress on strain will vary with individual differences in personality and with the goodness of fit between the demands and stresses of the job and the characteristics of the person. This second finding suggests a set of personnel procedures for improving the goodness of fit—namely, selection, placement, training, and job rotation. First, we will briefly discuss these personnel procedures because they are simpler and more familiar procedures. Then we will go on to consider the more desirable but more difficult possibilities of primary prevention, ending with an example of an experimental program of prevention designed to reduce several stresses in a specific organization.

PERSONNEL PROCEDURES FOR REDUCING STRESS

Selection and Placement

Our research suggests that certain types of persons are more susceptible to stress than others. Current selection procedures are typically devoted to preventing qualitative overload by assuming that the applicant has the required ability, training, knowledge, skill, and experience. One could extend these selection criteria by also choosing people on the basis of their tolerance for ambiguity, their ability to handle role conflict, or their resistance to the stress of responsibility. There are problems with this approach, however, since we lack adequate selection tests for measuring such traits and dispositions. Our tests have been used solely for scientific research and have not been adequately validated in studies where we predict in advance who will and who will not show strain under certain organizational stresses. This means that one might make errors in selection by relying on tests of this sort.

At any rate, special selection to prevent coronary heart disease is not necessary because the effects of stress and strain on this disease are probably very gradual. The new employee probably won't die on the job the first month even if his selection was a mistake. Thus, the organization has time to observe the employee's response to his current job, and to work on placement and promotion decisions on that basis. It is probably easier to diagnose a man's susceptibility to stress by watching him perform under stress than by giving him a battery of pre-employment tests.

Training

Another procedure for improving the fit of the person to the job involves training. He would be taught skill in performing his job more effectively and consequently with less effort and strain. He might be shown how to reduce overload by taking shortcuts in performing his tasks, or he could be provided with certain skills. His relations with others might be improved and his conflicts reduced by training him in techniques for getting along with people and handling conflict. Some training techniques such as role playing and sensitivity training are well known to management, but their effectiveness remains to be demonstrated (Campbell & Dunnette, 1968), especially for the purpose of reducing strain.

Job Rotation

This is yet another procedure to be considered in cases of high-stress jobs which cannot be easily restructured and where no one can handle the job without strain. In such cases, the exposure of any one person to these stresses is reduced by job rotation. Since jobs on organizational boundaries involve high stress, one might rotate people on and off these jobs to allow them to recuperate. One disadvantage of this procedure is that on the first rotation the new man will suffer the usual temporary stresses of a transfer: an increase in qualitative and quantitative work load and in role ambiguity. After he has had time to learn the new job, however, these stresses should disappear. There are, of course, limits to job rotation. Some people are "indispensable" and cannot be rotated (all the more reason to be concerned about their health). It is noteworthy that one of our most important and most stressful jobs, President of the United States, is subject to regular rotation.

REDUCING ORGANIZATIONAL STRESS

Here we need to consider the possibilities for reducing each of the stresses we have identified: role ambiguity, role conflict, quantitative overload, qualitative overload, interaction across boundaries and in foreign territories, responsibility for people, poor relations with others, and low participation. For each of these we must look for possible preventive actions directed at both the job itself and the wider organizational environment.

Changing the Stresses in the Job

Some job stresses—such as role ambiguity, role conflict, and poor relations with others—seem to be bad for both the health of the individual and the health of the organization. Managers have a special responsibility for establishing an unambiguous division of labor within the organization which is understood and accepted by all. At the same time, the organizational structure should be maximally flexible and responsive to local needs. Perhaps this can best be achieved by avoiding formal job descriptions imposed by the superior and instituting a program, already used successfully in one company, of discussions between each man and his supervisor for the purpose of jointly redefining the man's job. If such discussions are held frequently and successfully, less ambiguity and conflict, better interpersonal relations, and improved organizational coordination should result.

The stress of overload is bad for the individual, but high work loads may be good for the organization; so there is often conflict between employees and employers over work loads, work standards, and piece rates. However, where individual jobs are definitely overloaded, it is probably to the long-range advantage of all concerned to correct the inequity by reducing the overload and redistributing the work.

One might also change the job by institutionalizing certain procedures for reducing stress when it occurs. For example, Kahn et al. (1964) suggest that persons who experience a great deal of role conflict or overload should be given the right to convene those people who make excessive demands on them, confront them with the conflicting demands they are making, and work out some acceptable solution. Similarly, a person could be given the right to delegate work to other people or to ask for more work or responsibility if he is underloaded.

It should be recognized that giving people such rights is not always a simple matter, for there are strongly held norms and values specifying who should do what and how policies, procedures, and jobs should be changed. There may be resistance to changing norms about subordinates delegating work, redefining their jobs, or taking initiative to get more responsibility.

Changing the Wider Environment of the Job

A variety of such changes could be made. First, one could increase the resources available to the person to reduce overload and deadline pressures. More auxiliary help could be added. Immediate superiors could be trained in better management techniques to improve relations between the person and his superior and reduce role conflict. Better information transmission systems could be adopted to reduce role ambiguity.

Although many such environmental changes may be necessary to reduce stress, they may not be sufficient in and of themselves. If people are not *trained* to use their new rights or organizational resources, the structural changes may have little effect on them. Thus, many changes in the job or its environment will also require some changes in the person. Similarly, some changes in the person may have little effect if there are no structural changes in the job which allow the person to utilize his new skills, knowledge, or rights.

Large-scale changes in environment might also be adopted. If boundary stress is a problem, the number of boundaries within the organization, such as between different divisions, could be reduced by reorganization. Role ambiguity could similarly be reduced by reducing the number of hierarchical levels in the organization, thereby reducing the distances between organizational members who need to communicate with one another. New policies for the allocation of various forms of work load could also be introduced (such as work load on the basis of ability rather than role, with new roles added and subtracted to take up and let out slack).

Some of these larger system changes might follow models of "ideal" organizations suggested by Likert (1961, 1967), McGregor (1960), Argyris (1962, 1964), Katz and Kahn (1966), and others which are based on research in organizations. The implications of temporary work groups where roles constantly change to adapt to new organizational demands have been discussed by Burns and Stalker (1961) in *The Management of Innovation* and by Bennis and Slater (1968) in *The Temporary Society*. Both books lead the reader to conclude that organizations, particularly those in today's changing and unstable environments, have the best chance of adapting to new challenges from their environments if they utilize a flexible ("organic" rather than "mechanistic") structure of organization. This structure does not lock or freeze people into specific roles or jobs beyond the point where this is nonadaptive for the organization.

Using Participation to Reduce Stress and Strain

We have observed that low participation is related to psychological strains such as job dissatisfaction and job-related threat. We now wish to offer some advice on the use of participation, because there are ways of using participation which may have either no effect or may create even more strain and problems for management than if it is not used. This advice is based on some findings from research (French, Israel, & Ås, 1960; French, Kay, & Meyer, 1966) which, although inconclusive, nevertheless seem to be potentially too important to overlook.

We have already noted that one experimental program of participation worked best when the employee felt supported rather than threatened by his boss (French et al., 1966). Generalizing these findings a bit, we suggest that attempts to decrease stress by increasing participation should also provide a supportive supervisor and a cohesive and supportive group of co-workers. Such supportiveness will directly reduce psychological strain, and it will also increase the effectiveness of the participation.

Second, participation which is only *illusory*, as when management asks employees for their advice and then ignores it, may be perceived by the employees as an attempt at psychological manipulation. The end result of such an attempt by management to "win the hearts" of employees may be employee distrust of superiors, organizational sabotage, apathy, and turnover.

Third, participation in *trivial* decisions (should the company newsletter be on white paper or light-green paper?) are liable to have little, if any, effect on the employees. A fourth and related potential principle concerns *relevance*. If the aim is to reduce the stress of quantitative work load, then participation in decisions irrelevant to the work load are not likely to have ameliorative effects on strain created by quantitative overload. Participation, for example, in decisions about what hours the company cafeteria should operate to best meet the needs of employees would probably have little positive effect on strains caused by deadlines and other work overload.

Finally, the decisions which people participate in should be perceived as being *legitimately* theirs to make. If a group does not feel it is debating something within its area of freedom, the participants may feel anxious, threatened, even dissatisfied. Since strong norms or widely shared rules develop in organizations about who should decide what, it would not be uncommon to find people feeling that they were overstepping their bounds in making new kinds of decisions. Thus, increased participation may need to occur at a rate great enough for employees to perceive, yet not at a rate so great that they cringe in fear over new expectations they feel they have been saddled with.

In conclusion, the body of evidence we have reviewed here lends strong support to the notion that modern organizations have an impact on both the psychological and physiological health of their members. Many of the stresses that are fairly prevalent in national samples and in specific organizational settings appear to be linked in one way or another with strains which produce coronary heart disease. But the fact that coronary heart disease seems to be as much a part of organizational life as are other traits of organizations (such as size and structure) does not mean that steps cannot be taken to reduce the risk of disease. There are innovative measures available to management. Programs which involve the coordinated effort of management, medical personnel, and organizational psychologists can be developed. Careful evaluation of these programs can be carried out; and through such experimental programs, modern organizations can make potentially important contributions to both management and medical science, with benefits for both the individual's and the organization's well-being and strength.

REFERENCES

Ardrey, R. *The Territorial Imperative*. New York: Dell, 1968.

Argyris, C. *Integrating the Individual and the Organization*. New York: John Wiley & Sons, 1964.

Argyris, C. *Interpersonal Confidence and Organizational Effectiveness*. Homewood, Ill: Richard D. Irwin, Dorsey Press, 1962.

Bennis, W. G., and P.E. Slater. *The Temporary Society*. New York: Harper & Row, 1968.

Brooks, G. W., and E. F. Mueller. Serum urate concentrations among university professors. *Journal of the American Medical Association*, 1966, *195*, 415–418.

Brummet, R. L., W. C. Pyle, and E. G. Flamholtz. Accounting for human resources. *Michigan Business Review*, 1968, *20*, 20–25.

Burns, T., and G. M. Stalker. *The Management of Innovation*. London: Tavistock, 1961.

Campbell, J. P., and M. D. Dunnette. Effectiveness of t-group experiences in managerial training and development. *Psychological Bulletin*, 1968, *70*, 73–104.

Coch, L., and J. R. P. French, Jr. Overcoming resistance to change. *Human Relations*, 1948, *1*, 512–532.

Dreyfuss, F., and J. W. Czaczkes. Blood cholesterol and uric acid of healthy medical students under stress of examination. *Archives of International Medicine*, 1959, *103*, 708.

Dunn, J., and S. Cobb. Frequency of peptic ulcer among executives, craftsmen, and foremen. *Journal of Occupational Medicine*, 1962, *4*, 343–348.

French, J. R. P., Jr., J. Israel, and D. Ås. An experiment on participation in a Norwegian factory. *Human Relations*, 1960, *13*, 3–20.

French, J. R. P., Jr., E. Kay, and H. Meyer. Participation and the appraisal system. *Human Relations*, 1966, *19*, 3–20.

French, J. R. P., Jr., C. J. Tupper, and E. F. Mueller. *Work Load of University Professors*. Cooperative Research Project No. 2171, University of Michigan, 1965.

Friedman, M., R. H. Rosenman, and V. Carroll. Changes in serum cholesterol and blood clotting time in men subjected to cyclic variation of occupational stress. *Circulation*, 1958, *17*, 852–861.

Grundy, S. M., and A. C. Griffin. Effects of periodic mental stress on serum cholesterol levels. *Circulation*, 1959, *19*, 496.

Hinkle, L. E., Jr., S. T. Carver, M. Stevens, and S. Scheidt. Disorders of rate and rhythm as precursors of coronary death. Paper presented at the Conference on Cardiovascular Disease Epidemiology, March 1970.

Horwitz, C., and B. Bronte-Stewart. Mental stress and serum lipid variation in ischemic heart disease. *American Journal of Medical Science*, 1962, *244*, 272–281.

Kahn, R. L., D. M. Wolfe, R. P. Quinn, J. D. Snoek, and R. A. Rosenthal. *Organizational Stress: Studies in Role Conflict and Ambiguity*. New York: John Wiley & Sons, 1964.

Kasl, S. V., G. W. Brooks, and S. Cobb. Serum urate concentrations in male high-school students: A predictor of college attendance. *Journal of the American Medical Association*, 1966, *198*, 713–716.

Kasl, S., and J. R. P. French, Jr. The effects of occupational status on physical and mental health. *Journal of Social Issues*, 1962, *18*, 67–89.

Katz, D., and R. L. Kahn. *The Social Psychology of Organizations*. New York: John Wiley & Sons, 1966.

Levitan, U. Status in human organization as a determinant of mental health and performance. Ph.D. dissertation, University of Michigan, 1970.

Likert, R. *The Human Organization.* New York: McGraw-Hill, 1967.

Likert, R. *New Patterns of Management,* New York: McGraw-Hill, 1961.

Maier, N. R. F. *Psychology in Industry.* 3rd ed. Boston: Houghton Mifflin, 1965.

McClelland, D. C. *The Achieving Society.* Princeton, N.J.: Van Nostrand, 1961.

McGregor, D. *The Human Side of Enterprise.* New York McGraw-Hill, 1960.

Miller, J. G. Information input overload and psychopathology. *American Journal of Psychiatry,* 1960, *116,* 695–704.

Modigliani, A. *Embarrassment and Social Influence.* Ph.D. dissertation, University of Michigan, 1966. Ann Arbor, Mich.: University Microfilms, No. 67–8312.

Obradović, J., J. R. P. French, Jr., and W. Rodgers. Workers' councils in Yugoslavia. *Human Relations,* 1970, *23,* 459–471.

The President's Commission on Heart Disease, Cancer and Stroke. *Report to the President: A National Program to Conquer Heart Disease, Cancer and Stroke.* Vol. 1. Washington, D.C.: U.S. Government Printing Office, 1964.

Rosenman, R. H., M. Friedman, R. Strauss, C. D. Jenkins, S. J. Zyzanski, and M. Wurm. Coronary heart disease in the Western Collaborative Group Study: A follow-up experience of 4½ years. *Journal of Chronic Diseases,* 1970, *23,* 173–190.

Rosenman, R. H., M. Friedman, R. Strauss, M. Wurm, C. D. Jenkins, H. B. Messinger, R. Kositchek, W. Hahn, and N. T. Werthessen. Coronary heart disease in the Western Collaborative Group Study. *Journal of the American Medical Association,* 1966, *195,* 86–92.

Russek, H. I. Emotional stress and CHD in American physicians, dentists, and lawyers. *American Journal of Medical Science,* 1962, *243,* 716–725.

Russek, H. I. Emotional stress and coronary heart disease in American physicians. *American Journal of Medical Science,* 1960 *240,* 711–721.

Russek, H. I. Stress, tobacco, and coronary heart disease in North American professional groups. *Journal of the American Medical Association,* 1965, *192,* 189–194.

Sales, S. M. *Differences among Individuals in Affective, Behavioral, Biochemical, and Physiological Responses to Variations in Work Load.* Ph.D. dissertation, University of Michigan, 1969. Ann Arbor, Mich.: University Microfilms, No. 69–18098.

Sales, S. M., and J. House. Job dissatisfaction as a possible risk factor in coronary heart disease. To be published in *Journal of Chronic Diseases.*

Stamler, J., D. M. Berkson, H. A. Lindberg, W. A. Miller, E. L. Stevens, R. Soyugenc, T. J. Tokich, and R. Stamler. Heart rate: An important risk factor for coronary mortality, including sudden death—ten-year experience of the Peoples Gas Company Epidemiologic Study (1958-68). Paper presented at the Second International Symposium on Atherosclerosis, Chicago, November 1969.

Terreberry, S. *The Organization of Environments.* Ph.D. dissertation, University of Michigan, 1968. Ann Arbor, Mich.: University Microfilms, No. 69–12254.

Thomas, C. B., and E. A. Murphy. Further studies on cholesterol levels in the Johns Hopkins medical students: The effect of stress at examinations. *Journal of Chronic Diseases,* 1958, *8,* 661–668.

Wertlake, P. T., A. A. Wilcox, M. T. Haley, and J. E. Peterson. Relationship of mental and emotional stress to serum cholesterol levels. *Proceedings of the Society for Experimental Biology and Medicine*, 1958, 97, 163-165.

CHAPTER 5

ANDROGYNY AS
A STRESS-MANAGEMENT STRATEGY

Alice G. Sargent

Excessive levels of stress are a hazard of organizational life; the managerial style generally fostered and probably required by many organizations leads to undue stress and all of its consequences, both physiological and psychological. The physiological consequences include heart failure, stroke, high blood pressure, and ulcers; the psychological consequences include anxiety, tension, and feelings of isolation. People who are under extreme stress do not perform as well as they could either at work or in other facets of their lives; they reduce their capacity for pleasure and their ability to interact with others.

"TYPE A" BEHAVIOR

Excessive stress is particularly deadly for those with Type A personality characteristics, identified by cardiologists Friedman and Rosenman (1974). "Type A" people exhibit high-risk, coronary-prone behaviors and are two to three times more likely to develop coronary heart disease than are their low-risk, "Type B" counterparts.

In direct contrast to more relaxed, easygoing, Type B people, those with Type A personalities drive themselves relentlessly. Unfortunately, most organizations reward typical Type A behavior and expect their managers, in particular, to emulate the Type A behavioral model. Thus, in an effort to succeed in organizations, many men and more and more women have adopted personality characteristics that have dangerous implications for their physical and mental well-being.

The Type A personality traits warrant particular attention. Such people are constantly "on guard." They are unable to relax or to depend

---

Parts of this article will appear in A. G. Sargent, *The Androgynous Manager,* AMACOM, in press.

on others and so must rely exclusively on themselves. They cannot open themselves to new experiences or to real change. Their fear of change leads them to try to control events that are actually beyond their province of control.

Those with a Type A personality constantly work against time. Because they are always on the go, such people have difficulty waiting in lines or waiting for other people to complete their sentences. They often are perceived as rude because they do not wait for others to finish speaking. Since they do not hear what others say, their personal objectivity is inhibited. They often begin thinking about one activity before another is finished, priding themselves on their ability to work on many tasks concurrently. Their restless activity leads to scheduling problems and always rushing to keep up. Eventually their bodies and psyches must crack under this self-inflicted pressure.

Type A people exhibit superhuman behavior. They cannot admit vulnerability to others, dislike soft feelings in themselves, and deny that such feelings exist. People with Type A personalities are unable to maintain warm, close relationships with others. Therefore, they lack support systems and feel they must be the only ones to do the job. By ignoring nonverbal behavior, they tend to miss a lot of the content and context of communication.

In addition, they tend to ignore their own psychological needs. They do not effectively manage aggressive feelings and are feisty and challenging of others. They express high power needs, as opposed to the need for affiliation, and have difficulty controlling impulses. At the same time, they are egotistic and move conversations toward their own concerns. This characteristic behavior is coupled with impatience toward others' needs or points of view. Type A individuals also tend to ignore the practical significance of values; in other words, they do not deal with priority conflicts that clearly connote a value conflict, such as that between time and work on the one hand and family on the other. They typically evaluate in terms of quantity rather than quality: *Bigger* is seen as *better*. With their excessive focus on task, they cannot observe well and tend to be unaware of their environments; they lack awareness of the positive or negative aspects of their physical surroundings.

Type A behavior often is accompanied by fatigue and loss of interest in sex. People manifesting this behavior are tired but rarely sleep deeply. Pushing themselves becomes necessary and habitual. If sexual interest is maintained, it often is used as a release from tension rather than as a spontaneous or intimate response to another individual.

Often Type A people feel visible and vulnerable as a result of being the first ones to accomplish something new or to achieve a certain status.

This position is particularly stressful for women and minorities who find themselves alone in new situations. They are held accountable as role models for other members of their sex or race and feel that they must perform in a superhuman manner in order to prove that others like themselves can succeed.

Finally, Type A people avoid or are reluctant to express "feminine behaviors." For example, they would feel uncomfortable crying or expressing tender feelings; such behaviors would disrupt their rational, analytical work style.

ANDROGYNY AS A VIABLE STRATEGY

Proposed solutions to the problem of organizational stress experienced by Type A people have included emphases on proper nutrition; regular, vigorous exercise; life-style changes; and value and behavior shifts. Another area for further investigation as a possible solution is androgyny. *Andro* is Greek for *male*, and *gyn* is Greek for *female*; thus, *androgyny* refers to the combining of male and female characteristics and is based on the premise that all people, to some degree, possess both traditionally masculine and traditionally feminine behaviors. These behaviors are identified in the Bem Sex-Role Inventory (Bem, 1977). A conscious blending of these behaviors allows people to be both self-reliant and compassionate and to function effectively to get things done while maintaining their sensitivity toward others. Androgyny permits us to embrace and express all aspects of our individual personalities: aggression and tenderness, logic and emotion, the need to feel autonomous and the need to belong, self-interest and group interest.

Allowing ourselves to become androgynous is not synonymous with abandoning our masculinity or femininity. The man who expresses tenderness and nurturance toward others along with his masculine attributes becomes more fully human; the woman who is able to assert her needs and abilities while retaining her spontaneity and desire to nurture increases her growth and development as a person. Ultimately, both people increase their personal effectiveness in handling the stresses of life in general and organizational life in particular.

Therefore, in order to become androgynous and thereby alleviate much of the stress in their lives, Type A people need to develop the ability to express their personal feelings, accepting emotion and spontaneity as healthy and valid; promote close, interpersonal relationships through open and honest communication; and value their work as an outlet for self-fulfillment and affiliation with others.

INSTRUMENTAL AND EXPRESSIVE BEHAVIOR

Some of the new behaviors necessary for an androgynous style are classified as instrumental, or traditionally masculine, and expressive, or traditionally feminine. *Instrumental* behavior emphasizes rationality, and *expressive* behavior emphasizes emotionality. Most organizations value instrumental behavior much more highly than expressive behavior, whereas family relationships place a high premium on expressive behavior. This situation means that women re-entering the work force need to expand their repertoire of instrumental behavior. In contrast, some men and some career women wishing to enrich their home lives need to increase their expressive behavior. Both behaviors are critical to effective interpersonal problem solving, which, in turn, entails self-disclosure, brainstorming, and then choosing an alternative. With the increased focus on human-resource management in the marketplace, managers need to be able to set clear performance expectations with subordinates, develop training and career-development plans and opportunities, monitor performance effectiveness, and recommend for promotion. All of these activities include both instrumental and expressive aspects, which are defined in Table 1 provided by Peter Block and Neale Clapp of Block Petrella Associates. This table provides a glimpse at the areas of attitude and behavior in which change is necessary if men and women are to become androgynous.

Table 1. The Androgynous Manager

Attitude/ Behavior	Instrumental (Masculine)	Expressive (Feminine)
Purpose:	To solve problems, avoid failure, and achieve success	To allow self-expression, avoid loneliness, be acknowledged, and achieve a sense of belonging
Exchange:	Service, commodities, information, data	Empathy, feelings
Based on:	Data	Self-disclosure
Needs:	Control, power	Here and now—"let it be"
Time focus:	Future oriented (planning)	Flexible, less predictable
Structure:	Predictable, certain	Ambiguous
Avoid at all costs:	Surprise	Boredom

ANDROGYNY AND MEN

In the area of communication, men, particularly those with Type A tendencies, need to listen more and say less. Active listening is a skill that can be learned by truly focusing on what others are saying and becoming aware of nonverbal cues, instead of focusing on preparing responses. In addition, men can communicate physically by making warm contact and expressing approval. Given current mores, the sexual implications of physical contact and emotional warmth have to be dealt with openly and frankly.

Men can become aware of, accept, and express a wider range of feelings. Tender as well as tough feelings need to be considered acceptable; feelings are a basic and essential part of life and can serve as guides to authenticity and effectiveness for fully functioning persons, rather than as impediments to achievement. Among the feelings that need to be accepted and expressed is the need to be nurtured and supported when feeling hurt, afraid, vulnerable, or helpless. Hiding such feelings behind a mask of strength, rationality, and invulnerability leads to stress. Any feeling that demands expression will have a detrimental effect on the physical or emotional system if it is suppressed. Of course, sharing such feelings with others involves accepting risk and vulnerability. But if we accept vulnerability and imperfections as part of all persons, we can accept our own flaws and inadequacies, viewing them as potential avenues for personal growth; and we can begin to relax more.

With a more relaxed attitude, men can learn to fail at tasks without feeling that they have failed as men or failed totally in life. Men can be helped in accepting their faults if they learn that their individual identities are not defined totally by work and that all of us have the right to strive for self-fulfillment. Men need to assert this right rather than lock themselves into the role of provider, achiever, or hard-driving entrepreneur. In contrast to women, men would benefit from personalizing experience more, rather than assuming that objectivity is the only valid approach to life and relationships. Such a behavioral change might help to transform performance-oriented sexuality into more sensual, less goal-oriented sexuality.

Men's approach to other men is also important. They need mutual support systems in which they share competencies and feelings without competing with each other. By allowing close friendships to develop with men, it is possible to begin to ease out of the "rat race" that causes so much tension and stress. In dealing with other men, it seems necessary to confront and deal with homosexual fears so that they do not inhibit closeness.

In order to reinforce the foregoing behavioral changes and to abate the disruption that change produces, men need to nurture and support other men and women who also are struggling to change.

ANDROGYNY AND WOMEN

Women may need to pursue a behavioral pattern that is precisely the opposite of that which Type A men may need to pursue. This statement does not mean that women need to become masculine any more than the adoption of androgynous behavior implies that men should become feminine. The goal of becoming androgynous is to encompass within a person the characteristics, attitudes, beliefs, and behaviors that express the full range of what it means to be human. As women move into the world of management, they typically need to work toward developing the ability to forcefully direct task accomplishment; tempering their expression of feelings with appropriate use of logic, rationality, and analysis; promoting themselves within an organization by becoming more visible and entrepreneurial; and making their needs and opinions clearly known without acquiescing in the face of possible disagreement.

In order to communicate more effectively, women need to present themselves credibly by developing a fuller range of self-expression, such as forceful body posture, emphatic vocal tone, proper speech rate, and direct eye contact. It is essential that women learn to state exactly what they want to happen and that they face the risk of disagreement or rejection, especially at meetings; they need not abandon their viewpoints, even if the immediate response is not acceptance. Further, women can learn to stop such self-limiting behaviors as allowing interruptions while speaking or laughing after making a serious statement.

Another important area is effective feedback, or letting others know that their comments have been heard accurately but may not be agreed with. In other words, women need to question more the feedback they receive, instead of simply accepting it.

To be effective in the managerial world, women must be concerned with making a difference. Women will not establish a presence or be seen as leaders if they are ambivalent about using power in order to have an impact on others, to build alliances and to produce compliance, to get their viewpoints across through effective pro and con reasoning, to use contacts to build networks and coalitions, and to be proactive rather than reactive.

Of course, action entails risk. It means putting oneself on the line. To feel comfortable in taking forceful action, women need appropriate training in such areas as making decisions, developing analytical skills, and asserting themselves. They must develop a capacity to use creativity for synthesis, to grasp the "big picture," and to articulate the model. The typically masculine approach usually involves submerging feelings and fears about risk and simply taking action, whereas women may face a problem situation by reacting emotionally before they do something and losing valuable time in the process. Thus, women need to practice risk taking and *acting* rather than simply *reacting*.

These options broaden the behavioral repertoire for all of us in our organizational and home lives. Such a wide range of behavior is a lot to aspire to in one lifetime. None of us can do it all alone, but as we start to change we will discover that we are part of a larger community, hopefully grappling with reducing stress, with trying to be more authentic, and with trying to move beyond role behavior to a sense of balance and interdependence.

REFERENCES

Bem, S.L. Beyond androgyny: Some presumptuous prescriptions for a liberated sexual identity. In C.G. Carney & S.L. McMahon (Eds.), *Exploring contemporary male/female roles: A facilitator's guide.* San Diego, CA: University Associates, 1977.

Friedman, M., & Rosenman, R.H. *Type A behavior and your heart.* New York: A.A. Knopf, 1974.

CHAPTER 6

CORRELATES OF JOB STRESS AND JOB SATISFACTION FOR MINORITY PROFESSIONALS IN ORGANIZATIONS

David L. Ford, Jr.
Diane S. Bagot

ORGANIZATIONAL FACTORS AND REACTIONS TO JOB DEMANDS

Recent reviews of the leadership literature have examined various organizational variables and their effects on job satisfaction and job stress. Organizational level (Berger & Cummings, 1976); supervisory behavior (Kerr, Schriesheim, Murphy, & Stogdill, 1974); superior-subordinate sex interaction (Butterfield & Bartol, 1977); and role ambiguity (Rizzo, House, & Lirtzman, 1970) are but a few of the many organizational variables that have been investigated and discussed. Significant positive correlations with satisfaction with pay have been obtained for organizational level and job tenure (Lawler & Porter, 1966; Schwab & Wallace, 1974). However, when multiple correlations were employed, many of the relationships became nonsignificant or changed direction.

Herman, Dunham, and Hulin (1975) noted that organizational variables (e.g., tenure, job level, shift) accounted for four times more unique variance in job attitudes (including job satisfaction) than did personal variables (e.g., age, education, sex, marital status). These results are consistent with those reported by Herman and Hulin (1972), who found that three structural (organizational) variables consistently accounted for about two to three times as much attitude variance as did personal variables. Thus, there seems to be some basis for the conclusion that organizational variables explain a larger portion of satisfaction variance than do personal or individual difference variables.

Reprinted from: D.L. Ford, Jr., and D.S. Bagot. Correlates of Job Stress and Job Satisfaction for Minority Professionals in Organizations: An Examination of Personal and Organizational Factors. *Group & Organization Studies,* March 1978, 3(1), 30-41.

PERSONALITY VARIABLES, INDIVIDUAL DIFFERENCES, AND REACTIONS TO JOB DEMANDS

Several researchers have examined the effects of certain personal or individual difference variables as moderators of the relationships among role conflict, role ambiguity, and job satisfaction (Johnson & Stinson, 1975); job performance and job satisfaction (Steers, 1975); and task characteristics and job satisfaction (Wanous, 1974). Steers (1975) reported a positive relationship between job attitudes and performance for subjects with high achievement needs and no such relationship for subjects with low achievement needs. Wanous (1974) found that the strength of higher order needs (need for personal growth or challenge) was the best of three individual difference variables in moderating the relationships between job characteristics and specific job facet satisfaction and overall job satisfaction.

In a recent study Caplan and Jones (1975) examined the combined effects of job demands and personality on the subject's ability to cope with job stress. More specifically, the subject examined the role of the Type-A personality in the relationship between work stress and psychological and physiological strains. The Type-A personality is hard driving, persistent, involved in work, has a sense of time urgency, and is oriented toward leadership and achievement; Type-B personality characteristics are generally considered to be the opposite. Caplan and Jones took measures of stress, personality, and psychological strain (anxiety, depression, resentment) twice: at the initiation of a highly stress-inducing event (Time 1) and five months later (Time 2). In both instances a thirty-second reading of each respondent's heart rate was also taken. The results indicated that heart rate was significantly lower at Time 2 than at Time 1, that changes in subjective quantitative work load from Time 1 to Time 2 were positively correlated with changes in anxiety-tension, and, in turn, changes in anxiety-tension were positively associated with changes in heart rate. There also was a tendency for the relationship between changes in anxiety and heart rate to be higher for Type-A than for Type-B persons. The researchers concluded that stress indeed does have the greatest effects on the hard-driving, involved Type-A personality (Caplan & Jones, 1975).

Other researchers have suggested that employees having Type-A personality traits may contribute to their organizations—but at some cost to their own mental and physical health. For example, studies by Rogers (1975) and Ogilvie and Porter (1975) have highlighted the need to give increased attention to stress-induced coronary heart disease and its increasing toll on American men in middle age. These studies pointed to the relationship between organizational and Type-A personality traits. Studies by Friedman and Rosenman (cf. Rosenman, Friedman, Straus, Jenkins, Zyanski, & Wurm, 1970) have shown that Type-A persons suffer coronary attacks twice as frequently as Type-B persons.

Jenkins (1976), Russek and Russek (1976), and others have discussed similarities and/or interaction between Type-A personality traits and high need-achievement traits. Indeed, a person characterized by a high need for achievement might be defined as a Type-A personality. Studies show that emphasizing the achievement motive in the socialization of children can lead to an increased incidence of Type-A behavior, thus increasing the risks of heart disease (Jenkins, 1976).

ORGANIZATIONAL STRESS AND BLACK PROFESSIONALS

Job satisfaction could be described as the absence of conflict, well-defined tasks and roles, and an atmosphere in which mental health can prevail. (Mental health is defined by Gechman and Wiener, 1975, as functional effectiveness, well-being, mastery, and competence.) Job dissatisfaction is a function of many factors, including overwork, role conflict, status inconsistency, job immaturity, i.e., the absence of an environment in which mental health can flourish (House, 1974). Such an atmosphere generates tension in coronary-prone individuals.

Several recent studies concerned with black professionals in organizations have pointed up wide disparities between the career success and work experiences of black professionals and their white counterparts (Brown & Ford, 1977; Ford, 1976). Studies by O'Rielly and Roberts (1973), Slocum and Strawser (1972), and Milutinovich (1976) have reported lower satisfaction needs for black white-collar workers than for whites relative to specific aspects of their jobs. Other studies (Hamner, Kim, Baird, & Bigoness, 1976; Richards & Jaffee, 1972; Parker, 1976) suggest that performance ratings of blacks by whites may not accurately reflect the quality of their performance. It appears that in some cases the need fulfillment, performance, and satisfaction of blacks in organizations have suffered under white leadership. The effect these circumstances have had on the behavior and attitudes of blacks and other minorities in organizations is not known.

Equal opportunity and affirmative action programs in organizations were instituted as means of correcting past injustices. Often, in order for a black or other minority to be hired and/or promoted, he or she had to be much better than his or her white counterpart. Such requirements may have imposed a syndrome of overachievement and striving or, rather, Type-A personality, on blacks who desire to achieve and succeed in organizations. Of course, this is conjecture, but the implications are serious if it is true. Because Type-A persons are more prone to heart disease, the costs in terms of physical and mental health for blacks striving to get ahead could be high. Blacks are in double jeopardy because the incidence of hypertension (high blood pressure) is three times higher in blacks than in whites, and hypertension is strongly related to the incidence of heart disease (*Ebony Magazine*, 1974).

Research is not available to answer some of the questions raised. More research is needed on the relationships among organizational factors, job stress, hypertension, Type-A personality, and incidence of heart disease, especially among blacks. One study (Castle, Hendrickz, & Jones, 1976) reported the Type-A personality to be more pronounced among blacks, and it is the only such study of this nature that the authors were able to find. The results of a pilot exploratory study that investigated only a small segment of the possible relationships among these variables is reported in the following pages. The relationships between several organizational factors and perceived anxiety, stress, and job satisfaction were investigated for a small sample of black and Mexican-American professionals. Type-A personality and higher order needs were examined as potential moderators of the relationships. An additional comparison of black and Mexican-American subgroups was made to note any similarities in the relationships, because Mexican-Americans have historically encountered organizational experiences similar to those of blacks.

A Pilot Study

Sample

The sample consisted of twenty-two minority (thirteen black and nine Mexican-American) managerial, supervisory, technical, and clerical personnel from geographically dispersed subunits in the southern region of a large decentralized manufacturing and sales organization. Their ages ranged from twenty-five to thirty-three and 82 percent were male. The average time on the job was eighteen months, with a range from one to forty-two months. Questionnaires were administered to subjects under controlled conditions at a workshop convened by minority employees of the organization. Subjects were assured of the anonymity of their responses. The questionnaires measured the subjects' (perceived) leadership behavior of their superior, their job stress, job satisfaction, task structure, role clarity, job pressure, hierarchical level, propensity for Type-A personality behavior, higher order needs, race, and various other demographic items.

Measures: Dependent Variables

Job satisfaction. Job satisfaction was measured using the twenty-item short form of the Minnesota Satisfaction Questionnaire (Weiss, Davis, England, & Lofquist, 1967). This instrument measures global or general satisfaction and correlates well with other measures of job satisfaction such as the Job Descriptive Index. Reliabilities of .85 or better have been reported for the MSQ.

Job Stress. Job stress was defined as perceived on-the-job anxiety. Spielberger's twenty-item State-Anxiety subscale of the State-Trait Anxiety Inventory (Spielberger, Gorsuch, & Lushene, 1970) was employed to measure on-the-job anxiety. Respondents were requested to complete the subscale describing how they usually felt on their present jobs.

Measures: Independent Variables

Organizational Variables. Five organizational variables were included in the study. Each respondent's perception of his or her superior's leadership behavior was measured using House and Dessler's (1974) seven- and ten-item measures of instrumental and supportive leader behavior. Supportive behavior is defined as supervisory leader behavior that shows concern for subordinates' needs, well-being, and worth; instrumental behavior is defined as leader behavior that defines the roles of the leader and his subordinates, assigns specific tasks, and specifies procedures to be followed.

Task structure as an independent variable was measured using a ten-item scale developed by House and Dessler (1974). This scale measures the degree to which the task and execution and rules and procedures are simple, repetitive, and unambiguous. Role clarity was measured using Lyons' (1971) four-item scale, which measures the degree to which subjects are clear about how and what they are to do in their jobs. Organizational level was determined by whether subjects were supervisory/managerial (coded 1) or technical/clerical (coded 0). Finally, pressure was measured using a twelve-item scale developed by Caplan (1975) indicative of the time pressures and work load experienced by respondents on the job.

Moderator Variables

The strength of higher order needs was measured using an eleven-item instrument adopted with minor revision from Hackman and Lawler (1971). Higher order needs include the need for personal growth and development and the need for challenge (Alderfer, 1971). Propensity for

Type-A personality was measured using a scale developed by Caplan (1975). Race was coded as a dummy variable (1 = black; 0 = nonblack).

Analysis

Zero-order correlations were computed between each of the five independent variables and job satisfaction and job stress to determine the strength and direction of the relationships between the variables. Next, the personal variables of higher order needs, propensity for Type-A personality, and race were used as moderator variables for the same set of relationships. Racial subgroups included black and Mexican-American. High and low subgroups were formed for each of the other moderator variables via median splits on the respective scores. Correlations between independent and dependent variables were computed for each subgroup, and the significance of differences between correlations were examined according to the suggestions of Zedeck (1971). Due to the exploratory nature of the study, directional hypotheses were not posited. Rather, the results serve as a means of expanding the prior work of Caplan and Jones (1975), Jenkins (1976), Russek and Russek (1976), and others.

Results

The relationships of job satisfaction and job stress to organizational variables are included in Table 1. Job satisfaction was found to be significantly positively related to supervisor supportive behavior and supervisor instrumental behavior and negatively correlated with role clarity. The latter result is consistent with the findings of Brief and Aldag (1976) but inconsistent with the results reported by Schriesheim and Murphy (1976) and Lyons (1971). Job stress was significantly negatively correlated only with supervisor supportive behavior.

To test moderating effects of higher order needs, high and low HONS subgroups were formed. Significant differences between subgroup correlations were obtained only for the relationship between role clarity and job satisfaction. Under conditions of low need strength, role clarity was significantly negatively related to job satisfaction. This correlation changes to positive under conditions of high need strength (although the correlation itself is not significant). The strength of higher order needs did not moderate any of the job stress-organizational variable relationships. There was a tendency for leader instrumental behavior to be more positively related to job satisfaction and less negatively related to job stress under conditions of low need strength than high need strength; however, these differences were not significant (see Table 2).

Table 1. Zero-Order Correlations of Independent Variables with Job Satisfaction and Job Stress

Organizational Independent Variable	Satisfaction (n = 22)	Stress (n = 22)
	Correlated with	
Supervisor supportive behavior	.59***	-.41*
Supervisor instrumental behavior	.52**	-.32
Task structure	.13	.03
Role clarity	-.42*	.26
Organizational level	-.01	.02
Pressure	-.04	.16

*p<.10
**p<.05
***p<.01

Table 2. Correlations Between Independent and Dependent Variables for High and Low Need Strength Groups

Organizational Independent Variable	Satisfaction HONS High (n = 10)	Satisfaction HONS Low (n = 12)	Stress HONS High (n = 10)	Stress HONS Low (n = 12)
Supervisor supportive behavior	.49	.61**	-.36	-.43
Supervisor instrumental behavior	.21	.65**	-.52	-.19
Task structure	-.35	.04	.04	-.13
Role clarity	.36	-.82***a	.19	.30
Organizational level	.19	-.28	-.37	.11
Pressure	.28	-.14	.61**	.08

aHigh and low group correlations significantly different at p<.05.
*p<.10
**p<.05
***p<.01

Using propensity for Type-A personality as a moderator variable, it was found that for subjects classified as Type A, role clarity and job satisfaction were significantly negatively correlated, while for persons classified as Type B, this relationship was positive and nonsignificant. Propensity for Type-A personality failed to moderate any of the job stress-organizational variable relationships (see Table 3).

Table 3. Correlations Between Independent and Dependent Variables for Type-A and Type-B Personality Groups

Organizational Independent Variable	Correlated with			
	Satisfaction Personality		Stress Personality	
	Type A (n = 14)	Type B (n = 8)	Type A (n = 14)	Type B (n = 8)
Supervisor supportive behavior	.70***	.13	-.44	-.30
Supervisor instrumental behavior	.59**	.44	-.20	-.55*
Task structure	-.27	.04	.14	.41
Role clarity	-.62**	.17 a	.18	.44
Organizational level	.05	-.38	-.02	.34
Pressure	-.03	-.07	.13	.26

aHigh and low group correlations significantly different at $p<.05$.
*$p<.10$
**$p<.05$
***$p<.01$

When the job satisfaction-organizational variable and job stress-organizational variable relationships for black and Mexican-American respondents were compared, it was found that race moderated the relationship between role-clarity and job satisfaction and also moderated the relationships between supervisor supportive behavior and job stress and between organizational level and job stress. For Mexican-American respondents, the role clarity-job satisfaction relationship was significantly positively correlated; for black respondents the relationship was negative and nonsignificant. For Mexican-Americans, the relationships between leader behavior and job satisfaction were significantly positively correlated; for blacks these relationships were in the same direction but nonsignificant. The supervisor supportive behavior-job stress relationship was significantly moderated by race, with the relationship being negative and nonsignificant for blacks and significant and positive for Mexican-Americans. The same pattern held true for the organizational level-job stress relationship, except that the relationship was significant for blacks and nonsignificant for Mexican-Americans (see Table 4).

Table 4. Correlations Between Independent and Dependent Variables for Black and Mexican-American Groups

| | Correlated with | | | |
| | Satisfaction Race | | Stress Race | |
Organizational Independent Variable	Black (n = 13)	MA (n = 9)	Black (n = 13)	MA (n = 9)
Supervisor supportive behavior	.36	.85***	-.28	.70***b
Supervisor instrumental behavior	.31	.75**	-.48	-.25
Task structure	-.37	.21	.03	-.05
Role clarity	-.08	.73**	.06	.43
Organizational level	.21	-.50	-.52*	.30a
Pressure	.22	-.37	.20	.06

aHigh and low group correlations significantly different at p<.05.
bHigh and low group correlations significantly different at p<.025.
   *p<.10
  **p<.05
 ***p<.01

For the most part, many of the relationships examined in the present study were not significant. It appears that the organizational variables examined are at best moderately related to job satisfaction and slightly related to job stress. These results suggest that for the minority respondents in this study, stress generally is not significantly related to the organizational variables of leader behavior, task structure, organizational level, and pressure. Although the pattern of significant relationships across moderator subgroups was not consistent, it did appear that both leader supportive behavior and leader instrumental behavior were beneficial in helping respondents to achieve some level of job satisfaction and reduce experienced levels of job stress. Additionally, the relationship between role clarity and job satisfaction was consistently moderated by each of the moderator variables employed, indicating that as role clarity increases, job satisfaction decreases for Type-A persons and blacks; the opposite occurs for Type-B and Mexican-American subgroup respondents. Persons low in higher order needs exhibit a pattern similar to Type-A and black persons for the role clarity-job satisfaction relationship.

The results do little to provide insight or constructive assistance in answering the questions we asked initially. The expected strong relationships between organizational variables, job stress, and propensity for Type-A personality were not found. However, the questions raised should not be abandoned. Poor results from this study are due to the small sample size and some problems in the lack of sensitivity of the Type-A personality measure. Although the results were not too encouraging, they do represent a start toward addressing the need for research in this area. Hopefully, other researchers will follow.

REFERENCES

Alderfer, C. P. *Human needs in organizational settings.* New York: The Free Press, 1971.

Berger, C. J., & Cummings, L. L. *Organizational structure, attitudes, and behaviors.* Unpublished manuscript, Graduate School of Business, University of Wisconsin—Madison, 1976.

Brief, A., & Aldag, R. Correlates of role indices. *Journal of Applied Psychology,* 1976, *61,* 468-472.

Brown, H. A., & Ford, D. L. An exploratory analysis of discrimination in the employment of black MBA graduates. *Journal of Applied Psychology,* 1977, *62,* 50-56.

Butterfield, D. A., & Bartol, K. M. Evaluators of leader behavior: A missing element in leadership theory. In J. G. Hunt & L. L. Larson (Eds.), *Leadership: The cutting edge.* Carbondale, IL: Southern Illinois University Press, 1977.

Caplan, R. D. *Organizational stress and individual strain: A social psychological study of risk factors in coronary heart disease among administrators, engineers, and scientists.* Ann Arbor, MI: University of Michigan, Institute for Social Research, 1971. (University Microfilms No. 72-14822).

Caplan, R. D., & Jones, K. W. Effects of work load, role ambiguity, and type-A personality on anxiety, depression, and heart rate. *Journal of Applied Psychology,* 1975, *60,* 713-719.

Castle, W. M., Hendrickz, E., & Jones, J. J. Measuring emotional stress in Africa. *South African Medical Journal,* 1976, *17,* 1143-1146.

Ford, D. L. *Readings in minority group relations.* La Jolla, CA: University Associates, 1976.

Gechman, A. S., & Wiener, Y. Job involvement and satisfaction as related to mental health and personal time related to work. *Journal of Applied Psychology,* 1975, *60,* 521-523.

Hackman, J. R., & Lawler, E. E. Employer reactions to job characteristics. *Journal of Applied Psychology,* 1971, *55,* 259-286. (Monograph)

Hamner, W. C., Kim, J. S., Baird, L. L., & Bigoness, W. J. Race and sex as determinants of ratings of potential employees in a simulated work sampling task. Journal of Applied Psychology, 1974, 59, 705-711.

Herman, J. B., Dunham, R. B., & Hulin, C. L. Organizational structure, demographic characteristics, and employee responses. Organizational Behavior and Human Performance, 1975, 13, 206-232.

Herman, J. B., & Hulin, C. L. Studying organizational attitudes from individual and organizational frames of reference. Organizational Behavior and Human Performance, 1972, 8, 84-108.

House, J. S. Occupational stress and coronary heart disease: A review and theoretical integration. Journal of Health and Social Behavior, 1974, 15, 12-15.

House, R. J., & Dessler, G. The path-goal theory of leadership: Some post hoc and a priori tests. In J. G. Hunt & L. L. Larson (Eds.), Contingency approaches to leadership. Carbondale, IL: Southern Illinois University Press, 1974.

Jenkins, C. D. Recent evidence supporting psychological and social risk factors for coronary disease. The New England Journal of Medicine, 1976, 294, 1033-1038.

Johnson, T. W., & Stinson, J. E. Role ambiguity, role conflict, and satisfaction: Moderating effects of individual differences. Journal of Applied Psychology, 1975, 60, 329-333.

Kerr, S., Schriesheim, C. A., Murphy, C. J., & Stogdill, R. M. Toward a contingency theory of leadership based upon the consideration and initiating structure literature. Organizational Behavior and Human Performance, 1974, 12, 62-82.

Lawler, E. E., & Porter, L. W. Predicting managers' pay and their satisfaction with pay. Personnel Psychology, 1966, 19, 363-373.

Lyons, T. Role clarity, need for clarity, satisfaction, tension, and withdrawal. Organizational Behavior and Human Performance, 1971, 6, 99-110.

Milutinovich, J. S. A comparative study of work attitudes of black and white workers. In D. L. Ford (Ed.), Readings in minority group relations. La Jolla, CA: University Associates, 1976.

Ogilvie, B. C., & Porter, A. L. Business careers as treadmill to oblivion: The allure of cardiovascular death. Human Resource Management, 1975, 13, 14-18.

O'Rielly, C., & Roberts, K. H. Job satisfaction among whites and non-whites: A cross-sectional approach. Journal of Applied Psychology, 1973, 57, 295-299.

Parker, W. S. Black-white differences in leader behavior related to subordinates' reactions. Journal of Applied Psychology, 1976, 61, 140-147.

Richards, A. S., & Jaffee, C. L. Blacks supervising whites: A study of interracial difficulties in working together in a simulated organization. Journal of Applied Psychology, 1972, 56, 234-240.

Rizzo, J. R., House, R. J., & Lirtzman, S. I. Role conflict and ambiguity in complex organizations. Administrative Science Quarterly, 1970, 15, 150-163.

Rogers, R. E. Executive stress. Human Resource Management, 1975, 14, 21-24.

Rosenman, R. H., Friedman, M., Straus, R., Jenkins, C. D., Zyanski, S. J., & Wurm, M. Coronary heart disease in the western collaborative group study: A follow-up experience of 4½ years. Journal of Chronic Diseases, 1970, 23, 173-190.

Russek, H. T., & Russek, L. Is emotional stress an etiologic factor in coronary heart disease? Psychosomatics, 1976, 17, 63-66.

Schriesheim, C. A., & Murphy, C. J. Relationships between leader behavior and subordinate satisfaction and performance: A test of some situational moderators. *Journal of Applied Psychology*, 1976, *61*, 634-641.

Schwab, D. P., & Wallace, M. J. Correlates of employee satisfaction with pay. *Industrial Relations*, 1974, *13*, 78-89.

Slocum, J., & Strawser, R. H. Racial differences in job attitudes. *Journal of Applied Psychology*, 1972, *56*, 28-32.

Spielberger, C. D., Gorsuch, R. L., & Lushene, R. E. *Manual for the state-trait anxiety inventory.* Palo Alto, CA: Consulting Psychologist Press, 1970.

Steers, R. M. Effects of need for achievement on the job performance-job attitude relationship. *Journal of Applied Psychology*, 1975, *60*, 678-682.

Stresses and strains on black women. *Ebony Magazine*, 1974, *24*, 33-40.

Wanous, J. P. A causal-correlation analysis of the job satisfaction and performance relationship. *Journal of Applied Psychology*, 1974, *59*, 139-144.

Wanous, J. P. Individual differences and reactions to job characteristics. *Journal of Applied Psychology*, 1974, *59*, 616-622.

Weiss, D. J., Davis, R. V., England, G. W., & Lofquist, L. H. *Manual for the Minnesota satisfaction questionnaire.* Minneapolis: Industrial Relations Center, University of Minnesota, 1967.

Zedeck, S. Problems with the use of "moderator" variables. *Psychological Bulletin*, 1971, *76*, 295-310.

PART II
MANAGING STRESS

CHAPTER 7

EMERGENT AND CONTEMPORARY LIFE STYLES: AN INTER-GENERATIONAL ISSUE

Frank Friedlander

INTRODUCTION

As we are undergoing rapid change in our technological environment, so are we witnessing a rapid alteration in our social environment—and in the individual life styles prevalent in our society. Emerging life styles are most visible and impactful in the younger generation, but new life styles may be contagious—as youth sets new forms of living for itself, this may permit and encourage older generations to live differently also.

The general purpose of this study is to explore the diverse and emerging patterns of life styles within our social milieu. More specifically, it is to identify and develop measures of different life styles, and then to relate these to various age, educational, sexual, religious, and occupational data. This study is part of a larger research program to explore the relationships between people with different life styles and organizations with different kinds of structures and processes.

The focus upon the life styles of youth is not intended to point a finger at either the dominant culture or at an emerging group which deviates from traditional norms. Rather it serves as a basis for contrast and exposition of widely differing sets of values, and for prophecies of the future about the impact of these values.

One rationale for exploring youth life styles is that through the newcomer's eyes we can frequently gain a fresh perspective of what we

This study was supported in part by a grant from the National Institute of Mental Health, U.S. Public Health Service (Research Grant 5 R01 MH 20719).

Reprinted from: F. Friedlander. Emergent and Contemporary Life Styles: An Inter-Generational Issue. *Human Relations,* 1975, *28*(4), 329-346. Used with permission of Plenum Publishing Corporation and the author.

are—less biased by inculturation. The newcomer may point an embarrassing finger at the emperor's magnificent clothes. Those of us already living in an organization or social structure have already adapted to it and to a large degree accepted it as a way of life.

A second rationale for studying youth life styles is that the youth culture of today represents a potent force in influencing the future norms and values of our society. Today's youth culture will be tomorrow's middle-aged force in administering our governmental, industrial, community, religious, and familial organizations.

No claim is made that the next generation will follow in the footsteps of current youth—nor that contemporary youth norms and values will be maintained as its members become older and take on more responsible roles. But youth's current response to society—the kinds of experiences it is gaining, its increased personal and societal awareness, its new forms of organizational life—are all providing it with substance for a potentially new working and living structure. Erikson notes that the current generation may come back to some form of accommodation with the society as it grows older and accepts positions within the society. But its experience also "leaves a 'cultural deposit' which is cumulative consciousness and . . . is irreversible, and the next generation, therefore, starts from a more advanced position . . ." (Erikson, 1967, p. 863).

A third rationale concerns the repercussions of life style differences across generations. Understanding these differences may lead to a better understanding of the divergence between contemporary youth values and the institutional and organizational structures which older generations have built and maintained.

BACKGROUND

The concept of life style depicts the individual's patterns of preferences, values, and beliefs about himself in regard to the world around him. This includes his perspectives of how, who, and what he needs to relate to in order to learn, grow, and become an effective person. Thus, life style concerns an individual's set of beliefs about where and how he will obtain guidance, direction, love, respect, comfort, learning, and success. Life style is obviously not only an individual, but a cultural phenomenon. Sets of norms emerge which permit, encourage and reinforce different life styles. Furthermore, a single life style cannot be used to label an individual, for he is obviously a complex blend of different life style patterns. Finally, while life style is conceived as a relatively enduring pattern of preferences, values and beliefs, an individual's actual behavior may vary in different situations. Life style is intentionally defined as not necessarily reflected in behavior. Behavior is a function of not only the preferences and beliefs of a life style, and not only the situation in which an individual finds himself, but also the interaction of his life style pattern with the situation. Behavior is not always congruent with life style, and this incongruency is worth maintaining conceptually if we are to understand and help reduce it through situational or behavioral change.

The concept of life style as it is relevant in this research emerged from a study by Bier (1967) in which categories of life styles were inductively derived from three sources. The first of these encompassed values congruent with classical organization theory literature (e.g. Taylor, 1911; Weber, 1947); the second encompassed values congruent with human relations theories of organizations (Mayo, 1933; Lewin, 1951; Likert, 1967). A third category of values emerged from extensive interviews which Bier conducted with college students about to enter work organizations. These categories of values, beliefs, and preferences were thus derived inductively (Glaser & Strauss, 1967) through a literature search in the first two cases, and through interviews in the third case.

METHOD

A questionnaire was constructed drawing from the interview data presented by Bier and other authors concerned with youth values (Kenniston, 1965; Simmons & Winograd, 1966), and from the values inferred from the previously mentioned literature on human relations theory and classical organization theory. The domain of items thus spanned the variety of values which have emerged from major organizational eras of the past 50 years. Each era has produced and demanded its own set of personal values in organizational settings. Items were used which were thought to represent, specifically, these sets of values, preferences and beliefs. Item format consisted of responses to the question "To what extent does the statement represent your own attitude or preference?" Five multiple choices were offered ranging from "Completely" to "Not at all." This resulted in a 78-item questionnaire which was administered to about 1200 people.

Samples were selected to represent a wide variance on five major dimensions: age, sex, occupation, religion, and education. The age range was from 14 to 67 years, with an average age of 29; education ranged from 10th grade through Ph.D. level, with an average of college sophomore. Occupations included social service, sales, business, technology, science, cultural, and the arts. Four major religions included Protestant, Catholic, Jewish and atheist/agnostic.

Questionnaires were administered anonymously in small groups of from about 10 to 40 people, generally in the participant's work or school setting. Through taking the questionnaires, participants were provided with a framework for exploring their own life style and the organization structures in which they worked or learned. A self-scoring code sheet was provided so that participants could score their own questionnaires and receive immediate feedback. Results were then frequently discussed in small sub-groups of three to five. These discussions frequently indicated that participants found their life style dimension scores reflected their own self-perceived value system. In work groups that had worked together for extended periods of time, perceptions of the preferences and beliefs of working peers often were corroborated by life style dimension scores.

About 1200 people were asked to complete the questionnaire. Of these, 1154 usable questionnaires were obtained over a two-year period. In order to understand the underlying components of life style across a wide variety of social, economic, religious, age, and occupational groups, the responses to all 1154 questionnaires were subjected to a single factor analysis using a principal components solution and orthogonal rotations to varimax criteria. Initial community estimates were the squared multiple correlations.

RESULTS

Three factors emerged from the analysis which describe the underlying structure of life style. These are noted below in terms of the eight items which had highest loadings on each factor.

	FLS	SLS	PLS
	FLS	SLS	PLS
I. *Formalistic life style*	FLS	SLS	PLS
(a) I place a great deal of faith in law and order	.61	-.06	-.09
(b) I believe that my life will be most satisfying if there are some clear pathways for advancing and being rewarded	.60	-.10	-.03
(c) What is important is that I have a secure job and a comfortable home	.60	-.03	.03
(d) I find myself striving for greater advancement and prestige	.59	.02	.15
(e) I believe the world would be a better place if more people respected and abided by the law	.58	-.01	-.01
(f) I can grow and progress best in this world by finding out the way things ought to be done	.56	-.07	-.04

(g) I am responsible to those in positions of higher responsibility for my actions   .56 -.19 -.14

(h) I will do what is right when I am guided by the precedents and policies that have been established over the years   .54 -.05 -.07

This life style places a heavy reliance on higher authority for guidance in life. The authority is represented in a number of forms: law and order, precedent, and those in positions of higher responsibility. Fulfillment derives from upward mobility and from obtaining institutional symbols of success such as rewards for advancement, security, comfort, and prestige. The FLS tends to look upward and outward for guidance, direction, success criteria, and rewards.

		FLS	SLS	PLS
II.	*Sociocentric life style*			
	(a) In deciding how I want to live and act, I am most satisfied if I have some close friends or colleagues who will help me reach this decision	.07	-.57	.01
	(b) I can only get the really important things in life by working closely with friends and colleagues	.06	-.55	-.04
	(c) I place a great deal of faith in what my close friends say	.09	-.51	.09
	(d) I will do what is right when I am guided by the close relationships I have with others	.03	-.52	.09
	(e) I believe the world would be a better place if my colleagues and I were clearer on where we stand	.19	-.48	.04
	(f) I prefer that my actions be guided by discussion with others who are close to me	.07	-.44	.01
	(g) I believe that my feelings and emotions should be shared with others close to me	-.06	-.43	.24
	(h) I can grow and progress best in this world by learning and sharing with others	.01	-.42	.25

This life style looks toward close intimate relationships for guidance and direction. Friends and colleagues to whom he is committed are the primary choice for the SLS in reaching important decisions, for establishing working relationships, for sharing feelings, and for learning. His faith in his intimate relations with others provides the basis for his guidance and direction in life.

III. *Personalistic life style*	FLS	SLS	PLS
(a) In deciding how I want to live and act, I am most satisfied if I am completely free to make this decision myself	-.05	.07	.64
(b) I believe that my life will be most satisfying to me if I am completely free to choose how I want to live	-.03	.03	.59
(c) I prefer that my actions be guided by my own knowledge of what I want to do	-.01	.07	.54
(d) What is important is that I experience and discover who and what I am	-.12	-.27	.54
(e) I find myself striving for greater freedom and independence	-.01	-.11	.52
(f) I believe that my feelings and emotions should be experienced by me to the fullest	-.04	-.15	.52
(g) I can only get the really important things in life by doing what I want to do	-.11	-.06	.50
(h) I am responsible to only myself for my actions	.02	-.07	.42

To the extent that an individual is personalistic, he looks toward himself for guidance and direction. It is important to him to undergo a wide variety of personal experiences in order to experiment and discover who and what he is. Similarly, he needs to experience his own feelings and emotions to the fullest. Underlying these preferences and beliefs is a high value and need for personal freedom—freedom to decide how he wants to live, and to act through his own knowledge of what he wants to do. Related to this strong need for personal freedom is a sense of responsibility to only himself for his actions.

The underlying structure of life style, then, seems to be composed of three clearly distinct sets of preferences, beliefs, and values. The FLS tends to look upwards for guidance and direction from external authority such as precedent, rule, regulations, and those in positions of higher responsibility. The SLS tends to look to his small intimate peer group for guidance and direction, and the PLS looks within himself and his own set of experiences and feelings.

There are a number of previous trichotomies in the research literature which bear some semblance to the life style structure. Notable among these are the frameworks of McClelland, Atkinson, Clark and Lowell (1953) on power, affiliation, and achievement, Alderfer (1972) on existence, relatedness, and growth, Riesman, et al. (1961) on inner-directed and other-directed, and Schein (1965) on rational-economic man, social man, and self-actualizing man. The SLS has some similarities to McClelland's affiliation and power dimensions, while the FLS has some similarities to achievement. Alderfer's relatedness component seems close to the SLS dimensions, but there is only minimal similarity between the existence and growth components and, respectively, the FLS and PLS dimensions. Riesman's concepts of inner-directed and outer-directed have some parallels to the FLS and SLS respectively, although there is no analog to the PLS. Schein's trichotomy has some similarities, but his are more "assumptions about man" than life style orientations. In general, these frameworks and others (Maslow, 1954; White & Lippit, 1960; Bass, 1967) were developed in different settings, for different purposes, and do not reflect the range of preferences, beliefs, and values underlying the concept of life style.

Correlates of the Three Life Styles

Factor scores were computed for the eight highest loading items on each factor, thus providing each individual with three life style scores. Kuder-Richardson reliability coefficients for the three sets of factor scores were .78, .72, and .70, respectively. Factor scores were then correlated and/or compared with various biographic and demographic characteristics in order to gain a better understanding of the meaning of the three life styles. The mean and standard deviation for each of the three factor scores were as follows: $\overline{X}_{FLS} = 24.33$, $SD_{FLS} = 5.71$; $\overline{X}_{SLS} = 26.15$, $SD_{SLS} = 4.47$; $\overline{X}_{PLS} = 31.24$, $SD_{PLS} = 4.54$. The intercorrelations among the three life styles were all low, and ranged between .12 (FLS-SLS) to −.17 (FLS-PLS).

Life Styles as Related to Age

Both FLS and SLS were correlated significantly with age ($r = .28$ in both cases). PLS was negatively correlated with age ($r = -.21$). Thus there is a tendency for older individuals to be more formalistic, more socio-centric, and less personalistic. It should be noted that these are not longitudinal data; there is no reason to believe that those who are currently young will become more formalistic as they become older.

In order to understand these trends better the life style scores for each five year age bracket were computed and are compared in Table 1 and pictured in Figure 1. Although mean scores within columns in Table 1 are significantly different from each other, it is apparent from Figure 1 that the life style/age relationship is not all together linear. The formalistic component shows the most linear trend, starting at its lowest level in the teenage period and gradually increasing to a peak in the 58-62 year

Table 1. Formalistic, Sociocentric, and Personalistic Life Style Scores for Various Age Groups

Age	N	Life Style Scores		
		F	S	P
13-17	115	21.9	26.6	33.3
18-22	237	22.7	26.5	32.1
23-27	207	23.1	25.5	31.5
28-32	116	24.3	25.8	31.5
33-37	93	25.6	25.1	30.7
38-42	65	25.7	27.0	29.9
43-47	36	26.3	25.7	29.9
48-52	39	27.5	26.8	29.7
53-57	16	26.1	26.8	27.6
58-62	5	28.8	27.0	29.2
63-67	23	27.7	27.4	31.2
F (df = 11,941)		7.87	1.71	5.59
p		.001	.001	.001

bracket. The sociocentric component shows more irregularity; starting from a moderately high level in the teens, it drops off in the 23-27 year range, then gradually increases for the next 30 years of life, at least into the 60's. The personalistic dimension starts at its highest level in the early teens and declines steadily for the following 40 years reaching a low in the mid 50's, then it reverses itself and climbs steeply in the late 50's and 60's.

In terms of generation differences, youth can clearly be described as having very high personalistic and very low formalistic beliefs and preferences. This gradually reverses itself in the middle generations. Thus, individuals in their mid 50's are far more formalistic, and far less personalistic than the younger generation.

Life Style as Related to Education

Mean life style scores for each of nine educational levels were computed and are shown in Table 2. FLS is lowest among those who have gone as far as the high school years, and generally increases with greater education from tenth grade through an undergraduate college education. From this point on it declines regularly to some degree. The correlation between FLS and education is -.11 which increases to -.14 when age is partialed out. While these correlations are significant (p<.01), the non-linear trend between FLS and education seems to be of

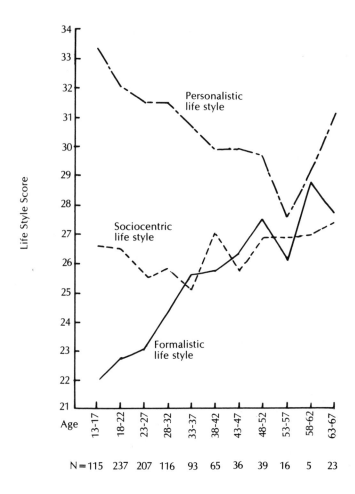

Figure 1. Life Style as a Function of Age

greater importance. SLS declines from tenth grade through the college junior level and then rises sharply during the first two years of graduate work. PLS is highest in the high school years, then declines consistently for the next five years of education and is lowest among those with a master's degree.

Education does seem to be related to life style, particularly from tenth grade high school through the master's degree. During this period, formalistic preferences and values steadily increase while sociocentric and personalistic preferences and values generally decline. From here through the Ph.D. level, PLS and SLS increase while FLS decreases.

Table 2. Formalistic, Sociocentric, and Personalistic Life Style Scores
for Various Educational Levels

Education Completed	N	Life Style Scores		
		F	S	P
10th grade - high school	18	20.28	27.50	33.11
11th grade - high school	38	21.50	26.95	33.18
12th grade - high school	63	22.13	25.98	33.43
College freshman	58	21.76	25.36	32.55
College junior	77	23.36	23.94	31.29
College senior	125	24.06	26.06	31.14
Grad school - one year	28	21.46	27.64	30.89
Grad school - two years	14	22.93	25.79	29.21
Grad school - three plus years	12	21.17	27.25	32.58
F (df = 8.424)		5.05	3.15	2.06
p		.001	.001	.001

Life Style as Related to Sex

Women are significantly more sociocentric and more personalistic than men, while men are clearly more formalistic than women. These results clearly fit the differentiated sex role emphasis that men and women receive from an early age. Block (1973) for example, found that the usual socialization process for boys starting early in elementary school reflects an emphasis upon the virtues of the Protestant Ethic: achievement and competition, control of feelings, and rule conformity. For girls, the emphasis is on close interpersonal relationships: to show and receive affection, to be expressive, aesthetic, and to reflect on life (Block, 1973). These different developmental patterns evidently become a strong part of the self-concept of the two sexes, and are reinforced consistently by the sex role stereotypes within our society.

Table 3. Formalistic, Sociocentric, and Personalistic Life Style Scores
for Women and Men

Sex	N	Life Style Scores		
		F	S	P
Women	251	22.9	26.6	32.5
Men	845	24.5	26.0	31.0
F (df = 8,424)		15.08	3.02	23.39
p		.001	.004	.001

Life Style as Related to Occupation

In order to explore the degree to which various occupational groups attract and maintain certain life styles, mean scores were computed for each of the eight occupational groups suggested and described by Roe (1956). University students formed a ninth group. Significant differences among the life styles are noted in all three cases in Table 4. The highest formalistic group is in the sales field, followed by business, technology and science. Those in the arts and entertainment fields scored lowest in formalistic, while students and social service professionals were also low. The highest sociocentric groups were scientists and social service occupations, while the lowest were those in sales and technology. Those in the arts and entertainment were the highest in personalistic life style, while those in sales, business and social science were lowest. In general, then, individuals with a high FLS are found predominantly in the business and technology areas, those with a high SLS in the science and social science areas, and those with a high PLS in the arts and entertainment fields.

Table 4. Formalistic, Sociocentric, and Personalistic Life Style Scores for Various Occupational Groups

Occupational Group	N	Life Style Scores		
		F	S	P
Social service	70	23.2	27.4	30.3
Sales	22	27.5	25.3	30.1
Business	191	26.2	25.6	30.3
Technology	180	26.1	25.3	30.6
Science	86	25.7	27.6	31.4
Cultural	38	24.3	25.7	31.7
Arts/entertainment	34	19.2	26.3	33.3
Students	269	22.5	26.4	31.7
F (df = 8,885)		16.75	3.47	3.72
p		.001	.001	.001

The levels which individuals have attained within each occupational group were also computed using the six level classification system of Roe (1956). Correlations were then computed between the level the individual has attained and his life style. To the extent that the individual's occupational level was high, he tended to be low on formalistic life style ($r = -.24$, p .001). When age is partialed out of this relationship, the FLS-occupational level correlation is reduced to $-.21$; when education is partialed out, the relationship is reduced to -.22. Thus, those with a high FLS tend to have a lower occupation level even when the effect of age or education is controlled. The correlations between occupational level and the other two life styles were not significant.

Life Style as Related to Religion

Religious affiliation and life style have significant relationships for the FLS and PLS, as indicated in Table 5. Protestants have the highest FLS score, while those with no religion (presumably atheist or agnostic) clearly have the lowest FLS. Jews have the highest PLS, while Catholics have the lowest. Here the cultural influences of religious background upon one's life style are apparent. There is a clear theme in the Protestant Ethic which stresses hard work and accomplishment and the rewards for these within and by the larger social order. Abiding by the respect for its rules, policies, and those with higher responsibilities are also obvious components of the ethic underlying Protestantism. Conversely, atheists and agnostics have no organized religion for purposes of guidance, reward, and to give respect. Judaism may provide an emphasis on personal choice, freedom, and initiative through its focus on a more personal God. On the other hand, Catholicism tends to discourage personal freedom, choice, interpretation, and decision in religious matters. Again, it is possible that individuals with certain life style patterns tend to join or reject specific religions on this basis; but it is more likely that the religious context in which an individual is born and raised provides a socialization process which inculcates his life style.

Table 5. Formalistic, Sociocentric, and Personalistic Life Style Scores for Various Religious Affiliations

Religion	N	Life Style Scores		
		F	S	P
Protestant	15	27.53	26.80	29.67
Catholic	29	25.07	26.89	28.28
Jewish	13	24.23	27.46	33.77
None	18	19.29	25.89	31.22
F (df = 3,71)		6.88	.38	6.40
p		.005	n.s.	.005

DISCUSSION

This study has found that the structure which underlies general sets of preferences, beliefs, and values across generations is composed of three dimensions. These have been termed formalistic, sociocentric, and personalistic life styles. Life styles were described both in terms of their component characteristics and through the relationships each life style has with an individual's age, education, sex, occupational group and level, and religion.

There are two important implications from these findings. One concerns the pervasive effect upon current life styles of the socialization processes within our changing cultural milieu. The second implication reverses the direction of causality. It raises issues of the potential repercussion of current and emerging life style patterns of contemporary youth upon future organizational and institutional structures.

Life Style as a Cultural Phenomenon

This study suggests that an individual's life style is integrally linked to his cultural milieu and social identity. Life style is clearly a generational issue, but it also stems from aspects of the individual's cultural upbring-ing (religion), socioeconomic status (education and occupational level), aspirations (occupational group), and sex. These are all sources of identity strength for the individual. Life style, then, can be thought of as both a culmination of and contribution toward an individual's identity pattern. The religious and socioeconomic background of one's family influences his educational and vocational aspirations, all of which impact upon his life style. Different religious, occupational, and educational experiences also provide the individual with different socialization experiences, culminating in different sets of preferences, values, and beliefs. Similarly, an individual's sex provides different occupational and educational opportunities, role stereotypes, and self concepts which may well impact upon his or her life style.

In general, it would appear that these aspects of the socialization process have a consistent and pervasive effect upon the preferences, beliefs, and values of individuals. The linear trends of life style pictured in Figure 1 may represent continual forces of socialization of the individual in reducing his personalistic tendencies and in increasing his formalistic tendencies. Yet there are also indications of reversals for individuals over the years. For example, sociocentric preferences seem to subside in the twenties and thirties, a period in which career aspirations are paramount. The subsequent and consistent increase in sociocentric life style begins around age 40, a period during which the individual often faces crises of career, identity, and life meaning.

But as the norms of our culture change over the years, so does the impact these norms have on life style change. A close look at Figure 1 indicates evidence that the generations born in the early 1900's are currently more personalistic than those born somewhat later. Members of this generation were adolescents and teenagers during the roaring twenties—a period of greater affluence, loosening morals, short skirts, flowing alcohol, and resounding jazz. These are characteristics which (if we substitute drugs for alcohol and rock music for jazz) have a marked resemblance to those of the 1960's and 70's.

Youth and Prophecy

This discussion has focused on the influences that our culture and its changes have had upon individual life styles. But life style itself influences the degree to which a person aspires toward educational, occupational and religious paths. Whether an advanced education, working in certain occupations, striving for a "higher" level within that occupation, affiliating with a certain religion are all worthwhile to the individual are at least partially influenced by his preferences, beliefs, and values—his life style pattern.

The life style pattern of youth as indicated in this study clearly reflects (1) a low trust in guidance from higher authority—law and order, precedent, those in a position of higher responsibility; (2) a low need for defining personal fulfillment as moving upward in accordance with the traditional meaning of success, advancement and reward; (3) a strong preference and value for self guidance, self exploration, self discovery based upon freedom to experience a variety of feelings and events.

If the younger generation maintains even a residual of these values, what implications might its preferences, beliefs, and values have upon future organizational structures and organization managers who place a high value on more formalistic life style patterns?

Other authors have noted that in youth there is a general distrust of involvement with conventional institutional roles and a desire to avoid institutional careers (Flacks, 1970). These are seen as constraints upon personal and social freedom, both for the self and others. Compared to college students in the late 1950's and early 1960's, recent college students show increased negativism toward authority figures in organizations, toward assuming managerial role prescriptions in large bureaucracies, toward accepting administrative responsibilities, toward competitive motivation and toward assuming masculine roles (Miner, 1971). Others have noted that youth seems to be turning away from the technological society—not its technology, but the effects of technology on humanness (Kenniston, 1963). It is turning away from the mechanistic organizational structure—again, not from organizational mechanics, but from the mechanization of man. Youth is moving away from public involvement and social responsibility toward private exploration and private satisfaction. They will eventually be in the system, but not support it. They are dedicated to their private leisure, rather than working for the system (Kenniston, 1963).

The formalistic life style is clearly congruent with most contemporary forms of organization. The hierarchical and bureaucratic nature of these forms fits the FLS's needs for guidance from authority and his concept of success as one of rising up in the organization. The emerging personalistic life style, however, will be committed neither to the organization, nor any group, but rather to the self. This life style may gravitate toward loose coalitions of similar people that provide excitement and rich experiences, but the norms of that group or organization must provide the personalistic with the freedom to do his thing—and to leave when he feels like it.

The organizational analogies for these life styles are, respectively, bureaucratic and autonomous (or anarchistic). If direct extrapolations are made for prophecy, we will see gradual change in our organizational and institutional frameworks toward anarchistic "do-your-thing" organizations, and away from bureaucracy. This applies not only to organizations as places to work, but families, religious organizations, and community groups as well.

In addition, we may see increasing conflict between generations which represent the conflicting formalistic and personalistic life style: values of authority, precedent, law and order, advancement, security, and prestige versus values of personal freedom and independence, personal experimentation, emotional experience, and responsibility to self. This value conflict will continue to be played out in all organizational settings—families, work places, churches, and communities.

REFERENCES

Alderfer, C. P. (1972). *Existence, relatedness, and growth.* New York: Free Press.

Bass, B. M. (1967). Social behaviour and the orientation inventory: A review. *Psychological Bulletin, 68,* 260-292.

Bier, T. E. (1967). Contemporary youth: Implications of the personalistic life style for organizations. Unpublished doctoral dissertation, Case Western Reserve University.

Block, J. H. (1973). Conceptions of sex role: Some cross-cultural and longitudinal perspectives. *American Psychologist, 28,* 512-526.

Erikson, E. H. (1967). Memorandum of youth. *Daedalus, 96,* 860-875.

Flacks, R. (1967). The liberated generation: An exploration of the roots of student protest. *Journal of Social Issues, 23,* 52-57.

Glaser, B. G. & Strauss, A. (1967). *The discovery of grounded theory.* Chicago: Albine.

Kenniston, K. (1965). Social change and youth in America. In E. Erikson (Ed.), *The challenge of youth.* Garden City, New York: Doubleday Anchor.

Lewin, K. (1951). *Field theory in social science.* New York: Harper.

Likert, R. (1967). *The human organization: Its management and value.* New York: McGraw Hill.

Maslow, A. H. (1954). *Motivation and personality.* New York: Harper.

Mayo E. (1933). *The human problems of an industrial civilization.* Boston: Harvard University, Graduate School of Business.

McClelland, D. C., Atkinson, J. W., Clark, R. A. and Lowell, E. L. (1953). *The achievement motive.* New York: Appleton-Century-Crofts.

Miner, J. B. (1971). Changes in student attitudes toward bureaucratic role prescriptions during the 1960's. *Admin. Sci. Quarterly, 16,* 227-238.

Riesman, D. (1961). *The lonely crowd.* New Haven: Yale University Press.

Roe, A. (1956). *The psychology of occupations.* New York: Wiley.

Schein, E. H. (1965). *Organizational psychology.* Englewood Cliffs, N.J.: Prentice-Hall.

Simmons, J. and Winograd, B. (1966). *It's happening: A portrait of the youth scene today.* Santa Barbara: Marc-Laird.

Taylor, F. (1911). *The principles of scientific management.* New York: Harper.

Weber, M. (1930). *The Protestant ethic and the spirit of capitalism.* New York: Scribners.

White, R. and Lippit, R. (1960). Leader behavior and member reaction in three "social climates." In D. Cartwright and A. Zander (Eds.), *Group dynamics: Research and theory.* Evanston, Ill.: Row Peterson.

CHAPTER 8

THE AFFLUENT DIET: A WORLDWIDE HEALTH HAZARD

Erik Eckholm
Frank Record

The stamp of each culture's cuisine is unique; the Americans have hamburgers, the French rich sauces, the Japanese raw fish. Nevertheless, when the basic nutritional components rather than the particular dishes of diets are analyzed, some pronounced international trends appear. One of the most conspicuous trends to emerge over the last century or so is a consumption pattern in the industrial Western countries that is sometimes called the "affluent diet."

The affluent diet flourishes only where incomes range far above subsistence level and where people have market access to a highly productive agricultural system—hence its name. Those with an affluent diet consume large amounts of animal proteins and fats in the forms of meats and dairy products; they substitute highly refined flour and sugar for bulky carbohydrates like whole grains, tubers, fruits, and vegetables; and, increasingly, they choose commercially manufactured foods over fresh, unprocessed products. Never before the present century have large numbers of people maintained such a diet.

The affluent diet is most deeply entrenched in North America, but it has taken hold in Western Europe, too. Japan and the Soviet Union, late starters in the transition away from traditional grain or potato-centered diets, are quickly making up for lost time. The "refined" meat-heavy diet is also enticing the well-heeled urban elite in Africa, Asia, and Latin America. At the marketplace and at the dinner table, people are proving that the appeals of meat, refined flour, and sugar transcend borders and cultural conventions.

Reprinted from: E. Eckholm and F. Record. The Affluent Diet: A Worldwide Health Hazard. *The Futurist,* Feb. 1977, 32-33; 36-42. Used with permission.

By the traditional measures of good nutrition, the affluent diet should be a healthy one. Protein supplies are generous; energy intake is adequate, though sometimes excessive; and key vitamin and mineral requirements are met. Viewed against the backdrop of humanity's long history of nutrient-deficiency diseases such as scurvy and pellagra, and of rampant present-day undernutrition, the affluent diet looks healthy indeed.

But nutritional appearances can deceive. Observed links between the way people in the industrial countries eat and the way they live and die have raised new questions about the soundness of the affluent diet. Such connections have forced nutritionists and doctors to view this diet from new angles, and to refigure the meaning of "good nutrition." They have also forced experts to evaluate a given diet within the context of a particular lifestyle. The conclusions springing from this reassessment are sobering, if not startling: like most "get rich quick" schemes, the quest for rich foods entails grave risks.

WESTERN DIET HIGH IN FATS

The most suspect characteristics of the affluent diet are its high levels of fats, especially animal fats, and cholesterol. Most people know that greasy fried foods, butter, and salad oil contain fats; fewer realize that much of our fat intake comes in less obvious forms. Meats, especially beef and pork (which contain more fat than do poultry and fish), as well as dairy products and vegetable oils, all add fat to the diet. Cholesterol, highly publicized because it has been associated with circulatory ailments, is most concentrated in eggs and liver. But it is also present in other animal products.

In the Western countries, fats have accounted for an increasing proportion of total caloric intake over the last century. Largely because they eat more meat and dairy products, people in the industrial countries consume far more fat than those, such as the Greeks, whose cuisines are visibly oil-laden. Fats sometimes account for 45 to 50% of the calories in a North American's diet; the national average is over 40% in many Western countries. In contrast, fats comprise less than a fourth of the food energy consumed in most poor countries.

The quantity of fat that people eat probably matters less than the kind of fat they eat. In particular, a high intake of saturated fats, those supplied mainly but not entirely by animal products, is thought to promote cardiovascular problems and, possibly, various forms of cancer. Unsaturated fats, plentiful in most animal and vegetable fat sources, seem to entail fewer health risks.

Average consumption of meats, including poultry, in the United States, Australia, and Argentina has now leveled off at close to 250 pounds (carcass weight) a year per capita. Citizens of France, West Germany, and Canada now each consume close to 200 pounds a year, while those in other European countries eat smaller but generally increasing amounts of meat. Among the richer countries, Japan lags conspicuously behind in meat consumption, but its per capita intake of 44 pounds in 1974 represented a spectacular 428% jump over the 1961 level. In contrast, average meat consumption in many low-income countries ranges below 20 pounds.

High in fats, the affluent diet is also low in whole grains. Ironically, *total* grain use in the developed countries has risen markedly over recent decades. At between one and two thousand pounds per capita, consumption is now two to five times that in poorer countries. But an increasing share of this grain is consumed indirectly, as meat from grain-fed animals. Thus we forfeit the possible benefits of whole grains to animals only to lard our diets. "Prime" beef, the highly marbled type for which consumers pay premium prices, exemplifies this changeover perfectly. Prime beef is produced by raising cattle on feedlots, where they consume about ten pounds of grain for every pound of meat added during their stay. Since grain-fed beef contains more fat than does range-fed beef, people pay extra for a product that, at current consumption levels in many countries, is more likely than less fatty meats to threaten their well-being.

Not only is direct grain consumption low in the affluent diet, but most of the fiber, or roughage, present in the outer layers of grain has also disappeared. In rich nations, wheat is usually milled into refined white flour. Raw or lightly cooked fruits and vegetables, which also provide roughage, are increasingly being passed over in favor of canned or frozen foods, which are often overcooked. Even the fruits and vegetables that are bought fresh are often peeled or overcooked. Unfortunately, reducing dietary roughage apparently alters the chemistry of digestion and the physical properties of body wastes, in turn possibly promoting a host of diseases of the digestive system.

CONSUMPTION OF REFINED SUGAR RISES

Starch intake has dropped precipitously along with the consumption of bulky foods and fiber in the affluent diet, only to be replaced by the dental scourge, refined sugar. In fact, global per capita sugar consumption has grown by half just since 1950, and the average person in the world now eats 44 pounds of sugar a year. Health problems other than tooth decay—painful and expensive as that is—have apparently grown along with the world's sweet tooth; high sugar intake is linked by many to diabetes and other diseases. Most traditional societies don't use refined sugar at all, and recipes calling for sugar were rare in Europe and North America a few centuries back. Today, high sugar consumption plagues all the developed and many of the less developed countries. Whether consumed in candy and soft drinks or in baked goods and manufactured foods, sugar has found a following. Cubans, Costa Ricans, Americans, Australians, and Israelis each down over a hundred pounds of sugar a year, while Western Europeans eat an average of 90 pounds each. By contrast, annual sugar consumption in Japan, Taiwan, and the Philippines, though climbing fast, is only about 50 pounds per person; and sugar intake in many poor countries is much lower still.

As the affluent diet has spread, so has a wide variety of heretofore rare diseases such as coronary heart disease, diabetes, diverticulosis, and bowel cancer. Confined largely to those leading the life-styles of the developed Western world, whether in Paris or Singapore, these ailments are sometimes collectively called the "diseases of civilization."

Medical detectives are slowly unravelling the intricate web of interconnections that link the affluent diet to the various diseases of civilization. Combined with a sedentary life-style, high calorie consumption leads to obesity, which in turn encourages diabetes, hypertension, and coronary heart disease. High intake of refined foods such as sugar and flour may encourage diverticulosis and a host of other conditions, while high salt intake facilitates the development of hypertension. Diabetes and hypertension, killers themselves, also greatly boost the risk of coronary heart disease and, in the case of hypertension, stroke. A diet high in animal fats fosters arterial problems that can lead to a coronary attack or stroke. Finally, fats may also be linked to the genesis of bowel, breast, prostate, and other types of cancer.

Both affluent diets and sedentary life-styles represent radical departures from the conditions under which humans evolved for millions of years. That our bodies should rebel is hardly surprising.

A MODERN EPIDEMIC: CORONARY HEART DISEASE

Seldom has one disease so dominated an era. Coronary heart disease, once a rare affliction even among the aged, is now the leading killer of the old and the middle-aged in many countries; and it sometimes takes the lives of the young as well. The affluent diet and sedentary life-styles are contributing to this trend, not only in the developed world, but also in the cities of the poor countries, where coronary heart disease is emerging as an important health problem.

All cardiovascular diseases together, including coronary and other heart diseases, strokes, arterial diseases, and others, account for about one-half of all deaths in the industrialized countries. Coronary heart disease, which involves the coronary arteries through which the heart supplies itself with blood, often culminates in a "heart attack" when the blood supply is cut off. This disease accounts for one in every three deaths in the United States, claiming annually some 700,000 lives. In Japan and France, cerebrovascular disease, or stroke, which involves an impaired supply of blood to parts of the brain, takes even more lives than does coronary heart disease.

World Health Organization data for 18 Western countries reveal increases in the incidence of coronary heart disease between 1950 and 1968 for every age group. Among those aged 35-44, the incidence rose by more than 50%, and among those 45-54, by more than 30%. In the United States, where coronary heart disease fatalities are more prevalent than in any other large country, the frequency of deaths from this disease for most age groups has tapered off somewhat since the early 1960s. Both changing life-styles and improved medical treatment of heart disease victims have probably contributed to this downturn.

In India, what sketchy information exists shows that the number of coronary heart disease patients in urban hospitals has been increasing steadily over the past 20 years. The incidence of coronary heart disease is on the rise in China as well. According to a WHO report, coronary heart disease, though still limited, occurs more and more frequently in Sri Lanka, Korea, Malaysia, and the Philippines, especially among people under 40.

Doctors at the Bir hospital in Katmandu, Nepal, have noted that the annual number of heart attacks increased from three to 30 between 1960 and 1973—an insignificant number, perhaps, by Western standards but enough to suggest that the changing life-style in the capital has had an influence. In the Ivory Coast, physicians have noted the emergence of coronary heart disease among the more affluent classes of Abidjan. One study of these urban heart disease patients found that nine of every ten victims were male and that their average age was only 53. In 17 out of 22 countries in North and South America, the disease is now one of the five principal causes of death. In ten of these countries, heart disease is the number one killer.

In Japan, coronary disease rates have tripled over the last 15 years. Yet the annual coronary death toll is still low compared to the toll from stroke, which accounts for one of every four deaths among those aged 75 or under. Compared to Europeans and Americans, the Japanese consume relatively little animal fat, and this dietary preference seems partially to protect them from coronary disease.

Though many factors influence heart-disease incidence, populations that eat large quantities of animal fat tend to have higher coronary death rates than those populations that consume smaller quantities of animal fat.

Socioeconomic levels also seem to correlate with the incidence of coronary heart disease. As median family income rises, death rates from coronary heart disease drop. Upper-middle and middle classes in the United States suffer from proportionately less coronary disease than they did before World War II, and both have lower coronary death rates than the poor.

Apparently, the rich in the United States are now more aware of the various risk factors associated with heart attacks than are the poor, and have adjusted their life-styles accordingly. But those in the lower economic classes have rushed to embrace the same affluent diets and sedentary life-styles that were once the exclusive privileges of the wealthy.

CHOLESTEROL-RICH FOODS AND ATHEROSCLEROSIS

Atherosclerosis, the partial blockage of arteries with tissue growth and fatty deposits, leads to coronary heart disease when the coronary arteries are affected. Since these arteries supply blood directly to the heart, a heart attack will result if they become sufficiently clogged. Any population suffering from a high incidence of atherosclerosis will almost certainly have high coronary heart disease rates as well.

The amount of fatty deposits in the arteries seems to be affected by the consumption of saturated fats and cholesterol. These food components appear to contribute to the chain of events that leads from a high cholesterol blood-count to atherosclerosis, and, finally, to a completely blocked coronary artery and a heart attack. Just what determines the level of cholesterol in the blood and how a high blood-cholesterol level is translated into atherosclerosis are as yet unanswered questions. But considerable evidence shows that a diet high in unsaturated fats lowers the cholesterol output of the body, while high intake of saturated fats, such as those in meat and dairy products, apparently stimulates the liver to produce more cholesterol. High consumption of meat, eggs, and other cholesterol-rich foods can raise cholesterol levels in the blood stream by about 10%.

The American Medical Association and medical authorities in Sweden, Norway, and the United Kingdom all exhort adults to reduce fat consumption. In their view, fats should supply less than 35% of total calories, as opposed to the 40-45% now common in these countries. Furthermore, according to the American Heart Association and others, most adult males should sharply reduce their intake of cholesterol. The daily level should not exceed 300 milligrams. (One egg contains 250 mgs. of cholesterol, while a three ounce cooked piece of beef, pork, or chicken contains approximately 85 mgs.)

In North America and Europe, 10% of all coronary deaths strike those under the age of 55, and over half involve people under the age of 75. Most of these probably could be prevented and certainly could be postponed by changes in diet and life-style.

"HOMO SEDENTARIUS" AND OBESITY

Human beings long depended upon their legs for transportation and upon their physical strength for the cultivation of food. The overwhelming majority of people consumed barely enough to survive while the privileged few ate rich, fattening diets. Restricted to the elite, obesity came to be regarded as a status symbol. The Roman senator's girth won him great prestige among the mass of underfed plebeians, and Aga Khan's yearly weighings were legendary among his people. Today in many of the less developed countries of the world the same attitudes still prevail. In Nepal, for example, obesity is a mark of distinction, and the present King would find it highly impolitic to go on a reducing diet.

In North America, Japan, many European countries, and in other developed nations around the world, the food supply is now more abundant than ever before. Most people from all social classes can get more than enough to eat; and with the emergence of the affluent diet, obesity is no longer the "privilege" of the elite. In fact, excessive fat has become the scourge of the lower class and, to the many Westerners who prize leanness, a mark of social disdain. "Doppelkinnepidemie," the double-chin epidemic, has blossomed in West Germany since the postwar economic miracle. In the United States, 10 to 20% of all children and 35 to 50% of the middle-aged are overweight.

The increased prevalence of obesity is not, however, solely a function of changing food supplies and of mercurial attitudes about the ideal weight. Combined with individual genetic susceptibility to obesity, two factors—caloric intake and expenditure of energy through physical activity—determine weight gains. In some rich countries calorie consumption has actually fallen since the turn of the century, but not as rapidly as the rate at which people exercise has declined. The aftermath of the Industrial Revolution, the age of the automobile and household appliances, has changed the way people live. Fewer and fewer jobs require physical work of any sort. Even the modern farmer, perched atop his tractor, can be overweight and out of condition. Millions of office workers get no exercise whatever, save a short walk or an occasional sprint to catch the rush-hour bus. Ours is a sedentary civilization, and the species of *Homo sedentarius* has migrated from the cities and the suburbs to the countryside. Examining the food consumption and exercise patterns of Americans, nutritionist Jean Mayer found that:

> Although our population has grown taller, we have grown heavier (and fatter) even faster—despite a slowly decreasing overall food intake. Clearly, the increased mechanization of our lives has diminished the level of physical activity much more rapidly than our caloric intake has dropped.

Obesity, often defined as the condition of being 20% or more over a desirable weight determined mainly on the basis of health statistics, is not randomly distributed throughout society. Rather, in developed countries, the condition seems to be concentrated in the lowest socioeconomic groups. A study performed in New York City showed that one of every three lower-class women was obese, compared to one in 20 among upper-class women. Obesity is more common among lower-class six-year-olds than among their upper-class counterparts.

OBESITY SHORTENS LIFE EXPECTANCY

Obesity is more than a social problem; it interests the medical profession because obese people run a higher risk of premature death than do people of normal or below-normal weight. For example, men who are 10% overweight have a one-third greater chance of dying prematurely from ailments such as coronary heart disease, high blood pressure, and diabetes than do those of average weight. Men more than 20% overweight are one and a half times as likely to die prematurely. In recent testimony before the U.S. Senate, Theodore Cooper, Assistant Secretary of Health, Education, and Welfare, estimated that one-fifth of all Americans are so overweight that their health is threatened. Hippocrates' dictum that the fat die sooner than the thin rings as true today as it did 2,000 years ago. Indeed, being slightly underweight actually confers some health advantages.

Fortunately, obesity and its ill-effects can usually be totally reversed. Diabetes and hypertension often disappear along with excess weight.

Data from life insurance companies show that when obese people lose and keep off weight, their life expectancy rises to what it would have been had they never been obese.

Crash diets undertaken at any age, however effective in the short term, are unlikely to be beneficial over the long term unless followed by increased routine physical activity and a permanent reduction in caloric intake. For many, a daily caloric excess equivalent to half a slice of bread or half a glass of beer can result in a weight gain of more than 40 pounds within ten years. A reduction in daily exercise by the equivalent of a ten-minute walk can have the same effect.

In the modern age of mechanical convenience and conveyance, many people engage in so little physical activity that simply eating to the point of feeling satisfied means eating excess calories. Studies show that, in the words of Jean Mayer, "decreasing activity below a certain limit will no longer be accompanied by a decrease in appetite." Thus attention must be given to both sides of the diet-exercise equation: *Homo sapiens* need not be *Homo sedentarius,* so long as his diet is commensurate with his level of physical activity.

SALT AND HYPERTENSION

Hypertension, or high blood pressure, is one of the most common illnesses in the world today. The prevalence of hypertension in the affluent nations is well recognized, but few seem to realize that this disease is now emerging in the sprawling urban areas of the world's poorer countries, too. Salt intake, genetic factors, stress, and urbanization all seem to be raising the incidence of hypertension in the boroughs of New York as well as in the *favelas* of Sao Paulo.

High blood pressure goes undetected in many people, but the ailments it promotes, including coronary heart disease, stroke, congestive heart failure, and kidney disease, are all too obvious when they strike. The extensive Framingham heart study showed that two out of every three middle-aged people with a history of stroke or coronary heart disease had above-normal blood pressure.

Hypertension can shorten its victims' lives. A 35-year-old American man with blood pressure 14% above normal for his age has lost about nine years of his life expectancy. A 45-year-old man whose blood pressure is 17% or more above normal is running twice the risk of a heart attack and four times the risk of a stroke that a man with blood pressure slightly lower than normal faces.

In nearly all cases the actual cause of hypertension is unknown. But dietary factors, especially salt intake levels, are now the subject of many medical studies. Past research has firmly established the link between high salt consumption and high blood pressure in rats. Though the evidence is only circumstantial, it strongly suggests that high salt intake contributes significantly to hypertension in humans as well.

The late Lewis K. Dahl, who studied hypertension in rats as well as in human beings, found that a low-salt diet drove down blood pressure levels not only for hypertensives in general, but also for obese people in particular. Obesity has been clearly established as a risk factor for both coronary heart disease and hypertension, and obese people who adopt special low-salt diets reduce their blood pressure readings long before they reduce their body weight. Studies of people in the Bahamas, South Africa, Japan, and Polynesia have all shown links between high salt intake and high blood pressure.

The average person in an industrial country consumes at least ten times more salt than the body actually requires.

DEVELOPING DIABETES

As the affluent diet has spread, the incidence of diabetes has risen throughout the world. In poor countries, diabetes appears to be mainly an urban disease; in rich countries, it afflicts urban and rural residents alike.

In the United States in 1900, diabetes was the twenty-seventh most common cause of death. In the mid-1970s, it has captured fifth place. According to the U.S. National Commission on Diabetes, the number of reported cases in the United States jumped 50% in the eight-year period from 1965 to 1973. If the heart diseases, circulatory problems, kidney disorders and other potentially fatal complications of diabetes are added to its annual direct death toll, diabetes emerges as the third most important killer, trailing only cardiovascular disease and cancer. In the United States and the United Kingdom, the disease is also a major cause of blindness.

Puerto Rico, which has undergone rapid economic growth and urbanization, now faces a serious public health threat from diabetes and other degenerative diseases. Even while Puerto Rico's overall health picture improved dramatically, diabetes rose from twelfth to eighth place as a cause of death between 1964 and 1974.

A rich urban resident in India, surveys show, is about twice as likely to develop diabetes as is his poor rural countryman. A similar trend among those people who have only recently been exposed to the affluent life-style of the capital city was discovered by a medical researcher in

Dakar, Senegal. The number of diabetics in Dakar's clinics increased from 21 to 963 between the years 1965 and 1970.

Obesity apparently facilitates the emergence of diabetes in those people who are genetically predisposed to the disease. Dietary influences tend to act as catalysts for diabetes in such individuals. George Cahill, Chief of the Joslin Diabetes Research Center in Boston, recently stressed the catalytic role of overeating, saying: "Overnutrition unmasks the diabetic. The greatest portion of the diabetes we have here in this country is frankly due just to overnutrition." A person who is 20% overweight is more than twice as likely to develop diabetes as is a person of normal weight.

Some researchers now suspect that the maturity-onset variety of diabetes can be induced by a sugar-laden diet. Not only does high sugar intake put direct stress on the insulin-producing system of the body, but it can also foster obesity. For those genetically susceptible to diabetes, reducing food consumption, eating less sugar, and losing weight may help prevent this unwanted offspring of the affluent diet.

DIET AND CANCER

People who think about a link between diet and cancer often think only about chemical food-additives. Synthetic additives pose real enough problems, but research over the last quarter century is pointing to other, as yet only dimly perceived, dietary factors that may influence cancer rates far more. Under suspicion are dietary aspects that, in some cases, were scarcely even considered by most nutritionists in the past: the degree to which foods are processed, the role of fats in the diet, food storage practices, deficiencies or surpluses of trace elements and vitamins, and even the type of preparation some foods receive.

Worldwide, all dietary factors together rival even tobacco as a contributor to cancer. Current evidence, says Ernst L. Wynder, president of the American Health Foundation, relates diet to "as much as 50% of all cancers in women and one-third of all cancers in men." Since about one in every four people in the industrial countries develops cancer, and one in five people dies from it, the toll of diet-related cancers looks large indeed.

Not surprisingly, dietary influences are thought to promote cancers of the digestive system, which includes the mouth, throat, esophagus, stomach, colon, and rectum. Less obviously, diet has also been associated with some cancer sites outside the digestive tract, such as the female breast and the male prostate gland. Both the quantity and quality of food consumed affect the body's hormonal secretions and overall metabolism, in turn affecting a surprising variety of organs.

Though more and more researchers are linking dietary factors with various kinds of cancer, scientists cannot agree upon the exact nature of those links. But growing evidence suggests that a high-fat diet does indeed contribute to the development of several important types of cancer, including those of the colon, rectum, breast, and prostate gland.

Some U.S. cancer researchers wonder whether their identification of the cancer risks associated with the high-fat, refined Western diet is certain enough to warrant publicizing the potential benefits of dietary changes. A growing number, however, now recommend the adoption of a "prudent diet" to help reduce cancer risk, much as heart specialists have long recommended dietary changes for potential heart attack victims without absolute proof of the benefits. The strength of the case for any given food's influence on cancer remains weaker than the cardiologists' dietary case. But the argument for trying to prevent cancer through dietary changes gains appeal in view of the happy coincidence in dietary directions called for by current knowledge of both heart disease and cancer. Reduced consumption of fats, especially animal fats, and increased consumption of whole grains, fresh fruits, and vegetables, appear to be just what the doctor should order.

OVERNUTRITION PROBLEM IGNORED BY WESTERN GOVERNMENTS

Against the menace of overconsumption, most developed countries have not yet begun to fight. Both medical communities and governments share responsibility for this failure. The overwhelming bulk of medical attention is devoted to the expert treatment of "crises" such as heart attacks, even though these seemingly sudden attacks are often the culmination of decades of nutritional abuse.

Governments, through their agricultural, economic, and educational policies, have at best usually ignored the problems of overnutrition. At worst they have actively promoted unhealthy consumption trends. Most nutrition education efforts dwell on the dwindling deficiency problems of the past rather than on the massive newer dangers of overnutrition, and key agricultural and economic decisions are made with scant regard for their impacts on health. Thus, faced with mountains of surplus butter, the European Economic Community Commission recently proposed taxing edible oils to make margarine as expensive as butter—in effect, to encourage higher consumption of saturated fats. In Great Britain, a recent Government White Paper on national food-production policy ignored health considerations while calling for increased output of milk, beef, and sugar beets. The congressionally-mandated involvement of the U.S. Department of Agriculture in promoting higher consumption of eggs by Americans provides another such example.

By subsidizing the further growth of food industries whose product, when consumed at current levels, is unhealthy, governments sanction the growth of huge industries with vested interests in promoting bad health. Here, a parallel to the detrimental—and, in many countries, government-subsidized—operations of the tobacco industry might be drawn.

The following changes for those on the affluent diet are recommended by most doctors and nutritionists studying overnutrition and its consequences:

1. Fat consumption should be reduced and held to under 35% of total calorie intake, in contrast to the 40-50% now common. Moderation in the consumption of meat, dairy products, and fried foods; a shift from beef and pork to poultry and fish; and a preference for grass-fed rather than grain-fed beef can help meet this goal.

2. Whenever possible, saturated fats should be replaced by unsaturated fats. In practice, this means substituting vegetable fats (such as margarine) for animal fats (such as butter).

3. Men especially should radically reduce their cholesterol intake by eating few eggs and only moderate amounts of other livestock products.

4. Sugar and salt intake should be sharply reduced.

5. Consumption of whole grains, potatoes and other starchy foods, and fresh fruits and vegetables should be increased.

6. Personal energy intake and energy expenditure need to be kept in balance, in part by calorie budgeting, and in part by engaging in more physical activity.

Changes like these do not come easily; for many they violate life-long habits and strongly ingrained notions about which foods are healthful and about which ones are tasty. And building exercise into a sedentary life-style is difficult for most individuals. Moreover, when people revise their consumption patterns, changes will ripple through the farm and food industries as well—changes unwelcome to those whose businesses are threatened.

ECONOMIC INCENTIVES FOR HEALTHY DIET NEEDED

A national strategy to counter overnutrition, like one to eliminate undernutrition, must involve a wide range of policies, not all of them directly linked to food and agriculture. In rich as in poor countries, the marketplace has its own set of priorities, and health is not one of them. The object must be to build a structure of economic incentives and institutions that encourages healthy food-production and consumption patterns.

Agricultural research, crop subsidies, taxes, meat-grading, international trade, and medical and general education are among the many concerns that a strategy against overnutrition must encompass. Since overnutrition and lack of exercise are part of the same problem, such topics as recreation and transportation policy enter into the picture as well. The construction of bicycle paths rather than parking lots for urban commuters would create, among other benefits, the opportunity for regular exercise and thereby perhaps reduce the incidence of obesity and heart disease.

NORWAY, SWEDEN DEVELOP NUTRITION POLICIES

Among the industrial countries, Sweden and Norway stand alone in their recent decisions to try to integrate modern dietary health concerns into national economic and agricultural planning. Particularly through a vigorous public education program, the Swedish Government has worked to reduce the amount of calories, fats, sugar, and alcohol Swedes consume and to increase the amount of exercise Swedes get. The Norwegian Government has proposed to its legislature a nutrition and food policy through which it hopes both to increase national self-sufficiency in food supplies and to cut the mounting national toll of cardiovascular and other diet-related diseases.

The Norwegian Government hopes to establish a broad array of subsidies, grants, price policies, and other incentives that will promote a stabilization of meat consumption (which has been rising over the last decade); an increase in fish consumption; a reduction in feed-grain imports; a preference for low-fat over whole milk; and a reversal of the decline in consumption of grains, potatoes, and vegetables. The educational potential of government agencies, private organizations, and schools will be enlisted to inform Norwegians about the health implications of their eating habits. Representatives of the eight different ministries, ranging from Fisheries to Agriculture to Foreign Affairs, whose activities should be influenced by the national nutrition and food plan will meet in a coordinating body. If the plan is implemented, Norway may not only better the health of its populace, but also reduce its agricultural trade deficit and reduce its claims on world food resources.

CASE AGAINST AFFLUENT DIET IS PERSUASIVE

Some people, especially representatives of threatened food industries, argue that strategies to alter the affluent diet cannot be justified on scientific grounds. A comprehensive review of dietary impacts on health, however, reveals a persuasive case for dietary change. The geography of the affluent diet and of the diseases it apparently promotes, together with the available experimental evidence, creates a powerful body of circumstantial evidence.against this diet.

With afflictions such as coronary heart disease, whose development spans decades and is obviously influenced by many forces, the exact causative role of any one factor necessarily remains elusive. Nevertheless, that aspects of the affluent diet promote atherosclerosis and heart disease, the leading killers in the West, has been proven beyond reasonable doubt. For other diseases, such as cancers of the bowel, breast, and prostate, our understanding of dietary influences is much less advanced. Yet the dietary changes called for by the leading theories of cancer causation are precisely those that help to reduce the threats of heart disease and obesity. It should not be surprising that the same dietary factors—those setting the modern Western diet apart from all others in human history—have been implicated in the origins of many different diseases.

Certainly more remains to be learned about diet and health, but, as D. M. Hegsted of Harvard University observes of problems of data and proof in this field, "one does not need to know all of the answers before one can make practical recommendations." The dietary changes that doctors are prescribing involve no foreseeable risks to the health of the population; quite the contrary, all evidence points to the great risks involved in clinging to our current diet. The only known risk associated with more prudent diets is to the food industries that would be affected. But, "while these industries deserve some consideration," observes Hegsted, "their interests cannot supersede the health interest of the population they must feed."

Though the health connection is sufficient by itself to justify programs to alter the diets of the affluent, two other considerations make such changes even more attractive. One is economy in personal food budgets. Reducing meat consumption and substituting vegetable for animal protein sources both save money. Grains, fresh fruits, and vegetables usually cost far less than processed, pre-prepared foods and snacks that tend to be overly refined and loaded with sugar, fats, and unnecessary additives.

Second, reducing overnutrition might contribute in a small way to reducing undernutrition. Widespread moderation in the consumption of fatty grain-fed livestock products—the production of which uses up over a third of the world's grain each year—can modify the terms of the global competition between rich and poor for available food and agricultural resources. The competition for agricultural products is sometimes overt, as in the recent case of Brazilian soybeans, but it is usually manifested more subtly in the competition for products in the world marketplace and, ultimately, in the allocation of land and capital.

Few potential social policies promise so many benefits and so few costs as the decision to alter the affluent diet. In the end, only individuals—who must change their behavior—can reduce overnutrition's toll. But governments have a responsibility to provide a structure of incentives and information that enhances rather than threatens the well-being of their populations. In the 19th century, as scientists became aware of the role of filth in propagating infectious disease, governments tried to provide clean water and sewage facilities. More recently, the responsibility of governments to combat undernutrition has been widely recognized. Today, our growing knowledge of the health consequences of overnutrition demands another step in the evolution of public health policies.

CHAPTER 9

CHOOSING THE RIGHT EXERCISE

Jane E. Brody

"You can achieve total fitness in four minutes a day." "Jogging isn't enough; you have to run if you want to be really fit." "If you're over fifty, you should stick to walking." "If you can't exercise every day, you'd better not do it at all." "Swimming is the best exercise." "If you're thin (or muscular) you don't need to exercise."

The list of myths and mistruths about exercise could go on and on. There are at least as many as there are miles in a marathoner's diary. And you might say, when it comes to exercise, a myth is as good as a mile.

For the millions of Americans who already have or eventually will succumb to the admonitions to get moving for the sake of their bodies and souls, the prevailing mythology has prompted confusion, anxiety and inappropriate decisions as to when and how to move.

Exercise can serve many purposes. It can enhance skills, improve flexibility, build muscle strength and tone, relieve tension, help in weight loss and maintenance and improve the body's general physiological condition, especially the ease with which the heart can supply oxygen to body tissues.

Particular types of exercise may serve some of these functions but not others. For example, bowling and golf can help you become more skillful at the game, strengthen certain muscles and expend energy (calories), but they rarely involve enough continuous activity to condition your cardiovascular system.

Isometric exercises, which clamp down on muscles, such as weight-lifting, water-skiing and arm-wrestling, will promote strong muscles but are useless—in fact, countereffective—as cardiovascular conditioners and may actually be harmful to persons with heart disease.

On the other hand, brisk walking may do little for your athletic skills or muscle strength, but it can be highly beneficial to your heart and figure.

Most people start exercising because they want to look better and feel better. Often, however, the chosen activity spurs a change or expansion of goals. For example, those who take up tennis to reduce tension or flab may find themselves huffing and puffing on the court. Realizing that they are "out of condition," they may start running or cycling to improve their bodies' ability to deliver oxygen to their muscles.

For others finding themselves gasping for breath after running half a block to catch a bus is an impetus to improve fitness.

In choosing an exercise, it's important to know what you hope to get out of it and whether that choice will help you achieve your goals.

Any type of exercise—from hanging laundry and scrubbing floors to badminton, skating, football or long-distance running—can help you control your weight. Weight gain represents an excess number of calories consumed over the number your body burns up for energy.

Any kind of motion involves the expenditure of more calories than your body uses at rest. The more you move, the more calories you burn. And the heavier you are to start with, the more calories it takes to move yourself a given distance. As an added benefit, moderate exercise improves the accuracy of your body's appetite control mechanism and more frequently decreases rather than increases appetite.

You don't have to sweat or exercise strenuously to use energy. In fact, walking a mile burns approximately the same number of calories as running a mile. At moderate ranges of activity, the difference, as far as calories are concerned, is that running a mile is faster and you may then have time to run a second mile and use up twice as many calories.

In addition to the calories burned while exercising, your body continues to burn calories at a higher rate for up to four hours after you stop exercising.

Some activities are intense energy guzzlers, using eight or more times the amount of calories your body burns at rest. These include running more than 5.5 miles an hour, cycling thirteen or more miles an hour, and playing squash and handball and skipping rope. But you can burn as many calories playing Ping-Pong or volleyball for an hour as you would running for half an hour.

This is not to say that Ping-Pong in any amount can be equivalent to running in total all-around exercise value. To maximize the likelihood of achieving a conditioning effect ("fitness" or endurance), the activity should use the large muscles in a rhythmic, repetitive, continuous motion—so-called isotonic exercises. While the amount of energy (calories) used depends only on the amount of work your body does, conditioning is a function of both the amount of work and the vigor with which it is done.

A cardiovascular conditioning exercise must also be aerobic—that is, it promotes the use of oxygen and is capable of being sustained for at least two minutes at a time without getting out of breath. Walking, running, cycling and swimming are aerobic exercises, but sprinting is not.

To condition the cardiovascular system the exercise should be performed at least three times a week for twenty minutes at a time during which the heart rate is within the individual's "target zone."

The target zone falls between 70 and 85 percent of the maximum rate your heart can achieve. The maximum heart rate (or pulse rate), counted as beats per minute, can be estimated for the average healthy adult as 220 minus your age in years. Take 70 percent and 85 percent of that number and you will have the pulse rate range that is your target zone.

To determine your heart rate while exercising, stop and immediately take your pulse, count the beats in ten seconds and multiply by six. As you become conditioned to a certain level of exercise, you may have to increase the rigor of your workout to keep your heart rate within the target zone. To avoid undue stress on your muscles and heart, every twenty-minute exercise session should be preceded by a five- to ten-minute warmup and followed by a five- to ten-minute cooldown period of less intense exercise (if you're a jogger, you might walk briskly during your warmup and cooldown).

A conditioning exercise should be done regularly, or the benefits will be lost rapidly. If you must stop for a week or more, resume at a lower level workout and gradually build up again.

Other factors to consider when choosing an exercise include:

- *Time available.* Running or indoor stationary cycling can be done at any time for thirty minutes or more. Organized sports tend to be more time-consuming and restrictive. For those short of time and who can take the rigor of the activity, rope jumping for ten minutes can provide a conditioning effect equivalent to thirty minutes of jogging.
- *Cost and convenience.* Tennis, for example, may involve driving miles to a court, paying high fees, searching for a partner and arranging schedules, all of which may discourage regular participation. The cost of a bicycle (indoors or out) may be prohibitive for some, but a jump rope can be purchased for a dollar or two. For most people, sex is convenient, inexpensive, and burns a lot of

calories, but to achieve a conditioning effect, the preorgasmic level of activity would have to be maintained for at least twenty minutes.

- *Your body's capabilities.* If you're uncoordinated, ball games or rope jumping may prove very frustrating. If you're tight-jointed, you may need flexibility-enhancing exercises (calisthenics) before you try running or tennis.

- *Age, health status and present physical condition.* The older the person, the less rigorous the activity he needs to bring his heart rate into the target zone. Beyond the age of thirty-five, you would be wise to check with your doctor before starting a rigorous exercise program. He may want to give you an exercise stress test to see what level of activity your cardiovascular system can tolerate.

   Beyond fifty, condition yourself first through a walking program before beginning more strenuous exercises. Beyond sixty, most people would be wise to avoid the more taxing exercises, such as jogging and competitive sports, and stick instead to walking, swimming and cycling. At any age, if you have been sedentary for years or are out of condition, start slowly and work up to more demanding activities. Anyone with a chronic illness or muscle or joint problems should consult his physician before starting to exercise.

- *Personal taste.* You're more likely to stick with an exercise that you enjoy, but you should give a new activity a trial of a month or two before deciding you don't like it.

Dr. Lenore R. Zohman, an exercise cardiologist at Montefiore Hospital in New York, advises that you think back to the activities you enjoyed as a youngster for clues to what you might like today.

"If you have an aversion to organized sports or strenuous activity," she said, "brisk walking for twenty to thirty minutes or climbing up twenty-five flights of stairs at a comfortable pace during a day can help you achieve physical fitness."

Dr. Zohman points out that contrary to popular belief, "there is no best exercise for everyone." Dr. John L. Marshall, orthopedic surgeon at the Hospital for Special Surgery in New York and physician for the New York Giants, recommends that the exerciser hone his skills at more than one.

This helps to develop muscle strength throughout the body, diminishes the chances of injury that can result when some muscles are developed at the expense of others, and provides alternative exercise if the main activity can't be done at a particular time. When it rains, the jogger or tennis player can jump rope or ride a stationary bicycle.

Before embarking on a serious exercise program, you might benefit from the descriptions of various activities provided in some popular books.

Dr. Zohman's pamphlet, "Beyond Diet ... Exercise Your Way to Fitness and Heart Health," is an excellent basic primer about exercises of all types and how to go about an exercise program. Single copies can be obtained free by writing to Mazola Nutrition Information Service Department ZD-NYT, Box 307, Coventry, CT 06238.

Other useful books include *Aerobics, Aerobics for Women*, and *The New Aerobics* by Kenneth H. Cooper, M.D., published in paperback by Bantam Books; *Running for Health and Beauty: A Complete Guide for Women* by Kathryn Lance (Bobbs-Merrill) and *The Perfect Exercise*, a book on rope jumping by Curtis Mitchell (Simon & Schuster).

MAXIMAL ATTAINABLE HEART RATE AND TARGET ZONE

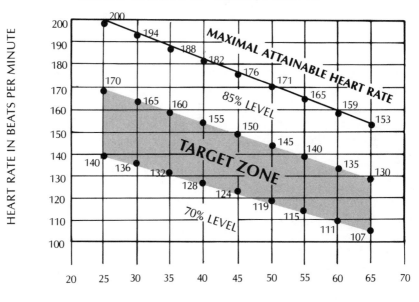

AGE IN YEARS

This figure shows that as we grow older, the highest heart rate which can be reached during all-out effort falls. These numerical values are "average" values for age. Note that one-third of the population may differ from these values. It is quite possible that a normal 50-year-old man may have a maximum heart rate of 195 or that a 30-year-old man might have a maximum of only 168. The same limitations apply to the 70 per cent and 85 per cent of maximum lines.

From Zohman, L.R., "Beyond Diet: Exercise Your Way to Fitness and Heart Health," CPC International, Englewood Cliffs, New Jersey, 1974. Used with permission.

VALUE OF VARIOUS EXERCISES

ENERGY RANGE[a] (Approx. calories used per hour)	ACTIVITY	BENEFITS
72-84	Sitting Conversing	Of no conditioning value.
120-150	Strolling, 1 mph Walking, 2 mph	Not sufficiently strenuous to promote endurance unless your exercise capacity is very low.
150-240	Golf, using power cart.	Not sufficiently taxing or continuous to promote endurance.
240-300	Cleaning windows Mopping floors Vacuuming	Adequate for conditioning if carried out continuously for 20-30 minutes.
	Bowling	Too intermittent; not sufficiently taxing to promote endurance.
	Walking, 3 mph Cycling, 6 mph	Adequate dynamic exercise if your capacity is low.
	Golf, pulling cart	Useful for conditioning if you walk briskly, but if cart is heavy, isometrics may be involved.
300-360	Scrubbing floors	Adequate endurance exercise if carried out in at least 2-minute stints.
	Walking, 3.5 mph Cycling, 8 mph	Usually good dynamic aerobic exercise.
	Table Tennis Badminton Volleyball	Vigorous continuous play can have endurance benefits. Otherwise, only promotes skill.
	Golf, carrying clubs	Promotes endurance if you reach and maintain target heart rate. Aids strength and skill.
	Tennis, doubles	Not very beneficial unless there is continuous play for at least 2 minutes at a time. Aids skill.
	Many calisthenics Ballet exercises	Will promote endurance if continuous, rhythmic and repetitive. Promotes agility, coordination and muscle strength. Those requiring isometric effort, such as push-ups and sit-ups, not good for cardiovascular fitness.

360-420	Walking, 4 mph Cycling, 10 mph Ice or roller skating	Dynamic, aerobic and beneficial. Skating should be done continuously.
420-480	Walking, 5 mph Cycling, 11 mph	Dynamic, aerobic and beneficial.
	Tennis, singles	Can provide benefit if played 30 minutes or more with an attempt to keep moving.
	Water skiing	Total isometrics. Very risky for persons with high risk for heart disease or deconditioned normals.
480-600	Jogging, 5 mph Cycling, 12 mph	Dynamic, aerobic, endurance-building exercise.
	Downhill skiing	Runs are usually too short to promote endurance significantly. Mostly benefits skill. Combined stress of altitude, cold and exercise may be too great for some heart patients.
	Paddleball	Not sufficiently continuous. Promotes skill.
600-660	Running, 5.5 mph Cycling, 13 mph	Excellent conditioner.
Above 660	Running, 6 or more mph	Excellent conditioner.
	Handball Squash	Competitive environment in hot room is dangerous to anyone not in excellent physical condition. Can provide conditioning benefit if played 30 minutes or more with attempt to keep moving.
	Swimming[b]	Good conditioning exercise—if continuous strokes. Especially good for persons who can't tolerate weight-bearing exercise, such as those with joint diseases.

a In all activities, energy used will vary depending on skill, rest patterns, environmental temperature and body size.
b Wide calorie range depending on skill of swimmer, stroke, temperature of water, body composition, current and other factors.

Adapted from "Beyond Diet . . . Exercise Your Way to Fitness and Heart Health," CPC International. Inc.

CHAPTER 10

MEDITATION HELPS BREAK THE STRESS SPIRAL

Daniel Goleman

It is a medical rule of thumb that among the patients a general practitioner sees on any day, half complain of symptoms directly stemming from anxiety. A majority of the rest have complaints that are at least partly caused by stress. The antianxiety drugs, tranquilizers such as Librium and Valium, are the number one prescriptions in America today, outdistancing antibiotics by far.

Social critics blame the hectic pace of industrial life: the crowding, the rush, the pressure. But industrialization itself is not to blame for the toll of stress; we are the victims of our reactions to its frantic pace.

Our bodies undergo the arousal physiologists label "stress" whenever a threatening or challenging event occurs. Stress can be triggered by any number of events. The screech of brakes as we stand vulnerable in a crosswalk can make our hearts race, and so can the unexpected sight of a loved one. Almost any unanticipated happening, or an anticipated one full of threat, causes the speeding up of bodily processes. Any kind of excitement is a stress in the physiologist's sense of the word.

TOO MANY CHANGES

Many normal life events cause stress, especially those that disrupt our everyday routines. Thomas H. Holmes, who is at the University of Washington School of Medicine in Seattle, has found that significant events of ordinary life—the death of a family member, the birth of a child, a change in jobs—can trigger illness because coping with these events puts demands on the body that weaken resistance.

The most strenuous life change is the death of a spouse. Marriage is in the middle of Holmes' list; and vacations, Christmas, and minor violations of the law are at the bottom. Holmes finds that the more adjustments required of a person at any one time, the more likely he is to get sick. While the ailments include back pains and other problems known to be psychosomatic, they also include ordinary diseases like colds and flu. Experiments with Navy men on the same ship showed that those with greater life-change stress came down with more and worse diseases three to six months later.

Hans Selye, an authority on stress research, says that we need a preventive measure to buffer us against the harmful effects of stress which will still allow us to enjoy a full and busy life (see "Stress: It's a G.A.S.," *Psychology Today*, September 1969).

Meditators, for instance, can withstand more life changes with less illness. Jessica Jo Lahr, a graduate student at Ohio State University, compared beginning and experienced meditators with a comparable group of nonmeditators. The meditators had experienced more life changes than nonmeditators, but had less illness. The experienced meditators had the most changes and the least illness of all. Apparently, the ability to handle stress increases with practice in meditation.

Much stress is purely psychological. Often we feel like victims of events, pawns in a game over which we have no control, but in which we must pay the price. University of Pennsylvania psychologist Martin Seligman (see "Fall Into Helplessness," *Psychology Today*, June 1973) has found that people who believe they are helpless react to normal life changes by becoming depressed. They feel pushed around by life no matter what they do.

MEDITATION AND CONTROL

People who chronically assume a helpless attitude have been studied by Julian B. Rotter (see "External Control and Internal Control," *Psychology Today*, June 1971). The chronically helpless are what Rotter calls "externals." They believe that personal rewards depend on the whim of external people and events rather than on their own actions. Such people see life changes as preordained fate, luck, or chance. Internals, on the other hand, believe that they control their own fates. Internals survive the slings and arrows of life better than the depression-prone externals. An internal person would be more likely to react to such setbacks as loss of job or divorce with action to set things right. He would look for a new job or seek a new mate. Externals react with passivity and paralysis to these same events, resigning themselves to their losses with a shrug and a sigh. Several studies have found that meditators, as a group, are much more internal than nonmeditators. Experienced meditators, furthermore, feel more in control of their lives than beginning meditators.

All of us, even externals, can take steps to master stress. The common way to overcome stress in our culture has been to take tranquilizers or barbiturates, but these chemical strategies have obvious drawbacks. For one, drug effects wear off, and the original anxiety reasserts itself. Another drawback is that many who turn to drugs to control stress-induced anxiety become addicted. Some people need such large doses that their everyday functioning is impaired. Sleeping pills used to overcome temporary insomnia, for instance, often become the cause of lasting sleep loss. Because of these and other negative side-effects of antistress drugs, there recently has been a large research effort to find effective non-chemical means to cope with stress. Meditation is one such antistress technique now under study.

MEDITATING INDUSTRIALIST

My interest in meditation changed from personal to professional while I was on a Harvard predoctoral fellowship in India. There I met a number of Indian yogis, Tibetan lamas, and Buddhist monks. I was struck by the relaxed warmth, openness, and alertness of these men, no matter what the situation. Each was the kind of person I enjoyed being with, and I felt nourished when I left them.

There were vast differences in their beliefs and backgrounds. The one thing they shared was meditation. Then I met a teacher of meditation who was not a monk, but an industrialist who had been one of the richest men in Burma. Though he had been highly successful, the executive found that his hectic pace took its toll in the form of daily migraine headaches. Medical treatments at European and American clinics had no effect on his headaches, and he turned to meditation as a last resort. Within three days of his first instruction, his migraines disappeared. In the '60s there was a military coup in Burma, and the new socialist government seized all of the millionaire's holdings, leaving him nearly penniless. He emigrated to India, where he took advantage of old business and family connections to start a new business. While his new enterprise was getting underway, he traveled throughout India giving 10-day courses in meditation. Some reservoir of energy allowed him to be both full-time meditation teacher and businessman. His example helped me to see that one needn't be a monk to meditate. You can separate the physical effects of meditation from its religious context.

When I returned to Harvard from India, I found that psychologist Gary Schwartz had begun research into meditation. He had found that meditators reported much lower daily anxiety levels than nonmeditators.

They had many fewer psychological or psychosomatic problems such as colds, headaches, and sleeplessness.

My personal experience, and these scientific findings, suggested that meditators were able to roll with life's punches, handling daily stresses well and suffering fewer consequences from them. With Schwartz as my thesis advisor, I designed a study to see how the practice of meditation helps one cope with stress.

BLOODY ACCIDENTS

I had two groups of volunteers come to our physiology lab. One group consisted of meditation teachers, all of whom had been meditating for at least two years. The other group of people were interested in meditation but had not yet begun to meditate. Once in the lab, each volunteer was told to sit quietly and either relax or meditate. If non-meditators were assigned to the meditation treatment, I taught them how to meditate right there in the lab. After 20 minutes of relaxation or meditation, the volunteers saw a short film depicting a series of bloody accidents among workers in a woodworking shop. The film is a standard way of inducing stress during laboratory studies, because everyone who watches it is upset by the accidents depicted in the film.

The meditators had a unique pattern of reaction to the film. Just as the accident was about to happen, their heart rates increased and they began to sweat more than the nonmeditators. To get ready to meet the distressing sight, their heart beats rose and their bodies mobilized in what physiologists call the fight-or-flight reaction. But as soon as the accident was over, the meditators recovered, their signals of bodily arousal falling more quickly than those of nonmeditators. After the film, they were more relaxed than the nonmeditators, who still showed signs of tension.

This pattern of greater initial arousal and faster recovery showed up in experienced meditators, whether or not they had meditated before the movie began. In fact, the meditators felt more relaxed the whole time they were in the lab. Rapid recovery from stress is a typical trait of meditators. Even the novices, who meditated for the first time that day in the lab, were less anxious after the film and recovered more quickly than the nonmeditators.

Meditation itself seems the most likely cause of rapid stress recovery. If the rapid recovery among experienced meditators had been the result of some personality trait common to the kind of people who stick with meditation, the novices would have been as slow to recover as were the people who relaxed.

My study may explain the lower incidence of anxiety and psycho-somatic disorders among meditators. People who are chronically anxious or who have a psychosomatic disorder share a specific pattern of reaction to stress; their bodies mobilize to meet the challenge, then fail to stop reacting when the problem is over. The initial tensing up is essential, for it allows them to marshal their energy and awareness to deal with a potential threat. But their bodies stay aroused for danger when they should be relaxed, recouping spent energies and gathering resources for the next brush with stress.

The anxious person meets life's normal events as though they were crises. Each minor happening increases his tension, and his tension in turn magnifies the next ordinary event—a deadline, an interview, a doctor's appointment—into a threat. Because the anxious person's body stays mobilized after one event has passed, he has a lower threat threshold for the next. Had he been in a relaxed state, he would have taken the second event in stride.

A meditator handles stress in a way that breaks up the threat-arousal-threat spiral. The meditator relaxes after a challenge passes more often than the nonmeditator. This makes him unlikely to see innocent occurrences as harmful. He perceives threat more accurately, and reacts with arousal only when necessary. Once aroused, his rapid recovery makes him less likely than the anxious person to see the next deadline as a threat.

The biggest appeal of meditation is the promise of becoming more relaxed more of the time. But some highly pressured members of society are not sure that relaxation is a good thing. When Harvard Medical School's Herbert Benson wrote an article in the *Harvard Business Review* urging businesses to give employees time for a meditation break, there was a flood of letters protesting that stress and tension were essential to good business management. A friend of mine, when told to meditate to lower his blood pressure, responded: "I need to take it easy, but I don't want to become a zombie."

Fortunately, meditation doesn't make zombies. The meditation pros I met in India and America were among the most lively people I've met anywhere. Our research into the effects of meditation on the brain explains why.

Meditation trains the capacity to pay attention. This sets it apart from other ways of relaxing, most of which let the mind wander as it will. This sharpening of attention lasts beyond the meditation session itself. It shows up in a number of ways in the rest of the meditator's day. Meditation, for example, has been found to improve one's ability to pick up subtle perceptual cues in the environment, and to pay attention to what is going on rather than letting the mind wander elsewhere. These skills mean that in conversation with another person, the meditator should be more empathic. Because the meditator can pay sharper attention to what the other person is doing and saying, he can pick up more of the hidden messages the other is sending.

All meditation techniques seem to be equally effective ways to lower the anxiety level and help handle stress. But different types of meditation retrain attention in different ways.

Some of my colleagues at Harvard—Gary Schwartz, Richard Davidson, and Richard Margolin—compared people trained in Transcendental Meditation (TM) with a group trained in a Gurdjieffian technique. This technique is named after George Gurdjieff, a turn-of-the-century Russian who brought to the West an amalgam of esoteric meditative techniques he collected on his Asian travels.

In TM the meditator listens in his mind to a Sanskrit sound, repeatedly starting the sound going mentally each time his mind wanders. The Gurdjieff training, like TM, includes techniques that improve the capacity to keep a single, subtle thought in mind. But Gurdjieff's students also apply this improved power of attention to learning an intricate series of dancelike movements, and to sensing specific areas throughout the body.

The Harvard group tested the TM and the Gurdjieff meditators one by one. They looked at brain-wave patterns while the meditator concentrated on the sensations in his own right hand, and then on a picture of someone sitting in a laboratory chair. The psychologists recorded signals from the part of the brain that controls vision and from the part that controls muscle movement. They found that when a Gurdjieff meditator attended to his hand, the muscle-movement center in his brain became active, as though preparing to order a movement. At the same time, the visual area of the brain became less active. When a Gurdjieff student looked at the picture, the opposite happened; the visual area became more active, the motor area quiet. No such differences appeared among the TM group, nor in a group of people who had never had meditation training of any kind.

The Gurdjieff meditators' brains showed cortical specificity, the ability to turn on those areas of the brain necessary to the task at hand while leaving the irrelevant areas inactive. This is the way the brain works when we are at our most efficient and alert. If too many areas are aroused too much, we get overexcited and perform poorly. If too few areas are active, we're groggy. The machinery of the brain and body works best when only those areas that are essential to the work at hand are activated. The Gurdjieff training developed this ability, while TM did not.

Both TM and Gurdjieff training prime the power of attention while relaxing the body. But only the Gurdjieff training applies this relaxed alertness to improving skills of sensory detection and muscle control. This same training combination is found in many Eastern martial arts. If his mind wandered, the karate master would break his hand, not the brick. Powerful concentration amplifies the effectiveness of any kind of activity, as athletes such as quarterback John Brodie will attest (see "Sport Is a Western Yoga," *Psychology Today*, October 1975).

The research evidence shows that one meditation technique is about as good as another for improving the way we handle stress. Meditators become more relaxed the longer they have been at it. At the same time they become more alert, something other ways to relax fail to bring about because they do not train the ability to pay attention. The combination of relaxation and concentration allows us to do better at whatever we try.

REFERENCES

Davidson, Richard and Daniel Goleman. "Attention and Affective Concomitants of Meditation" in *Journal of Abnormal Psychology*, in press.

Goleman, Daniel and Gary E. Schwartz. "Meditation as an Intervention in Stress Reactivity" in *Journal of Consulting and Clinical Psychology*, in press.

Goleman, Daniel. "Meditation and Consciousness: An Asian Approach to Mental Health" in *American Journal of Psychotherapy*, January 1976.

Leung, Paul. "Comparative Effects of Training in External and Internal Concentration in Two Counseling Behaviors" in *Journal of Counseling Psychology*, Vol. 20, pp. 227-234, 1973.

Schwartz, Gary. "Biofeedback: Self-Regulation and the Patterning of Physiological Processes" in *American Scientist*, Vol. 63, pp. 314-324, 1975.

CHAPTER 11

DEVELOPING AND USING A PERSONAL SUPPORT SYSTEM

Charles Seashore

One method of acquiring, maintaining, and demonstrating one's interpersonal competence is to have a network of supportive relationships which can be drawn on as needed to help one achieve one's particular objectives.

There are many different roles that other people can play which provide support to the individual. A well-developed support system therefore includes a variety of types of individuals and is not limited to people who are, say, close or good at listening or giving advice.

It is a skill to be able to establish, maintain, and effectively utilize a support system. As with all relationships, support systems can be difficult to establish, counter-productive and disappointing at times, and somewhat unpredictable; and they take energy to maintain. They can also be used as crutches which make an individual more dependent rather than more resourceful.

Keeping one's support system up-to-date and relevant to one's goals requires on-going assessment of the kinds of people who are currently available, letting go those who are not relevant or who in fact are sabotaging one's efforts, and building in new persons who could be of assistance.

Supportive people may or may not be aware that they are a part of your system, and they may or may not be aware of the other persons who are important in your life. The relationship may be close and personal or quite distant and impersonal. But it is important that they be useful and that the relationship be equitable and fair.

Reproduced by special permission from *The Reading Book for Human Relations Training,* Edited by Larry Porter, "Developing and Using a Personal Support System" by Charles E. Seashore, 1979, NTL Institute for Applied Behavioral Science. Also used with permission of the author.

It is not necessary that support systems be reciprocal. However, most of us do function as parts of other persons' support systems. It is an equally important skill to know how to *provide* support in a variety of ways. Analyzing how one becomes part of another's support system and how one leaves that relationship can provide a basis for increasing one's own interpersonal competence.

DEFINITION OF A SUPPORT SYSTEM

The definition given below is broken into phrases for the purpose of emphasizing and elaborating on some of the major issues involved in building an effective support system.

A support system is:

- a resource pool
- drawn on selectively
- to support me
- in moving in a direction of my choice
- and leaves me stronger

The resource pool consists of people, things, environments, and beliefs. However, here primary emphasis will be given to the issues concerning people and relationships. The notion of a resource pool raises several questions for us. It is important for us to be *aware* of those individuals who could be *potentially* a part of our support system. This requires some skills at scanning our world and keeping an open mind about the possibility that any given person may be a relevant resource. It is helpful to be *proactive* in reaching out to locate and identify people since it is unlikely that the appropriate people will all come to us. *Size* of the resource pool is important since larger and more complicated systems require a lot of energy to sustain, while very small systems may not have the range of resources that you may need. The composition or variety of people thus becomes an important criterion in building an effective system.

Drawing on people selectively requires skills in choosing appropriate persons and keeping those persons who are not particularly helpful from getting in the way. It involves taking the risk of asking for support and being rejected or let down. It may also occasionally require dealing with jealousy and competition among those people in the system who would like to be asked for assistance and feel left out when you call on someone else. Willingness and availability are also obvious requirements for those people we ask for support.

It is often difficult for many of us to ask others *to support us*. It may, for example, arouse feelings of guilt—we may think we're "imposing." It may feel like an expression of weakness or an admission of failure. It may go against our values or beliefs that altruism is more important than taking for ourselves. It also opens up the fear that we may become dependent on another person rather than being self-sufficient. It does require that we be open to help, that we be willing to make demands on other people, and that we be reasonably clear about the expectations that we have of them.

To move in a direction of my choice requires that I be able to distinguish my goals and directions from those of other people and organizations. Then I can move towards achieving *clarity* so that I am in a position to make a *declaration* of that direction that can be understood by others. It means making a commitment, even if it is only for a short time or is somewhat tentative.

Ideally, a good support system will *leave me stronger.* It confronts me with my own ambivalence about growth and often will generate new demands as others perceive my strength. I am also confronted with letting others know I can do certain things without them, which means I may lose some relationships.

FUNCTIONS OF SUPPORT SYSTEMS

Support systems can be used for several different purposes, depending on the situation confronting an individual:

• *Re-establishing Competence:* Particularly in times of high stress or major transitions, we may find ourselves functioning at a very low level of competence. This may be because of anxiety, the energy it takes to cope with a crisis, physical and emotional difficulties, or overload of demands on us by other people. A good support system can help us cope and return to our previous level of functioning.

• *Maintaining High Performance:* It can be equally important to have access to resourceful people when one is doing well in order to maintain that level of activity. Although it may be easier to use assistance when performing at a high level, many people tend to neglect their support systems at such times, finding it more difficult to ask for help.

• *Gaining New Competencies:* A somewhat different function of support systems is to assist in developing new skills. What is needed here is persons who can challenge, serve as teachers and models, and provide emotional support during periods when one may be feeling awkward or inept in dealing with new situations.

• *Achieving Specific Objectives:* Many of the objectives we strive for cannot be met without collaboration with and contributions from a number of persons. This often requires people who have skills and resources which we do not have or which we do not desire to develop.

These functions of support systems are focused primarily on the individual. They often can help an individual contribute to organizational goals and objectives, but it is equally important that support systems be used when individuals find themselves in conflict or opposition to the directions of other people, groups, or organizations. They should function in such a way as to maintain and develop the integrity of the individual, which may include changing the organization, creating conflict, or leaving a particular setting.

Support systems are particularly helpful in coping with the stress that accompanies transitions in relationships, roles and positions, or careers. Skills in establishing new support systems are essential for successful transitions into new environments.

DIFFERENT TYPES OF SUPPORT SYSTEM MEMBERS

Support system members can function in a number of different ways. Some people fill a variety of roles, while others may offer only a single type of support. The following list illustrates some of the different functions of support system members:

• *Role Models*—people who can help define goals for positions one might assume in the future. Role models not only show what is possible but are a source of valuable information about the opportunities and problems associated with a given role.

• *Common Interests*—people who share common interests or concerns can be especially important in keeping one motivated, and in sorting out those problems that are primarily those of the individual from problems imposed by the larger system and that require collective activity to bring about change in that system.

• *Close Friends*—people who help provide nurturance and caring, who enjoy some of the same interests, and who keep one from becoming isolated and alienated.

• *Helpers*—people who can be depended upon in a crisis to provide assistance. These people are often experts in solving particular kinds of problems and may not be the type with whom one would choose to have a close or personal relationship.

• *Respect Competence*—individuals who respect the skills one has already developed and who value the contributions that one makes in a given situation. They are particularly helpful during times of transition when one may be feeling unsure of oneself in developing new skills.

• *Referral Agents*—people who can connect one with resources in the environment through their knowledge of people and organizations. They can refer one to those places where one can obtain needed assistance.

• *Challengers*—people who can help motivate one to explore new ways of doing things, develop new skills, and work toward the development of latent capabilities. They often are people who one may not care for as personal friends, but who are abrasive and demanding.

SOME PRINCIPLES IN USING SUPPORT SYSTEMS

• *Parsimony*—An attempt should be made to keep the system as simple as possible to minimize the energy it takes to maintain it.

• *Maintenance*—It is wise to keep relationships current and up-to-date so that when you do need to draw on people, they are informed and appreciative of your need for their assistance.

• *Equity*—It is important that the relationship be one in which both sides feel that there is a fair arrangement, whether it be accomplished by returning help, payment of money, joint sense of accomplishment, or whatever else makes sense. Guilt can easily build up when there is a sense of indebtedness that cannot be repaid.

• *External Support Base*—The primary base of support for being competent should be external to the system in which one is using one's skills. This will enable a person to maximize his or her autonomy and to engage in conflict when it becomes necessary. Leaning on people inside the system in which one is trying to be competent often leads to a sense of dependency. (Paradoxically, when one is seen as having an external support group, it is more likely that people inside the system will also turn out to be supportive.)

• *Back-up Resources*—It is wise to have several places one can turn to for particular kinds of support to reduce the sense of vulnerability one feels should an individual be unavailable or unwilling to help in a given circumstance.

• *Feedback*—It is important that feedback be given both ways to check on how each person feels about the process of giving or receiving assistance. Helping often creates resistance and/or resentment and unless there is a means of keeping track of the process, the relationship is likely to erode over time.

CHAPTER 12

ON CONSUMING HUMAN RESOURCES: PERSPECTIVES ON THE MANAGEMENT OF STRESS

John D. Adams

Most of us like to assume that we can bounce back completely from a period of heavy stress at work by taking a day off or getting a good night's sleep. Evidence to the contrary is mounting, however, and it appears that we must pay some price for our stressful experiences, a cost that is difficult, at best, to recover. In other words, the human resources in our organizations (the way we operate them) are nonrenewable resources, much like fuels and mineral ores. Once consumed, they do not renew themselves.

Chronically stressful situations, especially those in which episodic or surprise stressors also are frequent, exert a wear-and-tear influence on the body, mind, and spirit of those who live or work in them. Eventually, an overload of stressful experiences can cause a person's resistances to drop, making individuals vulnerable to illnesses, chronic conditions (such as hypertension), depression, and feelings of apathy and alienation. Most organizations today give little or no attention to these outcomes— many actively deny them—because it is difficult to establish direct cause-and-effect linkages. The focus is most often on short-term objectives, such as "productivity today" and "quarterly goals," as opposed to and at the expense of the longer-term objective of human well-being. Those who "burn out," "rust out," or become less productive in other ways are transferred, shelved, or dismissed with little awareness on anyone's part of the reasons for the drop in productivity. It is still a "survival-of-the-fittest" world in which not everyone is expected to make it. This chapter explores some options to this viewpoint as they apply to managers at all levels.

Reprinted from: W.W. Burke and W.B. Eddy (Eds.), *Behavioral Science and the Manager's Role* (2nd ed.). San Diego, CA: University Associates, 1980.

STRESS IS UNAVOIDABLE

The first basic contention here is that life at all levels of management is excessively stressful due to factors that are inherent in the normal ways organizations choose to operate. An example is the result obtained when people are asked to review the following sets of descriptions and select the set that most typifies successful managers they know.

I	II
High achiever	Relaxed, easygoing
Competitive	Seldom lacks time
Aggressive	Speaks slowly
Fast worker	Steady worker
Pressure performer	Not preoccupied with achievement
Deadline oriented	Even tempered

Most people select Column I, or at least most of the terms in Column I. These two columns are from lists of Type-A and Type-B behavior traits identified by Friedman and Rosenman (1974). They and others have found that individuals whose behavior is characterized by Type-A traits (Column I) are two to three times as likely to experience a heart attack as those whose behavior is characterized by Type-B traits (Column II). Type-A behavior is now considered by doctors to be one of the major risk factors in coronary heart disease. Taken together, heart attacks and strokes account for nearly one-half of the deaths in this country, and a large proportion of them are related to prolonged experiences of stress.

The following statement from a senior manager in a large organization illustrates a commonly accepted point of view.

> The managers in the training department don't work until 7:30 every night like I do. I worry about that; I really do. No one can become president of this organization without extending himself!

Most organizations also exhibit very strong norms about how hard people work. Being forever in a position of rushing to keep even with the demands of one's job frequently is seen as desirable. I have done stress-management consulting with many organizations in which managers complain a lot about having "too much to do and too little time to do it." They actually desire this state of affairs. Usually, I say it is doubtful that any of them will use whatever time- or stress-management techniques I teach them to change this norm. After the protests die down, I ask them how they would describe a peer who states that she has her job under control and is not bothered continually by work overload, interruptions, surprise changes, and so on. The responses most often expressed include:

"lazy," "goof-off," "doesn't have enough to do," and "must be missing something." In other words, if someone actually applies good time- or stress-management principles and thereby gets on top of her job, she is going to be seen as a deviant from this basic, although highly stress-provoking, norm of contemporary organizational life.

Once again, the first basic contention of this chapter is that excessive levels of stress are an inherent part of the manager's daily environment.

STRESS IS COSTLY

The second basic contention of this chapter is that the costs associated with these high levels of stress are immense and largely hidden. Therefore, they are denied or ignored. In how many organizations is there direct acknowledgment that a heart attack suffered on the job was in large part caused by the organization itself? And if the heart attack happens at home or on vacation? There will be some acknowledgment that "Joe has been under a lot of stress lately," but seldom, if ever, will anything be changed in the organization to reduce stress levels for other "Joes." Ulcers and less climactic chronic conditions (e.g., hypertension, depression, high cholesterol, nervous tics, etc.) usually receive even less attention by the powers that be.

The main reason for this damage is that each stressor has a generalized effect on the body. Regardless of the cause of the stress—for example, work load or criticism from the boss—one's body responds in a predictable way. The autonomic nervous system and endocrine gland system, ordinarily the governors of this equilibrium, go into action to prepare the individual to fight the stressor or "get out of its way." The entire body is affected: the cardiovascular and respiratory systems speed up; the gastrointestinal system slows down; the muscles get stronger; and the immunological process prepares for a possible infection.

Setting all this in motion too often over a period of time has an erosive effect, which eventually may lead to some kind of physical, mental, or spiritual breakdown. Since individuals have unique heredities, habits, personalities, and past histories, Tom may develop ulcers, while Mary "catches" every virus that passes through town, and Geoffrey flies off the handle at unexpected moments. Although cause-and-effect linkages have not been established between specific stressors and specific dysfunctions, there is no longer any doubt that excessive stress levels do induce physical illness, mental distress, and spiritual malaise.

In a recent study (Adams, 1978), I found amount of illness to be correlated positively with the number of stressful events experienced by managers on the job. Correlated inversely with the level of chronic daily stress experienced by managers on the job were health, level of satisfaction, and feelings of productivity.

In other studies, University of Michigan psychologists (French & Caplan, 1972) have made similar findings in investigating stress and illness among employees of the National Aeronautics and Space Administration (NASA). Put most briefly, they have found consistently that factors such as role conflict and ambiguity, work overload, poor relationships, too much responsibility, and too little participation are correlated with the primary risk factors associated with coronary heart disease.

Conservative estimates, looking at the population at large, indicate that 10 percent of the people in this country are hypertensive and 10 percent have "alcohol-related problems." In most of these cases, the origins of both these problems now are considered to be stress related.

Although no meaningful estimate can be established, it is necessary to conclude that the costs associated with stress, in terms of ill health alone, are immense. In view of the fact that Americans spend $120 billion per year on health care, the implications of the following quote become clear (Lazarus, 1977).

> It has become increasingly apparent that stress is important as a factor in illness in general and in chronic illness in particular. Many present-day illnesses cannot be explained in terms of a single "cause." Research suggests that a significant portion of the population seeking medical care is suffering from stress-based illness.

The costs of securing, training, and orientating new employees also can be considered, at least partially, to be stress-related costs. For example, one new corporation is hurrying to get its production plant on line while it still is wrestling with the new technologies with which it is involved. As a result of the stresses associated with this fast-paced new effort, the organization has been averaging a 34 percent turnover of its operations people each year. Top management estimates that it costs $4,000 to recruit, orient, and train a new person. During 1978, approximately 1,000 new people were needed in the organization at a cost of over $4 million to get them job-ready.

To summarize, the first basic contention of this chapter is that excessive levels of stress are an inherent part of the manager's daily environment. The second basic contention is that the costs associated with these high levels of stress are immense and largely hidden. So, what does this boil down to? It is this—there is a general lack of awareness or consciousness among contemporary managers about the dysfunctional nature of most organizations relative to stress.

By and large, the most debilitating sources of stress are rooted in the norms of an organization, as illustrated in the "too much to do with too little time to do it in" norm. Since norms are more difficult to change than policies or procedures, it is unlikely that stress will be removed by policy changes or organizational decision making. What is needed is an increase of awareness (consciousness raising) followed by behavioral changes on a large scale. In other words, the first step must be to create a critical mass of consciousness about stress and its possible effects.

After they become more aware of stress, managers should learn more about managing their stresses and those of their employees. They need techniques both for immediate response to specific stressors and for developing long-term protection or buffering against the cumulative effects of stress. Ultimately, someone should develop a systems approach to the management of human resources that takes stressors and stress-management factors into account along with presently considered task factors. Such a systems approach might be called "holistic management" to the extent that it includes a physical (illness to wellness), psychological (depression to excitement), and spiritual (alienation to integration) balance in its consideration of stress.

THE EXPERIENCE OF ORGANIZATIONAL STRESS

Most approaches to stress management spend little time identifying where the stress is coming from in an individual's environment. However, an understanding of the sources of stress in one's life is an important prelude to developing a plan for effective stress management. Furthermore, understanding the organizational sources of stress is basic to developing processes for reducing or removing unnecessary stress. Where most stress programs focus only on the individual and her or his ability to withstand stress better (e.g., through meditation or "body work"), a complete approach also must consider altering stressful organizational norms and management practices. Therefore, as a consultant, I ask clients to identify their primary stressors in each of four sectors, as illustrated in Figure 1.

	On the Job	Away from Work
Recent Events	Type I	Type II
Ongoing Conditions	Type III	Type IV

Figure 1. Sources of Stress

Primary Stress Types (Stressors)

Types I and II are derived principally from the work of Holmes and Rahe (1967) and their colleagues at the University of Washington. They were instrumental in developing the now widely known social-readjustment rating scale, which predicts a growing likelihood of illness following periods of high change in an individual's life.

Stress Type I

Recent events on the job include changes for an individual, such as:

1. Major changes in instructions, policies, or procedures;
2. A requirement to work more hours per week than normal;
3. A sudden significant increase in the activity level or pace of work;
4. Major reorganization;
5. Etc.

A thirty-one-item list of such events has been developed by Naismith (1975). Each event has a point value reflecting the average amount of readjustment required for an individual to feel "back to normal" following the experience of that change event. In my research project (1978), I found the number of readjustment points accumulated by managers during a twelve-month period to be correlated significantly with the number of health conditions they were experiencing.

Stress Type II

Recent events away from work include changes for an individual, such as:

1. Restriction of social life;
2. Marriage;
3. Death of family member;
4. Serious illness;
5. Etc.

Following Holmes and Rahe, a list of change events such as this was developed by Cochrane and Robertson (1973). Here again, each change event has a certain number of points associated with it, reflecting the average amount of readjustment required to get back to normal. In my project (1978), the number of readjustment points accumulated by managers was again correlated with the numbers of health conditions they reported.

To summarize, events (both on and off the job) cause disruptions for us. Whether or not we are conscious of it, these events trigger a chain reaction intended to restore equilibrium, because a certain amount of readjustment is always necessary. The more often we trigger the stress response, the more likely it is that we will become ill. In most cases, specific kinds of stress cannot be linked to specific illnesses. However, with too much stress, our inherent tendencies to become ill or psychologically distressed, whatever they are, are more likely to come to the surface.

Types III and IV (Figure 1) are derived principally from the work of French and Caplan (1972) and their colleagues at the Institute for Social Research at the University of Michigan. This group of professionals has worked extensively with NASA in the study of day-to-day or chronic stress and its effect on health and well-being.

Stress Type III

On-the-job conditions include daily pressures on an individual, such as:

1. Too much work, too little time;
2. Feedback only when performance is unsatisfactory;
3. Conflicts between his unit and others it must work with;
4. Unclear standards and responsibilities;
5. Etc.

These kinds of stressors are similar to the primary sources of stress identified by French and his colleagues: work overload, role ambiguity and conflict, responsibility level, poor interpersonal relationships, and lack of participation. It is safe to say that most people in most large organizations today can readily identify with these conditions—and few are surprised that too much of them can be debilitating.

In my research study (1978), I found the frequency with which managers were experiencing these conditions to be correlated positively with the number of chronic health conditions they reported and correlated negatively with their felt work effectiveness and their felt satisfaction and growth. It has already been pointed out that this type of stressor is frequently normative in nature. Thus, changing negative norms, to the extent that is possible, can lead to lower levels of chronic stress at work.

Stress Type IV

Away-from-work conditions include pressure on an individual, such as:

1. Pollution;
2. Noise;

3. Concern over the economy;
4. Anxiety about children's activities;
5. Etc.

Here again, the frequency with which managers experience these and other conditions as stressful is correlated (though less strongly) with the number of chronic health conditions they report. This type of stress has had much less attention from researchers than the other three.

In summary, daily conditions cause pressures that, even after a person becomes accustomed to them, can cause illness and lower feelings of satisfaction, growth, and work effectiveness. When change events occur on the job in large numbers to people already working under highly stressful conditions, the incidence of sick leave, accidents, and inattention to work increases rapidly.

The overall format I have devised to guide my work on stress is portrayed by Figure 2. The types of stressors are listed at the top of the diagram.

Situational Givens

The context or the inherent givens of a situation may serve to diffuse or to intensify stress, depending on their nature. These givens include:

1. The personal characteristics and background of the individual;
2. Quality and amount of support; and
3. Organizational factors.

First, individuals inherit strengths and weaknesses or develop them through good or bad personal habits, accidents, or abuses. Furthermore, our behavioral orientations both predispose us to certain types of stress (e.g., needing close direction but working in an ambiguous role) and influence how we might break down (e.g., people who are more driven, competitive, deadline and achievement oriented—Type-A behavior—are more likely to have heart attacks). With an awareness of one's orientations and idiosyncrasies, one has more choices available relative to avoiding overly stressful situations.

Secondly, people who work in an environment lacking in social support are likely to have more health and emotional problems than people working in more supportive settings.

Thirdly, the nature of the organization one works in can either heighten or reduce stress levels. Factors such as the number of deadlines, manner of facing crises, and the frequency and nature of client demands all should be considered for their role in increasing or decreasing stress.

Usually we cannot change these three factors much (personality, quality of support, nature of organization), but the manager needs to

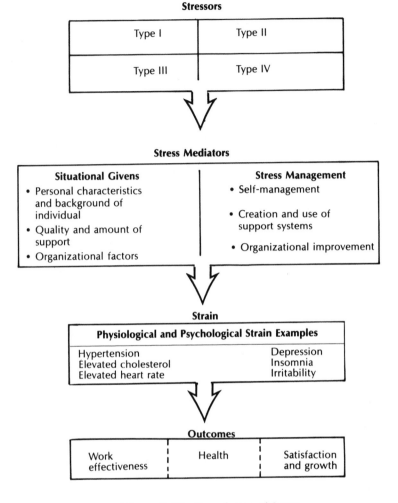

Figure 2. The Experience of Stress

develop an understanding of how they affect stress levels in order to promote effective stress management.

Stress Management

A different sort of mediating variable has to do with how well the individual manages his own stress in each of these same three areas: within himself, in relation to others, and within the organizational context. Training in this area, first in mixed groups of managers and then in face-to-face work groups, seems to be the most promising approach to managing the high levels of stress in contemporary organizations. Both long-term (preventive) and immediate (responsive) stress-management techniques are needed to protect an organization's human resources from the effects of stress. Although most stress-management training focuses on one basic technique (e.g., progressive relaxation or meditation), it is important to cover a variety of techniques in cafeteria style and encourage individuals to develop stress-management plans suited to their own situations and preferences.

SUGGESTIONS FOR STRESS MANAGEMENT

In addition to managing stress effectively for themselves, it is important for managers to understand the organizational stress process well enough to assist others with their experiences of stress. Some options for both of these facets of stress management are offered here.

Self-Management

The paragraphs that follow represent the broad range of techniques that may be used both for buffering oneself against the impact of stress in the long run and for responding directly to stressors in the short run.

First, every manager should be enhancing her or his self-awareness continually. Knowledge of our own idiosyncrasies, preferences, and needs enables us to make more choices that avoid stressful situations. If, for example, an individual prefers to work alone, participative management can be a stressful experience. On the job, we can enhance our self-awareness with feedback from trusted colleagues and during performance reviews. Away from work, self-awareness can be developed by reading, introspection, feedback from family and friends, psychological tests, therapy, and participation in a variety of kinds of groups. Generally, we all are surrounded with information that could enhance our self-awareness, if we would only pay attention to it.

In a study involving a large number of managers, Burke (1971) identified ten of the most frequently used responses to job stress and tension; these are listed in Figure 3.

Howard (1975) has used these same coping responses in a separate study of differences among managers in their ability to protect their health when under stress. He listed the responses in rank order according to how frequently each is used, as shown in the first column of Figure 3. The reader might benefit from noting which of the ten items he or she uses. The second column shows rank order according to how many

Rank by Use (%)	Rank by Symptoms	Coping Responses
1 (64)	6	Change to engrossing nonwork activity
2 (49)	4	Talk it through on the job with peers
3 (41)	9	Analyze situation and change strategy
4 (40)	2	Compartmentalize work life and home life
5 (35)	3	Engage in regular physical exercise
6 (26)	7	Talk it through with spouse
7 (25)	1	Build resistance through healthful life-style habits
8 (25)	5	Withdraw physically from the situation
9 (24)	8	Work harder
10 (15)	10	Change to a different work task

Figure 3. Managers' Coping Responses to Job Stress and Tension

---

symptoms of chronic ill health were experienced by people who had practiced each of the responses.

In the "Rank by Use" column, the number one item is the most widely used response. In the "Rank by Symptoms" column, the number one item has the lowest average number of symptoms experienced by those who regularly use that response. The implication of this ranking of symptoms is that some of the coping responses are more likely to protect health in the face of stress than others.

It should be noted that the five most effective coping strategies (i.e., having the fewest symptoms associated with them) are of a "work smarter" type: (1) build resistance through healthful life style; (2) compartmentalize work life and home life; (3) engage in regular physical exercise; (4) talk it through on the job with peers; and (5) withdraw physically from the situation.

The five less effective strategies (i.e., having the most symptoms associated with them) are more of a "work harder" or "nose-to-the-grindstone" variety: (6) change to engrossing nonwork activity; (7) talk it through with spouse; (8) work harder; (9) analyze situation and change strategy; and (10) change to a different work task.

In Howard's study (1975), those coping strategies that involve taking care of oneself and dealing directly with stressors appear to lead to relatively fewer symptoms of illness than do strategies that involve attempts to overwhelm the stressors with higher energy outputs. The responses dealing with healthful life-style habits and exercise include some of the most important long-term health maintenance habits: *nutrition, exercise, relationships,* and *relaxation.*

Nutrition

A glance into the typical manager's "lunch box" is likely to reveal a deficient or marginally balanced diet. Most managers have little awareness of good nutritional principles; few of them get three sound meals a day, including a balance of meats, dairy products, fruits and vegetables, and cereals and grains. Although these four food groups are necessary to ensure that people get sufficient vitamins, minerals, protein and fiber, one or more of the groups often is overlooked.

On the other hand, there are marked tendencies for managers to: eat on the run; consume foods that are high in refined starch, fat, salt, sugar and chemical additives; drink too much alcohol and caffeine; and rely too often on overcooked, heavy, restaurant meals. Good nutritional habits are necessary in the long run to combat the effects of stress.

Exercise

Relatively few managers engage in any regular exercise program; although, happily, this situation does seem to be changing. Most management roles do not require anywhere near the physical exertion human bodies are designed for, or indeed require, to maintain full health. Therefore, the manager who does not have any regular nonwork activities requiring sustained exertion is at risk.

In order to improve cardiovascular fitness to the levels needed to combat stress, an individual's pulse should be elevated to around 130 beats per minute and that pace should be maintained for twenty to thirty minutes an average of three times each week. This creates what is referred to as the aerobic effect, which improves the efficiency of one's cardiovascular system and lowers the resting pulse rate. Some long distance runners, for example, have heart rates below fifty beats per minute. Activities that create this effect include: running, swimming, vigorous walking, rowing, bicycling, jumping rope, and sports that are not marked with pauses or time-outs (e.g., hockey, soccer, rugby).

Kenneth Cooper (1970) has developed tables for measuring an individual's progress in several different aerobic activities. He also suggests training programs and provides training tips for beginners. One of his most important points is that those who are planning to start jogging, for example, should have a complete physical, including the treadmill stress test, prior to beginning. This will give one additional assurance that a running or other heavy exercise program will not be dangerous—or it will rule out this exercise if some unknown heart problem is uncovered.

Relationships

Most managers give too little attention to maintaining high quality relationships. Numerous studies (e.g., Berkman, 1977; Cassel, 1976; French & Caplan, 1972) have emphasized that maintaining solid interpersonal relationships is important to continued good health in the face of prolonged high levels of stress. Often, managers who are working vigorously to advance their careers keep themselves so busy with work matters that they have little time or energy remaining for developing ongoing relationships with others, either on or off the job. In most organizations, there is little encouragement to do so and, frequently, the inherent nature of the system pits the manager against his peers and potential friends in a no-holds-barred competition for the next promotion.

We all need supportive relationships in order to feel connected, to be challenged, to gain access, to be respected, to exchange ideas, and so on. For reasons not yet clearly known, when we lack such relationships for too long, the risk of our developing stress-related physical and psychological conditions increases.

Relaxation

The final dimension of personal stress management to be included here is relaxation. It seldom is legitimate for one to take a half-hour rest break on the job, even though such a practice would enhance performance considerably more than do coffee breaks. Tremendous progress has been made in understanding the effects and potential of relaxation techniques such as meditation (e.g., Benson, 1975). Such activities still are rather foreign to the American culture and definitely do not fit into the image of the American manager. As a consequence, very few managers practice one of these remarkable restorative and protective techniques.

The following is a superficial and yet revealing test of the potentials inherent in easily learned relaxation techniques:

> Simply close your eyes and take ten slow deep breaths. Each time you exhale, count silently—"one" after the first breath, "two" after the second breath, etc.—up to ten. If you lose count or find yourself "working" on thoughts as they pass through your mind, start your count over. When you are finished, you should feel relaxed (your blood pressure will go down temporarily, too, if it tends to be high) and ready to concentrate fully on your next activity.

Twenty minutes of uninterrupted relaxation could have a tremendous impact on most managers' work effectiveness, as well as increasing their ability to withstand stress.

This section has looked at some ideas that managers can implement for themselves—self-management—to confront stressors directly and protect themselves from prolonged stress. The next step is to consider some things managers can do for others who are experiencing too much stress on the job.

Stress in Others

First of all, how can we recognize that another person may be experiencing too much stress, when we often do not even notice when we are getting overloaded ourselves? Sometimes it takes another person to point it out to us. The "signals of stress" list shown here, although not complete, provides some clues of behaviors displayed by a person who is experiencing high levels of stress. These behaviors are the ones most frequently identified by participants in several stress-management workshops as being signals of stress. They are similar both to behaviors identified in studies of burnout among human-service professionals and to characteristics of system overload.

SIGNALS OF STRESS

1. Disregarding low (or high) priority tasks;
2. Giving reduced amount of time to each task;
3. Redrawing boundaries to shift or avoid responsibilities;
4. Blocking out new information;
5. Being superficially involved; appearing to give up;
6. Expressing negative or cynical attitudes about customers/clients;
7. Appearing depersonalized, detached;
8. "Going by the book";
9. Being overly precise; intellectualizing;
10. Displaying inappropriate humor;
11. Stealing or using other means of "ripping off" the organization;
12. Obviously wasting time; being "unavailable" much of the time;
13. Being late for work; frequently being absent.

When any of these signals appear as *new* behaviors, they are probably signs of excessive levels of stress. Learning to identify these symptoms is the first step toward helping others manage their stress more effectively. The second step involves understanding what is involved in coping with Type I (episodic) and Type III (chronic) sources of stress.

Coping with Episodic Stressors

A Type I (episodic) stressor is experienced as stressful by individuals to the extent that it takes them by surprise. For example, in a department in which a major new policy is simply announced as an accomplished fact and imposed, more stress will be induced than in a department in which the manager has helped her people understand that the new policy is coming, why it has been developed, and how it will apply to them. When it arrives, the "low-stress manager" helps her people try out the policy and, if necessary, sound off about it. Although the aforementioned example is overly simplified, it does communicate the essence of reducing the impact of Type I stressors—full two-way communications. The more information we have about an event, the less we will be taken by surprise by it and, therefore, the less stress we will experience as a result.

Coping with Chronic Stressors

Type III (chronic) stressors, such as ambiguous work roles, are more pervasive in their impact than the Type I (episodic) stressors because they are there every day. Also, the chronic stressors are rooted most often in the norms of the organization rather than in its policies or procedures, and they are, therefore, more difficult for the manager to address and change.

It is possible, however, to remove some of the stressful norms in any organization. The first step is to identify them. Second, everyone in a given work unit should acknowledge that a particular norm ought to be changed. As an example, recall the "too much to do and too little time to do it" norm mentioned earlier. Even though this norm is identified and acknowledged to be a cause of stress in a unit, if some of the other members of that unit are unwilling to change their behaviors relative to this norm, then the unit's manager cannot afford to change her behavior and risk being seen as underemployed or lazy.

Many of these stressors require actions other than behavior change. For example, depending on the nature of the chronic stressors that have been identified, a work unit may need to engage in team building, role negotiation, conflict management, the establishment or revision of job descriptions, management by objectives, problem solving, and so on. As the reader who is familiar with intentional organizational change processes will recognize, organization development techniques are particularly suited to dealing with Type III stressors.

Organization development, however, is not enough by itself. People ordinarily will not mobilize to face the stressors inherent in their organizations without an awareness of what stress is, where it comes from, and what it can do. Furthermore, they need to know what they can do about stress. This suggests that some form of education and training is needed. Whatever approach is taken, the objective must be to create a critical mass of consciousness about stress, without which changes are unlikely.

And finally, the organization, if it is to respond effectively, must build a holistic approach to its management of human resources—making sure that people are given encouragement and opportunities to replenish their physical, mental, and spiritual energies. Some examples of what this might mean include: management by objectives, plans that include personal-development objectives; quiet relaxation rooms; nutritional-awareness programs; exercise programs with changing areas; the hiring of a physical-exercise trainer; stress counseling associated with an annual physical examination; yoga instruction; availability of fruits and juices at meetings and seminars; and ongoing stress-education programs.

REFERENCES

Adams, J. D. Improving stress management: An action-research-based OD intervention. In W. W. Burke (Ed.), *The cutting edge.* San Diego, CA: University Associates, 1978.

Benson, H. *The relaxation response.* New York: William Morrow and Co., 1975.

Burke, R. J. Are you fed up with work? *Personnel Administration,* 1971, January-February.

Cassel, J. The contribution of social environment to host resistance. *American Journal of Epidemiology,* 1976, *104*(2), 107-123.

Cochrane, R., & Robertson, A. The life events inventory. *The Journal of Psychosomatic Research,* 1973, *17*, 135-139.

Cooper, K. *The new aerobics.* New York: Bantam Books, 1970.

French, J. R. P., & Caplan, R. D. Organizational stress and individual strain. In A. Marrow (Ed.), *The failure of success.* New York: AMACOM, 1972.

Friedman, M., & Rosenman, R. H. *Type A behavior and your heart.* New York: Knopf, 1974.

Holmes, T. H., & Rahe, R. H. The social readjustment rating scale. *The Journal of Psychosomatic Research,* 1967, *11*, 213-218.

Howard, J. H., Rechnitzer, P. A., & Cunningham, D. A. Coping with job tension—effective and ineffective methods. *Public Personnel Management,* 1975, September-October, *4*(5), 317-326.

Lazarus, R. S. *Proceedings of the National Heart and Lung Institute* (now Heart, Lung and Blood Institute) *Working Conference on Health Behavior,* 1977 (DHEW NIH77-868). Washington, D.C.: U.S. Government Printing Office, 1977.

Naismith, D. *Stress among managers as a function of organizational change.* Unpublished doctoral dissertation. The George Washington University, Washington, D.C., 1975.

CHAPTER 13

IMPROVING STRESS MANAGEMENT: AN ACTION-RESEARCH-BASED OD INTERVENTION

John D. Adams

Concerns for the impact of stress on the health of managers and on their sense of well-being and productivity are very high in most organizations these days. Increasingly, senior managers are becoming aware—both in financial and in human terms—of the costs of their fast-paced, deadline-oriented ways of operating. The pace of change and the daily pressures of life in general serve to compound the pressures of work, often with costly results.

The United States Clearinghouse for Mental Health Information, for example, recently reported that U.S. industry has had a seventeen-billion-dollar annual decrease in its productive capacity over the last few years due to stress-induced mental dysfunctions. Similarly, other studies estimate even greater losses (at least sixty billion) arising from stress-induced physical illnesses. The need for increased competence in stress management is clear. Some more specific examples of the "costs" of stress include:

1. Over twenty million people in the U.S. have hypertension. About the same number are alcoholic. (Each is estimated, conservatively, to afflict one in ten persons.)

2. Nearly 35 percent of all deaths in this country are due to myocardial infarctions (heart attacks). Another 11 percent are due to strokes.

3. Side effects or abuse of drugs is the eleventh leading cause of death in the U.S.

Portions of this paper are adapted from the original action research report by Adams and Margolis, 1977.

Reprinted from: W.W. Burke (Ed.), *The Cutting Edge.* San Diego, CA: University Associates, 1978.

4. Eleven percent of U.S. doctors abuse alcohol and/or drugs.

5. An alcoholic executive (5 to 8 percent) costs his or her organization an average of four thousand dollars per year in lost time, waste, and so on.

6. Hundreds of thousands of persons are killed or badly injured in unnecessary industrial accidents each year.

7. Occupational factors are estimated to be involved in 150,000 cancer deaths per year.

8. Estimates of the number of suicides per year in the U.S. vary from 25,000 to 50,000. One attempted suicide in eight is "successful."

9. We spend over 120 billion dollars per year on health care.

One of the basic premises of the approach to stress management described in this paper is reflected in the growing use of the term "behavioral medicine," which emphasizes that the individual, and not his or her physician, must become *responsible* for his or her own health and well-being. The following quotation from a National Institutes of Health conference perhaps sums up the issue of responsibility best:

> Most medical schools, and therefore medical students, (now) place highest value on physical diagnosis (of existing symptoms,) secondary value on selecting the appropriate treatment of diagnosed conditions and little or no value on the importance of effective communication with patients in the interests of increasing client understanding of and responsibility for his own health ... Methods must be developed for teaching health habits that are likely to maintain or improve health, e.g., exercise, nutrition, rest and relaxation, and avoidance of smoking. (Weiss, 1977, pp. 19-20, 22)

This approach is the one described in this paper. If "medical" is changed to "OD" and "health" to "organizational," the quotation could become an admonition to organization development professionals. In any event, this approach is highly compatible with organization development and other participative planned-change processes. In many instances, awareness of the consequences of prolonged high levels of stress has caused managers to become committed to organization development programs they previously had resisted as being unrelated to their objectives. Stress awareness helps to bring unity to mind and body and clearly demonstrates the connections between stress level, health, satisfaction and personal growth, and productivity. Stress management requires both effective personal habits and effective (in the OD sense) organizational habits.

This paper describes a stress-based action research intervention carried out over a two-year period in a metropolitan hospital.

WHAT IS STRESS?

Very few specific cause-and-effect statements can be made about either stress-induced illnesses or stress-reducing practices. A large and growing number of population studies give percentages, i.e., numbers of people affected per thousand. These are likely to be accurate predictors on an organization-wide basis, but they cannot tell you, as an individual, that *your* high-pressured life style will lead definitely to a heart attack or that changing your health habits definitely will prevent one. We can say that a person's *chances* of having a heart attack are two-to-three times greater than those of someone whose life style is less stressful and that people who eat a well-balanced diet are likely to have better health than those whose diet is deficient in basic nutrients or is comprised mainly of fats, refined white flour, and sugar.

The stress response is a nonspecific physiological and psychological chain of events triggered by any disruption to one's equilibrium or "homeostasis." It is the same reaction regardless of the stressor; yet each unique individual's outward reaction to stress may be slightly different from another's. The chain of events leading to the re-establishment of equilibrium involves the autonomic nervous system and the endocrine system. These systems combine to speed up cardiovascular functions and slow down gastrointestinal functions, thus equipping a person to "fight or take flight." The triggering of this response frequently over prolonged periods of time causes wear and tear on one's system, increasing the risk of illness or emotional dysfunction. It increases the likelihood that *latent* disease and emotional distress will become manifest. How much stress it takes to trigger this or which illness will occur is different for each person and is based on factors such as heredity, personality, habits, and past accidents and illnesses. We all need some stress in order to be alert and productive, and we each have a unique point at which more stress becomes destructive. Lazarus (Weiss, 1977, p. 51) states that:

> It has become increasingly apparent that stress is important as a factor in illness in general and in chronic illness in particular. Many present day illnesses cannot be explained in terms of a single "cause." Research suggests that a significant portion of the population seeking medical care is suffering from stress based illness.

The manager's personal challenge is to seek *enough* stress, yet to manage his or her stress levels when they go beyond stimulating top performance. As a manager, the challenge is to minimize the amount of unnecessary stress he or she creates for others. For example, changes that are surprising are more stressful than changes that are anticipated and understood. Unilateral announcements about major decisions or policy changes generally are found to be high stressors in departments in which there is low participation and poor communication.

Most approaches to stress management spend little time identifying where the stress is coming from. Understanding the sources of stress is an important prelude to developing a plan for effective stress management. Organizational sources of stress must be identified before processes can be developed for reducing or removing unnecessary stressors. Most stress programs focus only on the individual and his or her ability to withstand stress, e.g., through meditation or "body work"; an OD approach must *also* consider altering stressful organizational norms and management practices. Clients must be helped to identify their primary stressors in four areas, as illustrated in Figure 1.

	On the Job	Away from Work
Recent Events	Type I	Type II
Ongoing Conditions	Type III	Type IV

Figure 1. Sources of Stress

Stress sources I and II are derived principally from the work of Holmes and Rahe (1967) and their colleagues at the University of Washington. They were instrumental in developing the now widely known Social Readjustment Rating Scale, which predicts the growing likelihood of illness following periods of great change in one's life.

Type I stress is recent events on the job, including changes such as: (a) major changes in instructions, policies, or procedures; (b) being required to work more hours than usual per week; (c) a sudden, significant increase in the activity level or pace of work; and (d) a major reorganization. A thirty-one-item list of such events has been developed by Naismith (1975). Each event has a point value that reflects the average amount of readjustment required for one to feel "back to normal" following that change event. In the project described herein, I found the number of readjustment points accumulated by managers during a twelve-month period to correlate significantly with the number of health conditions they experienced.

Type II stress includes recent events away from work, such as: (a) a restriction of social life, (b) marriage, (c) the death of a family member, and (d) a serious illness. Following Holmes and Rahe (1967), a list of change events such as these has been developed by Cochrane and Robertson (1973). Again each change event is assigned a certain number of points that reflect the average amount of readjustment required to "get back to normal." The number of readjustment points accumulated by managers was correlated with the numbers of health conditions they reported.

Results showed that events (both on and off the job) cause disruptions. A chain reaction is triggered in order to restore equilibrium; a certain amount of readjustment is necessary. The more often we trigger the stress response, the more likely it is that we will become ill. Although specific kinds of stress cannot be linked in most cases to specific diseases, with too much stress our latent tendencies to become physically or psychologically ill are more likely to surface.

Stress sources III and IV are derived principally from the work of French and Caplan (1972) and their colleagues at the Institute for Social Research at the University of Michigan. This group of psychologists has worked extensively with the National Aeronautics and Space Administration in the study of day-to-day (or chronic) stress and its effects on health and well-being.

Type III stress includes on-the-job conditions and daily pressures such as: (a) too much work to do in too little time, (b) feedback only when performance is unsatisfactory, (c) conflicts between one's work unit and others with which it must work, and (d) unclear standards and responsibilities. These kinds of stressors are similar to the primary sources of chronic stress identified by French and his colleagues: work overload, role ambiguity or conflict, territoriality, poor-quality relationships, and lack of participation. It is safe to say that most working people today can readily identify with these conditions; few people would be surprised to hear that too much of these stressors can be debilitating. In our project, I found the frequency with which managers were experiencing these kinds of conditions to be correlated with the number of health conditions they reported and to be negatively correlated with their feelings of work effectiveness and satisfaction and growth. This type of stressor is frequently normative in nature. Thus, eliminating negative norms can reduce levels of chronic stress at work.

Type IV stress includes nonwork conditions and pressures such as: (a) pollution, (b) noise, (c) concern over economy and/or personal financial stability, and (d) anxiety about children's activities or choice of friends. Here again, the frequency with which managers experience such conditions as stressful is correlated, though less strongly, with the number of health conditions they report. While this type of stress has had much less attention from researchers than the other three, it is often the one that managers want most to explore.

In summary, daily conditions cause pressures that—even after one becomes accustomed to them—can cause illness and lower satisfaction, growth, and work effectiveness. When on-the-job change *events* occur in large numbers to people already working under highly stressful *conditions*, the incidence of sick leave, accidents, and inattention to work increases rapidly.

PROJECT DESIGN

The format devised to guide our work on stress is portrayed in Figure 2. The mediating variables (context of situation and stress management) may serve either to intensify or to diffuse the impact of the sources of stress (stressors).

The context or "givens" of a situation include: (a) the personal characteristics and background of the individual; (b) situational factors; and (c) quality of support. People inherit strengths and weaknesses and develop them through good or bad personal habits, accidents, illnesses, or abuses. Further, behavioral orientations both predispose us to certain types of stress (e.g., one may need close direction but work in an ambiguous role) and influence how we might break down (e.g., highly motivated, competitive, and achievement-oriented people are more likely to have heart attacks). If one is aware of one's orientations and idiosyncrasies, one is more able to avoid overly stressful situations. The nature of the work organization can either heighten or reduce stress levels for employees. Factors such as the number of deadlines, the way in which crises are faced, and the frequency and nature of client demands all need to be considered for their roles in increasing or decreasing stress. In addition, people who lack social support at work are likely to have more health and emotional problems than people who work in supportive environments. Usually, we cannot change these three context factors (personality, nature of organization, and quality of support) appreciably; but a manager needs to understand how they affect stress levels in order to promote effective stress management.

The second mediating variable is how well an individual manages his or her own stress (see the Appendix). Whereas the context of the situation is often difficult to change, individuals can learn to assess their present behavior patterns and make changes that will buffer the effects of stress relatively easily. Training in this area, first in groups of managers and then in face-to-face work groups, seems to be the most promising approach to managing the high levels of stress in contemporary organizations. Both long-term (preventive) and immediate (responsive) stress-

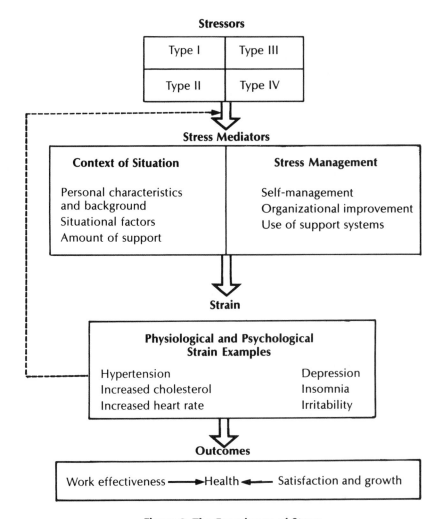

Figure 2. The Experience of Stress

management techniques are needed to protect employees from the effects of too much stress. Although most stress-management training focuses on one basic technique, e.g., progressive relaxation or meditation, it is important to introduce a variety of techniques and to encourage individuals to develop stress-management plans suited to their own situations and preferences.

Depending on whether the context of a situation intensifies or diffuses stress and on how effectively the individual manages stress, high or low levels of *strain* will result. Chronically high levels of strain over a period of time can lead to health changes, lowered satisfaction, and decreased productivity. *Concerns* over prolonged strain responses can themselves become stressors (see dotted line in Figure 2).

A questionnaire was developed and used to collect data from middle managers responsible for almost every phase of operation in the hospital in which our action-research was conducted. Each section of the questionnaire was designed to yield a total score or rating. These were then ranked to permit comparisons. Following the diagram in Figure 2, the sections of the questionnaire were:

1. Stressors
   (a) Type I stressors: Recent organizational change events
   (b) Type II stressors: Recent life change events
   (c) Type III stressors: Ongoing stressful work conditions
   (d) Type IV stressors: Ongoing stressful conditions away from work
2. Predicted mediators
   (a) Physical exercise
   (b) Nutritional awareness
   (c) Self-awareness (life-style orientations as developed by Friedlander, 1975)
   (d) Self-management awareness (self-management, creation and use of support systems, management practices)
   (e) Age, race, and sex
   (f) Amounts of time in present position and at hospital
3. Level of strain experienced (irritability, sleep difficulty, changes in eating and drinking patterns, apathy, depression, disorientation, etc.)
4. Outcome variables
   (a) Felt effectiveness (deadlines, quantity, quality)
   (b) Felt satisfaction and growth (general, learning on the job, sense of accomplishment)
   (c) Health conditions (see the Appendix for a tally of the conditions reported in this project)

For the most part, the data analysis consisted of comparing each variable with the others by calculating the rank-order correlations. Respondents also were asked to name their "top three stressors" in each of the first four sections; this resulted in lists of what the managers felt to have been the most stressful events and conditions in the hospital and away from work. Only on-the-job stressors, however, were addressed in follow-up activities.

FINDINGS

Some of the more general findings are:

1. The hospital managers perceived that they were under a great deal of stress.

2. Most respondents (thirty-two of forty-five) were not able to articulate any significant stress-management repertoire (see the Appendix).

3. The stressors that apparently have the most pervasive impact on respondents are, actually, informal norms (stress type III) rather than specific organizational change events.

4. Stress levels are correlated, at significant levels, with:
   (a) level of strain,
   (b) number of health conditions,
   (c) felt satisfaction and growth, and
   (d) felt effectiveness.

5. Most respondents had poor exercise habits (only 20 percent engaged in regular exercise).

6. A surprising number of respondents had poor dietary habits (40 percent had well-balanced diets, 50 percent had marginally balanced diets, and 10 percent had very poorly balanced diets).

7. Good exercise and dietary habits were associated with low numbers of reported health conditions.

Organizational Change Events (Type I Stress)

The following list of stressors was developed by pooling the respondents' choices of the three most stressful events affecting their work during the previous twelve months. A total of 107 selections was made by the respondents. Of those, seventy-one were included in the following list of eight (of thirty possible) events.

RANK	ORGANIZATIONAL CHANGE EVENT
1.5	Major or frequent changes in instructions, policies, or procedures.
1.5	Required to work more hours per week than normal because of crises, deadlines, etc.
3	Sudden significant increase in the activity level or pace of work.
4	New supervisor.
5.5	New subordinates.

RANK	ORGANIZATIONAL CHANGE EVENT
5.5	Major (department-wide) reorganization.
7	Sudden significant change in the nature of work.
8	New co-worker.

Work load and the necessity to adapt to changed policies and new people were experienced as the most stressful events at work. Such changes are bound to occur and often are beneficial in the long run. However, there are ways to implement needed changes so that they do not induce high levels of stress. Changes usually provoke stress in proportion to the degree in which they take people by surprise. Non-stressful introduction of change should be a primary responsibility of every manager and supervisor.

Organizational-change-event scores are correlated positively with the number of health conditions reported ($r = 0.33$, $p \leq 0.025$). This finding indicates that those who experience more changes on the job also experience more health conditions. Those who experience fewer changes have fewer health conditions.

People with higher organizational-change-event scores who had lower sociocentric scores reported fewer health conditions ($r = 0.49$, $p \leq 0.025$). The people included in this finding comprise the upper 50 percent of the sample of organizational-event scores. Among these people, those with lower sociocentric orientations (Friedlander, 1975) tend also to experience fewer health conditions. A low sociocentric score indicates a relatively low tendency to seek guidance from peers, participation, and consensus management.

People with higher organizational-change-event scores who had higher strain scores reported higher numbers of health conditions ($r = 0.62$, $p \leq 0.005$). The people included in this finding also comprised the upper 50 percent of the scores for organizational change events. Those with higher change scores who also reflected high strain scores experienced higher numbers of health conditions. By the same token, those with lower strain scores experienced fewer health conditions.

It appears from the above that an accumulation of significant changes at work requires sufficient adaptive energy to lead to health changes. Comparisons of organizational-change-event scores with felt satisfaction and growth and felt effectiveness did *not* lead to significant correlations. The change events probably happen sporadically enough so as not to affect longer-term feelings of satisfaction and productivity. However, they still trigger the internal stress response and thereby, eventually, exact their toll.

People with high sociocentric scores are oriented toward reaching decisions participatively and prefer to adopt new ways of behaving through consensual procedures. The organizational change events do not lend themselves to these processes since they are usually thrust upon the employee, often taking him or her by surprise. Those with lower sociocentric scores, therefore, seem to be less impacted by change events events (as they are presently implemented at the hospital we studied).

Ongoing Working Conditions (Type III Stress)

The following list of stressors was developed by pooling the respondents' choices of the top three daily stressors affecting their work. Respondents noted a total of ninety-four selections. Of those, fifty-eight were for the following list of eight (of twenty-six possible) chronic conditions.

RANK	ONGOING WORKING CONDITIONS
1	Too much to do with too little time in which to do it.
2.5	Feedback only when my performance is unsatisfactory.
2.5	Lack of confidence in management.
4	Other demands for my time conflict with each other.
5	Unsettled conflicts with the people at work.
6.5	Spending time "fighting fires" rather than working to a plan.
6.5	Conflicts between my unit and others with which it must work.
8	Lack of clarity about what is expected of me.

Ongoing working conditions written in as "other" and selected as most stressful fell into the following categories:

1. Problems with supervisor (department head, head nurse, or assistant administrator);
2. Problems with peers (poor patient care, apathy, covering for others, troublemakers, destructiveness); and
3. Personal work problems (trying to keep everyone satisfied, unable to obtain needed information, forced to attend low-priority meetings, rumors about self, no time for professional development).

The studies conducted by French and Caplan (1972) found that the primary chronic organizational stressors were role ambiguity and conflict, work load, territoriality, poor relationships, and lack of participation. The list above contains many similarities and conveys a picture of a hectic pace of work and of people who are under a great deal of tension.

Few of the chronic conditions investigated in this study are mandated by policy; rather, they are mostly normative. Norms are unexpressed expectations for behavior or shared habits that strongly influence how work gets done. *Dysfunctional norms are the principal sources of daily on-the-job stress.*

Just as they are not mandated by policy, norms usually cannot be removed by decision making or bureaucratic changes. Changing norms requires intensive efforts on a level-by-level and unit-by-unit basis. The cost-benefit ratio of this much effort must, of course, be assessed. The findings that follow are a first step toward making such an assessment.

Ongoing working-conditions scores are correlated with strain scores ($r=0.51$, $p\leq0.005$). There is a strong positive correlation between the amount of daily work stress and the amount of strain that a manager experiences. The next two findings suggest that higher strain scores increase one's chances of experiencing a larger number of health conditions.

Strain scores and number of health conditions are correlated ($r=0.30$, $p\leq0.025$).

Ongoing working conditions are correlated with the number of health conditions reported ($r=0.30$, $r\leq0.025$). This finding, closely related to the previous two, suggests that higher levels of daily stress lead to larger numbers of health conditions.

Ongoing working-conditions scores are inversely correlated with felt satisfaction and growth ($r=-0.37$, $p\leq0.025$). In addition to affecting health, this suggests that higher levels of daily stress are likely to reduce feelings of satisfaction and growth on the job. Similarly, the finding below indicates that higher levels of daily stress are likely to lead to lower feelings of work effectiveness.

Ongoing working-conditions scores are inversely correlated with felt effectiveness ($r=-0.25$, $p\leq0.10$).

Ongoing working-conditions scores are inversely correlated with formalistic scores ($r=-0.46$, $p\leq0.005$). This finding suggests that people who have low formalistic scores (unlikely to look to the system for guidance and direction) experience relatively higher levels of daily stress. This suggests the bureaucratic nature of the hospital and predicts that those with a preference for working within set procedures and guidelines experience less daily stress. The next finding is related to this one in that those who scored in the upper 50 percent of the daily-stress scores who were also low in their formalistic orientation felt less satisfied with their work.

Those with both higher ongoing working-conditions scores and lower formalistic scores tend also to have lower felt-satisfaction and growth scores (r=0.42, p≤0.05).

Ongoing working-conditions scores are correlated with personalistic scores (r=0.25, p≤0.05). As was the case with *low* formalistic scores, this finding suggests that *high* personalistic-oriented ("do your own thing") people experience relatively more daily stress in the hospital system. Here again, we find that a higher level of stress seems to lead to more reported health changes. In addition, with higher levels of ongoing stress, both felt effectiveness and felt satisfaction and growth decline. Thus, the ongoing working conditions appear to be more pervasive in their impact than the organizational change events. As before, the amount of strain experienced also increases with increasing levels of chronic stress.

People with high formalistic scores tend to look to the authority, the policy, the system, and so on, for direction and guidance. From these data, we can infer that those managers and supervisors who have higher formalistic scores are likely to experience less daily stress; those with lower formalistic scores are more likely to feel less satisfaction and growth on the job. This is probably because most of the jobs in the hospital must fit into a set pattern; therefore, people most willing to work through the system are likely to be less stressed and more satisfied.

People with high personalistic scores prefer to set their own personal standards for performance and to "chart their own courses." These tendencies, at the hospital, seem to lead to higher levels of daily stress. People with less orientation toward behaving in this self-directed manner experience lower levels of daily stress. Once again, we may surmise that people who work through the established system will experience less stress than those in the same setting who have a continuous preference for independent action.

Additional Findings

Major follow-up interventions were derived from two additional findings.

Those who engage in regular, vigorous exercise report fewer health conditions than those who engage in little or no exercise. This finding predicts the importance of *vigorous* regular exercise for maintaining good health. Moderate exercise, in this project, was not significantly better than little or no exercise in maintaining one's health.

Those who regularly eat a well-balanced diet report fewer health conditions than those whose diets are marginally or poorly balanced. As with exercise, those with well-balanced diets appear to be more likely to enjoy relatively good health than those with marginally balanced or poorly balanced diets.

FOLLOW-UP: RECOMMENDATIONS AND ACTIONS

"Stress" has a negative connotation in America. For managers, stress connotes an inability to perform according to standards. When we say of an executive that he really seems to be under stress, we are usually referring to the fact that his performance is slipping.

It is not suggested, however, that a corporate goal should be to eliminate stress from organizational life. A crucial aspect of any manager's job is the intentional creation of stress as a dynamic motivating force in the organization. The point is that this stress should be planned and controlled. It is the uncontrolled effects of organizational stress that may be costly to both the organization and the individual employee.

Since we largely are dealing with norms that are hard to change, one cannot expect that the mere distribution of the above findings will lead to any changes in behavior if no follow-up actions are taken. It is necessary for management to take specific responsibility for implementing educational and change programs concerning stress.

Changes in behavior and in the basic ways in which people approach their work are needed to create normative change. If whatever changes are needed do not take place first at the top levels of the organization, they cannot be expected to take place at any other levels of the organization. To quote Suojanen and Hudson (1977, pp.7-8):

> The behavior of both the superior and the subordinate can be addictive, and this can repeat itself all the way down from the level of the chief executive officer of the organization to that of the most junior supervisor. If we bear in mind the fact that the behavior of top management dictates the behavior of the other members of the organization and if this behavior is addictive, then the end result often will be an enterprise in which members appear to be "busy" in every respect but which is falling down totally in overall performance. . . . Until the senior manager takes the first step, the other members of top management cannot take it. Organizational behavior change must wait until all members of the top management have begun their individual programs of change.

Although an individual's ability to cope with stress is greatly influenced by his or her personal style, support from the social environment (family, friends, colleagues, mentors), and the person's unique situation (financial status, geographic location, past history), enlightened management can do a great deal to reduce harmful levels of stress at work. The following suggestions are based on the findings of our study and were made to the senior management of the hospital. While many have been implemented, a follow-up study has not yet been conducted to assess the results.

Understand the Origins of Stress

The first step is to identify the sources of stress and whether a stressor is one that can be controlled better. For example, since work load is producing negative consequences, it is recommended that the hospital do an analysis of individual positions in order to determine if some redistribution of work is possible.

If actual work load is not the problem, the chances are that there is a problem with the manager's ability to organize his or her work and time or with the way in which he or she chooses to delegate work. Educational activities can help managers learn these skills; good coaching and performance feedback from executives can support the improvement of these managerial practices. The development of job descriptions and performance standards where they are missing or inadequate also helps to reduce stress. Time management and effective feedback programs can also be developed.

Changes in policy cause stress when (a) the change is unilaterally imposed without consultation and (b) the people affected see no functional justification for the change. What appears to be a logical and simple change in procedure coming from one division can cause a ripple effect of stress elsewhere when the change is unannounced and unexplained.

Unpredictable work flow results in employee dissatisfaction (from having to adjust to rapidly changing work practices). More seriously, it can result in dependence on people with whom there is little face-to-face contact and on environmental conditions over which the employee has no control (e.g., frequent patient transfers, use of contract nurses, heavy reliance on part-time and on-call people). Consequently, in many work units employees have erratic or infrequent work contacts with one another—especially across shifts.

How managers appear to cope with these stressors is quite revealing. The "fire-fighting" climate in the hospital we studied resulted from these stressors and appears to focus on vertical relations at the expense of good lateral and diagonal communications. Under stress, vertical relations tend to become more work related while lateral communications tend to become more superficial and complaintive. In addition, managers under stress frequently reduce contacts with various groups in order to concentrate on the problem area. This usually has a negative consequence because it reduces the manager's collegial support at a time when he or she needs it and denies him or her an opportunity to gain a broader and more varied perspective of the problem. In order to support increased lateral and diagonal dialogue among managers, it was recommended that department heads and supervisors in the hospital get together in periodic quasi-social work sessions on a monthly basis. The completed management development program did much to support lateral communications, and a similar new program has now been undertaken.

Sensitivity to the effects of sudden change should be encouraged at all levels of management. The introduction of change in any policy or procedure should be done carefully. The people to be affected by the change should be educated about the what and why of the change before it actually goes into effect, since the amount of stress that accompanies a change seems to be a function of the degree of surprise or unfamiliarity present when one learns about the change.

Reduce Role Ambiguity and the Negative Effects of Role Strain

In examining stressful working conditions (type III stress), there was a high degree of apparent role ambiguity experienced by managers. Role ambiguity is defined as uncertainty regarding what is expected of one in one's job.

In a recent study, Beehr (1976) found that role ambiguity was strongly related to four psychological role strains: job dissatisfaction, life dissatisfaction, low self-esteem, and depressed mood. Further, Beehr found that even with role ambiguity on the job, when there were certain situational characteristics associated with the people in those roles, the role strain was significantly modified. Group cohesiveness, or a *support group,* had a significant lessening effect on role strain. People working in cohesive groups were found to be less likely to internalize the blame for having an ambiguous role; thus, they were less likely to have a lowered sense of self-esteem and/or a depressed mood. People in noncohesive groups were less likely to have the social supports required to "talk out" their problems and tended to blame themselves for the ambiguity. While lowered self-esteem is less likely in a cohesive group, job dissatisfaction is related more strongly to role ambiguity in noncohesive groups as well.

The strongest and most consistent moderator of the relationship between role ambiguity and role strain was the lack of autonomy in the Beehr study. Consequently, it was recommended that a climate supporting the building of peer-support groups and an increase in the degree of managerial autonomy should be reinforced by the hospital management.

The management-by-objectives program already contemplated will help to support increased autonomy because management boundaries will become well defined. Although assistant administrators have been working with department heads on defining job expectations, developing performance standards, and providing ongoing performance feedback, a similar process has *not* been ongoing between division leaders and assistant administrators. It was suggested that the job-clarification process must be started at the top and that doing so will have a high impact on follow-through at lower organizational levels.

Improve Information Flow

This is important so that more people will understand what is happening around them and whether or not developments will affect them. To a large extent, the level of stress is related to the flow of information in the hospital. Information often is not conveyed fully or is distorted as it passes through the manager-supervisor levels. This creates tension as different units or departments begin to interpret a decision or policy in different ways. The organizational change events tend to be more stressful to the extent that they come as surprises. As mentioned previously, if the reasons for policy changes, needs for extra work, reorganizations, and the like are discussed thoroughly, their advent will cause less stress. Too often, managers and supervisors decide that such discussions would be a waste of time or not worth the effort. Likewise, there are few attempts to integrate or ease the transitions involved in introducing new supervisors, subordinates, and peers into a given work setting. These changes would be less surprising to people if there were more sharing of information and advanced planning. To insure improvement in communication problems of these kinds, the top management of the hospital has agreed to meet with the first-line supervisors on a quarterly basis to clear up misunderstandings, misinterpretations, and rumors. Communications are also dealt with in depth in the re-created management-development training programs.

Information flow is again implicated in reviewing ongoing work conditions. As noted previously, many people are unclear about what is expected of them and receive only negative performance feedback. In addition, the "firefighting," conflicts, and work-load stressors are often caused by managers' lack of understanding of what information they need from their subordinates and what information their subordinates need from them. All of this, then, is probably the main reason why the number-two daily stressor is "lack of confidence in management."

Provide Individual Help to Managers as a Protective/Preventive Measure

The above measures will, if consistently implemented over the long term, reduce the level of episodic and daily stresses in the work environment. Some stress will always be present, however, and occasionally it will be intense enough over a period of time to become destructive. Therefore, people need to learn how to protect themselves. Several protective/preventive measures are being implemented at the hospital.

1. For the detection of physiological and psychological strains from stress, employee health physicals will be required every year. The current physical will be supplemented with more comprehensive blood work and appropriate counseling. Both the manager and his or her boss will be informed if a presumed stress-related condition is found.

2. A counseling and/or referral service to sources of help within or outside the hospital will be developed.

3. Managers will be taught to identify stress problems and symptoms in themselves and in their subordinates through training programs and follow-up work on the job. These programs will be scheduled regularly.

4. Managers will be required to take vacations. A large number of employees, as well as managers, in the hospital take little or no vacation. Some time off will be strongly encouraged.

5. Outlets will be provided through regular vigorous exercise by means of an exercise club and sports activities such as bicycling, running, basketball, and tennis. Yoga classes may be offered on a weekly basis.

6. Educational activities on both nutrition and exercise will be developed and provided. Spouses may be invited. The first such program, combining nutritional awareness with techniques for dealing with tension headaches and backaches, has been very well received. Fresh fruit is now available as an alternative to donuts in all meetings and seminars.

7. Ongoing training in stress management will be continued. This provides an overview of stress and how to deal with it. Self-awareness is considered the first step to improved personal stress management.

8. Stress will be monitored. The stress research will be repeated on a twelve- to eighteen-month basis to evaluate progress.

As the reader familiar with organization development will have noticed, the follow-up activities described here fit nicely into a broader developmental context. The stress-provoking norms in most organizations tend to be both pervasive and persistent. Thus, it is important to the success of any stress-related follow-up program that it be explicitly managed, that it be granted adequate resources that are applied completely and consistently, and that the amount of time required to make complex changes in personal and organizational habits not be underestimated.

APPENDIX

1. The following stress-management techniques are included in the organizational training programs associated with this project. Others are encouraged to add to the list from their own experiences.

 I. Self-management
    A. Vigorous regular exercise
    B. Balanced nutritional habits
    C. Letting-go techniques (relaxation, meditation, etc.)
    D. Awareness of own preferences and idiosyncrasies
    E. Personal planning (time management, life planning, etc.)
 II. Support systems
    A. Diagnosing present sources of support
    B. Identifying needs for improved support
    C. Action planning for improving key relationships
III. Altering stressful organizational norms and management practices
    A. Diagnosing sources of stress
    B. Developing alternatives for reducing unnecessary stress
    C. Identifying and managing distressed employees

2. Respondents were asked to check which conditions, from a given list, they had experienced during the past year. Chronic conditions, e.g., hypertension, were to receive one check mark and episodic conditions, e.g., influenza, one check mark for each occurrence.

   43 = number of respondents

   20 = number making four or fewer check marks

   299 = total number of check marks

   69 Tension headache

   52 Diarrhea or constipation

49 Common cold

28 Backache

15 Infection

14 Allergy

10 Influenza

 9 Arthritis

 7 Rheumatoid arthritis

 7 Migraine headache

 6 Surgery

 5 Hypertension

 5 Accidents

 5 Palpitations

 4 Dizziness

 3 Sinusitis

 2 Ulcers

 2 Anemia

 2 Severe psychological problem

 1 Each: diabetes, laryngitis, benign
   tumor, kidney stone, tonsillitis

REFERENCES

Adams, J. D., & Margolis, J. *The impact of organizational stressors on hospital managers and supervisors.* Unpublished report to senior management, GSCH. Washington, D.C., 1977.

Beehr, T. A. Perceived situational moderators of the relationship between subjective role ambiguity and role strain. *Journal of Applied Psychology,* 1976, *61,* 1.

Cochrane, R., & Robertson, A. The life events inventory. *Journal of Psychosomatic Research,* 1973, *17,* 135-139.

French, R. P., & Caplan, R. D. Organizational stress and individual strain. In A. J. Marrow (Ed.), *The failure of success.* New York: AMACOM, 1972.

Friedlander, F. Emergent and contemporary life styles: An inter-generational issue. *Human Relations,* 1975, *28,* 329-347.

Holmes, T. H., & Rahe, R. H. The social readjustment rating scale. *Journal of Psychosomatic Research,* 1967, *11,* 213-218.

Naismith, D. *Stress among managers as a function of organizational change.* Unpublished doctoral dissertation, The George Washington University, 1975.

Suojanen, W. W., & Hudson, D. R. Coping with stress and addictive work behavior. *Atlanta Economic Review,* March-April, 1977, pp. 4-9.

Weiss, S. M. (Ed.) *Proceedings of the National Heart, Lung and Blood Institute Working Conference on Health Behavior.* Department of Health, Education and Welfare, National Institutes of Health (77-868), 1977.

PART III

MAKING PERSONAL LIFE-STYLE CHANGES

CHAPTER 14

GUIDELINES FOR STRESS MANAGEMENT AND LIFE STYLE CHANGES

John D. Adams

Some of the primary factors which mediate the experience of stress are very difficult, at best, to change. These include an individual's personality, inherited characteristics and past history; the quality of the interpersonal support inherent in his or her environment; and the nature of the organization in which he or she works. Each of these, depending on its make-up, can either heighten or diminish the impact of stressors on the individual.

The stress mediating effect of each of these areas has been well documented. Unfortunately, none of these factors are amenable to change. Personality change is very difficult and you cannot change your heredity or past history at all. Likewise, it is difficult or impossible to change your interpersonal environment from, say, cut throat competition and "every man for himself" norms to norms of caring, openness and support. And thirdly, the fact that the organization in which you work experiences massive seasonal changes, is governed by tight deadlines or exists in a turbulent technical or economic environment also is difficult to alter. The basic problem is that these three factors—personal, interpersonal and organizational—are the primary mediators of stress, but are not amenable to change.

Happily, within each area there are things which can be done by individuals to manage stress effectively. These are shown in Figure 1. Elsewhere (Adams, 1978, 1979).

Self-management means taking care of and nurturing yourself, both in an immediate (responsive) and in a long term (protective) sense. Some of the most effective self-management areas are summarized in Figure 2.

Reprinted from: J.D. Adams. Guidelines for Stress Management and Life Style Changes. *The Personal Administrator*, June 1979, 35-38; 44. Used with permission.

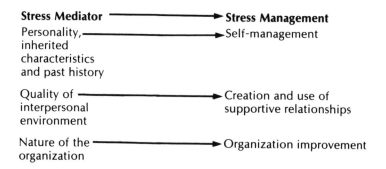

Figure 1. The Management of Stress

Good Nutritional Habits
1. Balanced diet
    • Sufficient vitamins, minerals, protein, complex carbohydrates and fiber
    • Minimized consumption of sugar, salt, saturated fats, refined white flour and chemical additives
2. Regular meals
3. Maintenance of recommended weight
4. Moderate use of alcohol and caffeine
5. No smoking

Good Exercise Habits
1. Regular aerobic exercise to improve cardiovascular fitness
2. Regular recreational exercise for tension reduction and diversion

Self-Awareness
1. Understanding of personal needs, preferences and idiosyncrasies
2. Assertive behavior and role negotiation.

Letting Go Techniques
1. Regular relaxation habits (e.g., meditation, prayer, healing visualization)
2. Seeking closure on tasks and interpersonal situations—finishing unfinished business

Personal Planning
1. Effective time management day to day
2. Life and career planning for the long term

Figure 2. Self-Management Techniques

It should be immediately clear that effective self-management requires a healthful life style. This listing will indicate that significant changes in life style are needed by many, if not most, readers.

The creation and use of supporting relationships should be self explanatory. While no studies have yet indicated that the presence of supportive relationships will, in any way, *prevent* stressful experiences, numerous studies have found that the absence of such relationships leaves people more vulnerable to the ravages of prolonged stress (see, for example, La Rocco and Jones, 1978 for a review). It is clear that we need others to help us test reality, share our successes and problems, gain respect from, learn from, provide us with linkages and access to others, pull us out of ruts, etc. If an individual has relationships which provide these kinds of processes, he or she is better equipped to deal with stressors head on.

Again, there are implications for life style change. When you examine your present relationships with intimates, friends and acquaintances, you are likely to find gaps, inconsistencies and conflicts which detract from an adequate level of support. Further, you may usually assume that unless you take the initiative to improve a relationship or create a new one, inertia and evolution will prevail in their usual slow to change ways. The simple procedure of identifying one thing to do—one action step—to improve or create each needed supportive relationship will give you an indication of how much change is needed here.

The approaches to *organizational improvement* which will affect stress levels on the job most effectively include: full two-way flow of information, identification and change of stress-provoking norms, team building, role clarification, stress education, annual physical examinations which include stress assessment and counseling and the establishment of clear objectives and performance standards for all employees.

These tasks require the involvement or participation of large numbers of people. Put another way, a "critical mass of concern" must be created in the organization before significant stress reduction is possible. This is because the most persistent and pervasive sources of organizational stress are embodied in the form of unverbalized social habits or norms such as: "We only get feedback when we screw up"; "We've got too much to do and too little time"; "My unit and others with which it must interface are forever in conflict"; and "No one knows what is expected of them." Nearly everyone in a given organization unit participates, either tacitly or overtly, in maintaining such stressful norms. In order to bring about changes, nearly everyone also must be involved in identifying these norms and in making the commitment to changing them.

The literature on organization development is descriptive of the many techniques and processes available which will facilitate making the kinds of organizational changes needed to reduce stress levels at work. The remainder of this article, however, focuses on *individual change* for improved stress management.

Actually, it would be more accurate to say that the remainder of this article focuses on some guidelines for facilitating healthful life style changes, since such changes are difficult for many people. Few of the stress management techniques outlined in the previous paragraphs are "new information" to people. Nearly everyone already knows that the techniques listed as good stress management habits in the self-management and supportive relationship sections are good ideas. They are just good common sense that has been around for a long time. Why is it, then, that so many people ignore them or, when faced with them, decide not to make any significant changes; opting for the likelihood of poorer health and shorter lives?

I think there are some clear reasons for this. First, we are "programmed" by the media, our educations and some sectors of the medical profession to "live the good life" and rely on technology and drugs to fix us up when we begin to fall apart. Second, there is not a widespread understanding of how significantly an unhealthful life style can shorten one's life or impair one's health.

In another vein, many stress management programs fail because they promote a single "one best way" technique. It is clear that each individual is unique in his or her personality, heredity, past history and so on. Therefore, what is stressful for one person may not be for another. Also, different people will tend towards different kinds of physical and psychological manifestations as a result of prolonged stressful experiences. And finally, a technique that is particularly useful in managing one person's stress may be boring and/or useless to another. I think you need to be presented with a range of proven stress management techniques to try out and choose from.

But there are problems here also. When presented with an array of techniques for stress management, there are two frequent negative outcomes. Many people throw up their hands, feeling overwhelmed by the options and don't do anything different. Others rush to make "wholesale" changes in their life styles, only to become quickly overloaded and then retreat to their former ways of doing things. When several changes in life style are attempted all at once, they tend to be added on to an already full schedule. It is common for people to conclude "I don't have time to run three times a week, meditate twice a day, prepare healthful meals and work on improving relationships—I'm already too busy!"

And finally, many people are not willing to take explicit responsibility for their own health and well-being. Without a sense of personal responsibility, people are not likely to adopt any behaviors which will lead to improved stress management.

There are several guidelines which seem to help when you are seriously considering making changes in order to achieve a less stressful and more healthful life style. By following these guidelines, a *gradual process* of life style change can take place which is not overwhelming at any one time in its pace or magnitude.

Mobilization is necessary. In order to make gains in stress management, an *explicit* personal decision or commitment is very important. Often, this mobilizing decision comes as a result of some "shock," either to one's self or to a relative or close friend (e.g., ulcers, hypertension, emotional crisis and other stress related conditions). A shocking discovery or experience of this nature is not always necessary, but a self-responsible commitment to action *is* necessary.

Knowledge. Once a person has mobilized, he needs information about what does and does not work. There are many fads around relative to each of the stress management areas and, without adequate information, separating the good from the bad is very difficult. Further, in most of the self-management areas, there are professional disagreements (e.g., to take vitamins or not). It is important that you study the various facets of the issues in order to make informed and responsible life style choices.

Patience. When people discover how poorly they are managing their stresses, they often want to correct their perceived deficiencies immediately. Unfortunately, this often is not possible. For example, everyone knows people who have gone on one or another of the crash diets to lose a lot of weight very quickly. Even if they succeed in losing the desired amount of weight (and do not damage themselves in the process), they generally gain all the lost weight back. The only proven way to lose weight is *very gradually,* using a balanced diet with reduced caloric intake. The same principle applies to all stress management techniques. There probably will be no apparent differences from one day to the next. Improvements in health and well-being accrue very slowly.

Life long learning. You do not become a good stress manager or adopt a healthful life style as a result of reading one book or attending one seminar. A book or a seminar may be a starting point, but the overall process must be one of continual learning. It is never finished, because there are always new sources of stress and new ways of dealing with them.

Don't fight it if you can't win. Many of us bring a lot of unnecessary stress onto ourselves by "tilting at windmills"—be they corporate, societal or personal. We do not need to become ego-involved with every policy, cause, issue and traffic jam we come across! Most of us could do ourselves a big service by learning to distinguish between the battles that are worth fighting and those that are not.

The previous five guidelines—mobilization, knowledge, patience, life long learning and don't fight it if you can't win—are somewhat generally oriented towards getting started and towards a set of attitudes appropriate for improved stress management and life style change. The remaining seven guidelines are more directly related to specific life style change efforts.

Move towards the environment. When you experience heavy or prolonged stress, the natural tendency is to withdraw and pull inward. While this may be a good temporary response to an intense stressor, it runs counter to long term learning and development. Taking initiatives, reaching out and extending yourself—moving towards the environment in a positive and thoughtful way—seem necessary to making specific changes. Withdrawing may be a short term necessity but, in the long run, it maintains the status quo.

Project orientation. The best way to make life style changes *is not,* as was pointed out before, on a wholesale or shotgun basis. The most effective approach to such changes time and again has been shown to be what may be called a "one step at a time" approach. With this approach, the individual decides upon a *manageable* change project, such as eating no sugar or meditating, and tries out the change on a regular basis *for a minimum of three weeks.* After this period, he or she makes a determination about whether or not to continue with the change. If they decide to make the change permanent at that point, they enter into a period of stabilization of, say, two months prior to undertaking a new project. In this way, life style changes are neither overwhelming nor are they "added on" to existing practices. Rather, the change process tends to become one of exchanging new activities and habits for old ones.

Take calculated risks. Other people do not want or expect you to change. If, for example, you become determined to manage your time effectively and, in doing so, have a period of unavailability each day, others will resist this and pressure you to return to your old open door ways. Stress management and life style changes often have interpersonal risks associated with them. Relationships with bosses, peers, subordinates, family and friends all are likely to be affected by personal changes. It is best to break major changes that have major risks associated with them down into a series of gradual steps, each of which has a more manageable risk associated with it.

Don't work uphill. This guideline is closely related to the previous two. There is a greater chance for successfully integrating a personal change if the change project itself is not too pervasive. To put this another way, take on "easier" changes early (e.g. not using the salt shaker anymore or keeping a daily "to do" list for the first time) and save the bigger changes (e.g., giving up tobacco or alcohol) for later. Early success experiences help to build momentum. Building on early successes will make the tackling of the more difficult changes later on a lot easier.

Maintain an optimistic bias. This means you should develop an attitude in which you expect to succeed. Expectations have a way of becoming self-fulfilling. If you expect to succeed at something, your chances of doing so are much higher than if you expect to fail. If you take a one step at a time approach in which you take calculated risks and build on your successes, it should not be too dificult to develop and maintain an optimistic bias.

Open to new information. It is natural to notice how many Fords are on the road whenever we buy a new Ford. Likewise, whenever we try out a change, we'll notice other people who also practice (or avoid) the habit we're trying to adopt and we're likely to "find" more articles related to it, hear about it more on TV and so on. It also is natural eventually to take the changed habit for granted and stop noticing information related to it in the environment around us. When this happens, we are no longer learning, but are setting the habit "in concrete." In general, I think it is a good idea to maintain an open mind and a sense of relativity and flexibility about personal changes we make so that further changes in the area, should they be appropriate, will be easy.

Build and use support. Life style changes, both on and off the job, are difficult to make and maintain. We often can facilitate these changes by including others in them. For any given change project being contemplated, it is a good idea to ask yourself "are there others I should include, or ask for help or guidance?" Three questions we should ask in doing this are:

1. What sort of support, if any, do I need for this change project?
2. Who or what can provide that support?
3. Are there specific "contracts" I need to make with others relative to my intended change?

Making life style changes which will equip us to better withstand the stressors we encounter (and probably help us maintain our health) takes time. While the "instant" culture fostered by technology and the media tend to reinforce the notion that we can be what we want to be anytime we choose, the reality is that most people cannot incorporate personal change this fast. As regards life style changes, our chances for success are much better if we make small "one step at a time" changes on the one hand and think in terms of what we want our life style to be, say, five years from now on the other.

REFERENCES

Adams, J. D. "Improving Stress Management," *Social Change.* NTL Institute, Rosslyn, VA, 8(4), 1978.

Adams, J. D. "On Consuming Human Resources: Perspectives on the Management of Stress," in *Behavioral Science and the Manager's Role* (2nd ed.). W. W. Burke and W. Eddy (Eds.), University Associates. San Diego, CA, 1980.

La Rocco, J. M. and Jones, A. P. "Co-Worker and Leader Support as Moderators of Stress-Strain Relationships in Work Situations," *Journal of Applied Psychology.* 63(5), 1978.

APPENDICES

A VARIETY OF IDEAS
FOR RESPONDING TO STRESS

Participants in stress workshops frequently request a list of simple suggestions they can follow to reduce the stress in their lives or cope with it better. Unfortunately, there are no simple or universally effective solutions to the problem of stress management. We are all unique, and what works well for some of us may be totally ineffective for others.

However, each of the techniques that follow represents an approach that has worked well for someone somewhere; some of them, at least, should be effective for you, too. Add to the list wherever you can.

1. *Become knowledgeable about stress.*

   • Understand the process and effects of stress.
   • Identify your major sources of stress.
   • Anticipate stressful periods and plan for them.
   • Develop a repertoire of successful stress-management techniques, and practice them.
   • Learn to identify the opportunities for personal growth inherent in periods of stress.
   • Find the level of stress that is best for you, remembering that both insufficient and excessive stress are potentially harmful.

2. *Take a systematic approach to problem solving.*

   • Define your problem specifically, delving beyond symptoms. Divide it into manageable components that can be dealt with easily.
   • Gather sufficient information about the problem to put it in perspective.
   • Discover why the problem exists for you.
   • Review your experience with the present problem or similar ones.

- Develop and evaluate a set of alternative courses of action.
- Select a course of action, and proceed with it.

3. *Come to terms with your feelings.*

- Differentiate between your thoughts and your feelings.
- Do not suppress your feelings; acknowledge them to yourself, and share them with others.
- Learn to be flexible and adaptive.
- Honestly appraise your personal liabilities.
- Accept your feelings.

4. *Develop effective behavioral skills.*

- Do not use the word *can't* when you actually mean *won't* (for example, "I *can't* stop smoking").
- When you have determined what needs to be done with your life, act on your decisions.
- Use free time productively.
- Be assertive.
- Manage conflicts openly and directly.
- Avoid blaming others for situations.
- Provide positive feedback to others.
- Learn to say *no.*
- Deal with problems as soon as they appear; if you procrastinate, they may intensify.
- Evaluate the reality of your expectations, avoiding both the grandiose and the catastrophic.
- Learn to let go of stressful situations and take breaks.

5. *Establish and maintain a strong support network.*

- Ask for direct help, and be receptive to it when it is offered.
- Develop empathy for others.
- Make an honest assessment of your needs for support and your satisfaction with the support you presently receive.
- List six people with whom you would like to improve your relationship, and in each case identify one action step you will take toward such improvement.
- Rid yourself of dead or damaging relationships.
- Maintain high-quality relationships both on and off the job.
- Tell the members of your support network that you value the relationships shared with them.

6. *Develop a life style that will buffer against the effects of stress.*
   - Regularly practice some form of each of the following types of exercise: vigorous, stretching, and recreational.
   - Engage regularly in some form of systematic relaxation.
   - Use alcohol in moderation or not at all.
   - Do not use tobacco.
   - Obtain sufficient rest on a regular basis.
   - Maintain your recommended weight.
   - Eat a balanced diet.
   - Avoid caffeine.
   - Avoid foods high in sugar, salt, white flour, saturated fats, and chemicals.
   - Plan your use of time on both a daily and a long-term basis.
   - Seek out variety and change of pace.
   - Take total responsibility for your life.
   - Maintain an optimistic attitude.
   - Find a holistic physician, undergo laboratory tests to establish a physiological base line, and plan for improving your wellness.
   - Do not dwell on unimportant matters.

7. *Concentrate on positive spiritual development.*
   - Adopt the attitude that no problem is too monumental to be solved.
   - Engage regularly in prayer or meditation.
   - Establish a sense of purpose and direction.
   - Seek spiritual guidance.
   - Learn to transcend stressful situations.
   - Believe in yourself.
   - Increase your awareness of the interdependence of all things in the universe.

8. *Plan and execute successful life-style changes.*
   - Expect to succeed.
   - Approach projects one step at a time.
   - Keep change projects small and manageable.
   - Practice each change rigorously for 21 days; then decide whether to continue with it.
   - Celebrate your successes; reward yourself.

SUGGESTED READINGS

I. UNDERSTANDING STRESS

Adams, J.D., Hayes, J., & Hopson, B. *Transition: Understanding and managing personal change.* London: Martin Robertson, 1976. (New York: Universe Books, 1977.)

Blue Cross. *Stress.* Free booklet available through the public relations department of local Blue Cross offices.

Dychtwald, K. *Bodymind.* New York: Pantheon, 1977.

McCamy, J.C., & Presley, J. *Human life styling: Keeping whole in the twentieth century.* New York: Harper & Row, 1975.

McQuade, W., & Aikman, A. *Stress.* New York: Bantam, 1975.

Pelletier, K.R. *Mind as healer mind as slayer.* New York: Delacorte, 1977.

Selye, H. *Stress without distress.* New York: J.B. Lippincott, 1974.

II. CREATING AND USING SUPPORT SYSTEMS: INTERPERSONAL RELATIONSHIPS

De Saint-Exupery, A. *The little prince.* New York: Harcourt Brace Jovanovich, 1973.

Harris, T.A. *I'm ok—you're ok: A practical guide to transactional analysis.* New York: Harper & Row, 1969.

Kirschenbaum, H., & Glaser, B. *Developing support groups.* San Diego, CA: University Associates, 1978.

Seashore, C., & Seashore, E.W. Managing stress by building support systems. In R.A. Luke (Ed.), *The Dallas connection.* Washington: National Training and Development Service, 1974.

III. ORGANIZATIONAL FACTORS: NORMS, PRACTICES, AND POLICIES

Cooper, C.L., & Payne, R. (Eds.) *Stress at work.* New York: John Wiley & Sons, 1978.

Kahn, R.L., Wolfe, D.M., Quinn, R.P., Snoek, J.D., & Rosenthal, R.A. *Organizational stress: Studies in role conflict and ambiguity.* New York: John Wiley & Sons, 1964.

IV. SELF-MANAGEMENT: NUTRITION

Ballentine, R.M. *Diet and nutrition.* Glenview, IL: Himalayan Institute, 1976.

Cheraskin, E. *Psychodietetics.* New York: Bantam, 1976.

Davis, A. *Let's eat right to keep fit* (Rev. ed.). New York: Harcourt Brace Jovanovich, 1970.

Kirschmann, J.D. *Nutrition almanac.* New York: McGraw-Hill, 1975.

Lappe, F.M. *Diet for a small planet* (Rev. ed.). New York: Ballantine, 1975.

Prevention. A monthly magazine from Emmaus, PA: Rodale Press.

Williams, R.J. *Nutrition against disease.* New York: Bantam, 1973.

V. SELF-MANAGEMENT: EXERCISE

Cooper, K.H. *The new aerobics.* New York: M. Evans, 1970.

Hittleman, R. *Richard Hittleman's Introduction to yoga.* New York: Bantam, 1969.

Iyengar, B.K. *Light on yoga* (Rev. ed.). New York: Schocken, 1977.

Leonard, G. *The ultimate athlete.* New York: Viking, 1975.

Root, L., & Kiernan, T. *Oh, my aching back: A doctor's guide to your back pain and how to control it.* New York: David McKay, 1973.

Smith, D. *The east-west exercise book.* New York: McGraw-Hill, 1976.

VI. SELF-MANAGEMENT: LETTING-GO TECHNIQUES

Benson, H. *The relaxation response.* New York: William Morrow, 1975.

Downing, G. *The massage book.* New York: Random House, 1972.

Downing, G. *Massage and meditation.* New York: Random House, 1974.

Keyes, K., Jr. *Handbook to higher consciousness* (5th ed.). Berkeley, CA: Living Love Center, 1975.

Lamott, K. *Escape from stress: How to stop killing yourself.* New York: G.P. Putnam's Sons, 1974.

Lowen, A. *Pleasure: A creative approach to life.* New York: Penguin, 1975.

Naranjo, C., & Ornstein, R.E. *On the psychology of meditation.* New York: Penguin, 1977.

Yogi, M.M. *Transcendental meditation.* New York: Penguin, 1969.

VII. SELF-MANAGEMENT: SELF-AWARENESS

The Boston Women's Health Book Collective. *Our bodies, ourselves* (Rev. 2nd ed.). New York: Simon and Schuster, 1976.

Friedman, M., & Rosenman, R.H. *Type A behavior and your heart.* New York: A.A. Knopf, 1974.

Ornstein, R.E. *The psychology of consciousness* (2nd ed.). New York: Harcourt Brace Jovanovich, 1977.

Ram Dass, B. *The only dance there is: Thoughts along the spiritual way.* New York: Doubleday, 1974.

VIII. SELF-MANAGEMENT: PERSONAL PLANNING

Bolles, R.N. *What color is your parachute? A practical manual for job-hunters and career changers.* Berkeley, CA: Ten Speed Press, 1977.

Kirn, A.G., & Kirn, M.O. *Life work planning* (4th ed.) New York: McGraw-Hill, 1978.

Lakein, A. *How to get control of your time and your life.* New York: David McKay, 1973.

Mackenzie, R.A. *The time trap.* New York: AMACOM, 1972.

Webber, R.A. *Time and management.* New York: Van Nostrand Reinhold, 1972.